# The Chancellorsville Campaign

# The Chancellorsville Campaign

## March - May 1863

David G. Martin

COMBINED
BOOKS

First published in the United States of America in 1991 by
Combined Books, Inc.

For information, address:
Combined Books, Inc.
151 East 10th Avenue
Conshohocken, PA 19428

Special thanks to the United States Army Historical Institute
for allowing us to reproduce valuable photographs from their
extensive collection.

*Library of Congress Cataloging-in-Publication Data available*

ISBN 0-938289-06-3

Printed in Hong Kong.

# Contents

*Washington Artillery in action on Marye's Heights.*

# Introduction

Chancellorsville has long been considered to be Robert E. Lee's greatest battle, a tactical masterpiece in which he out-generaled and outfought an enemy army that was over twice as big as his own. In the year since he had taken command of the Army of Northern Virginia, Lee had won victory after victory, so earning the love of his soldiers and fearful respect from his enemies. None of his victories would be greater or harder won than Chancellorsville, which was fought in early May 1863. At the opening of the campaign Lee was encamped on the battlefield of Fredericksburg, scene of his easy victory over Ambrose E. Burnside the previous December. Supply difficulties and a Yankee threat from Norfolk had forced Lee to weaken his command by detaching Lieutenant General James Longstreet with two divisions to the Suffolk area of Virginia. Across the Rappahannock River from Fredericksburg, the Union *Army of the Potomac*, now led by Major General Joseph E. Hooker, was reinforced and rejuvenated for yet another campaign against Richmond. At the opening of the campaign Hooker secretly divided his army and gained a strategic advantage over Lee by swinging around the Confederate left flank west of Fredericksburg. Lee quickly responded by dividing his own much smaller force to meet Hooker head on in the scrub forest near Chancellorsville known locally as "The Wilderness." Only a reinforced division was left to hold the old lines at Fredericksburg. When Hooker decided to put his army in a defensive posture, Lee made one of the boldest decisions of his career and divided his army yet again, sending his trusted lieutenant "Stonewall" Jackson with half of the army's infantry on a wide flank movement against Hooker's right wing. The move worked masterfully, though it was not without a few tense moments. On the evening of 2 May, Jackson's troops came crashing through the woods to rout the Union *XI Corps* and its supports. Fierce fighting continued the next day as Lee pressed his advantage and pushed Hooker back. Now a new crisis arose for the Confederates as Union Major General John Sedgwick crossed the river at Fredericksburg and routed the weakened defending line posted there. Lee dealt with this new threat without hesitation and defeated Sedgwick at Salem Church on 4 May after a great deal of hectic maneuvering. Hooker, who was weakened by a wound, gave no aid to Sedgwick and then retreated across the Rappahannock, against the advice of his better generals. Thus the campaign came to a close with the two armies occupying the same positions they had held a week earlier before all the fighting started. The victory was indeed a magnificent triumph for Lee, but a costly one. Once again he had defeated the Yankees but had not managed to destroy their army. The soldiers he lost in battle were becoming increasingly difficult to replace, while the enemy's manpower pool seemed endless. One of Lee's casualties was irreplaceable—the hero of the Confederacy, Stonewall Jackson, had been accidentally wounded by his own men at the height of the battle, and died a week later. Jackson's loss definitely soured Lee's victory, and forced a major reorganization of the army and its command structure. When Lee decided to use his great victory at Chancellorsville as a spring board for his greatest strategic gamble of the war, a second invasion of the North, he knew he would have to rely on several untested commanders in key positions. The after effects of Chancellorsville would definitely play a key role in the performance of the Confederate army at Gettysburg.

*Confederate skirmishers opposing Sedgwick's advance through Fredericksburg early on 3 May.*

# CHAPTER I

# The Army Under Burnside

## December, 1862 - January, 1863

*J*anuary 1863 was not a happy time for the soldiers of the Union *Army of the Potomac*. Since the summer of 1861 they had been beaten in campaign after campaign as they attempted to defeat the Confederates and capture the enemy capital at Richmond. First Irvin McDowell had been routed at First Bull Run, and then George McClellan was driven back from the gates of Richmond. Then John Pope was defeated at Second Bull Run, and a reinstated George McClellan needed an extraordinary stroke of good luck to catch Lee and then fight a drawn tactical battle at Antietam. Most recently Major General Ambrose E. Burnside had achieved a strategic surprise over the enemy by a quick march from Warrenton to Fredericksburg, but he lost his temporary advantage when necessary bridging material failed to arrive on time. By the time he was able to cross the Rappahannock River two weeks later, Confederate commander Robert E. Lee had had plenty of time to gather his army and fortify a strong defensive line. Instead of backing off, Burnside stubbornly adhered to his campaign plan and assaulted Lee's prepared lines on 13 December 1862. It was one of the most one-sided battles of the war, a bloody defeat that cost Burnside 13,000 casualties and gained him no advantage whatever.

Following the battle of Fredericksburg, Burnside withdrew across the Rappahannock to lick his wounds. Lee, who had lost about 5000 men at Fredericksburg, remained in his old lines with a force of about 70,000. As Burnside began regaining his confidence, he developed a new strategy to outflank Lee's position by crossing the Rappahannock at Muddy Creek, seven miles below Fredericksburg. During the week before Christmas he constructed roadways to the crossing point and ordered artillery positions to be selected nearby. Supplies were prepared and stowed in wagons, and on 26 December the troops were ordered to prepare a three day's supply of cooked rations, a sure sign that a march was imminent. All the officers were directed to be ready to move out on a moment's notice.

In order to draw Lee's attention away from the projected crossing at Muddy Creek, Burnside determined to send a cavalry foray against the river crossings upstream (west) of Fredericksburg. Some units were to feint in the direction of Warrenton and

*The bombardment of Fredericksburg by the Federals on 11 December 1862.*

Culpeper, while eight chosen regiments under Brigadier General W. W. Averell struck for Raccoon Ford on the Rapidan. Averell wanted to develop the feint into a major raid—if he made it safely across the Rapidan, he could try to cut the railroad lines west and south of Fredericksburg, and then could head east to the safety of the Union lines at Suffolk.

Averell's expedition was underway on 29 December and reached Kelly's Ford on the Rappahannock the next day. We will never know how far he could have pushed his raiding party, for he was recalled on the 30th under some rather strange circumstances. On the evening of the 30th, just as he was preparing to begin his movement to Muddy Creek, Burnside received the following curt telegram from President Lincoln in Washington. It was sent at 1530 that afternoon and read as follows: "I have good reason for saying that you must not make a general movement of the army without letting me know." Burnside dutifully recalled Averell's cavalry, and telegraphed the president that he would come to Washington the next day to discuss the situation. He thought that the president might be attempting to better coordinate Burnside's movements with those of the other forces in the theater.

Lincoln, had a quite different agenda for his meeting with Burnside on 1 January 1863. In the previous few days he had received disturbing news from the *Army of the Potomac* that morale was terribly low and neither the men nor their officers trusted Burnside to lead them into another battle. Matters came to a head when two brigadier generals of the *VI Corps*, John Newton and John Cochrane, came to Washington after Christmas to complain about Burnside. It seems that there was a large group of officers in the army, many of them supporters of twice deposed Major General George B. McClellan, who did not care at all for Burnside. The bloody disaster at Fredericksburg only cemented their low opinion of him. Newton and Cochrane were just two of the lower level dissidents. They shared their dislike of Burnside with two of their superiors Major General William F. "Baldy" Smith (commander of the *VI Corps*), and Major General William B. Franklin (commander of the *Left Grand Division*), and had received encouragement to take their complaints to Washington. The two brigadiers intended to see two members of Congress with whom they were familiar—Senator Henry Wilson of Massachusetts, chairman of the Senate Military Committee, and Congressman Moses F. Odell of New York, a member of the Joint Committee on the Conduct of the War. However, these two worthies were not in the capital because Congress was recessed for the holidays. Cochrane, who had been a U.S. congressman from New York City before the war, now decided to pay a call on William H. Seward, former governor of New York who was presently serving as Lincoln's secretary of state. Their comments about the army's leadership so disturbed Seward that he took the two generals for an interview with the president. This was higher than Newton and Cochrane had intended to go with their complaints. At first they gave the impression that they were two self-serving officers seeking advancement by carping at their distressed superior. Cochrane, though, spoke long and well to dispel this appearance and insisted that their only motive was patriotism. Newton was at first less direct; he said later that he found it difficult to tell the president "that the whole trouble was that the privates had no confidence in General Burnside." Eventually he did blurt out that he thought the army might be completely destroyed if it met another defeat along the Rappahannock. Before leaving, the two generals strongly urged Lincoln to investigate the condition of the army himself. The president was to believe their allegations since the two generals did not appear to be pushing for their own advancement nor were they making a strong case for the advancement of another candidate to supplant Burnside.

The statements made by Newton and Cochrane had so disturbed the president that he issued the 30 December telegram already mentioned directing Burnside not to make any unauthorized movements. He was prepared to discuss the situation openly with Burnside when the general arrived in Washington, and even directed Edwin M. Stanton, the secretary of war, and Major General Henry W. Halleck, to be present at the meeting held on the morning of 1 July.

General Burnside, as might be expected, was not at all pleased to hear the criticisms made of his leadership and the army's condition. He insisted that Lincoln reveal the identity of his two informants which the president refused to do because he wanted them to be cashiered for insubordination. Halleck supported Burnside on the cashiering issue, but no consensus was reached on the general problem, and the inconclusive meeting broke up.

Burnside's ego was considerably abused by the course of the meeting, so much so that he felt it necessary to restate his position in a letter he wrote to the president later on 1 January. Here he also took up the offensive by making charges against the competency of Secretary Stanton and General Halleck: "The Secretary of War has not the confidence of the officers and soldiers, and I feel sure that he has not the confidence of the country....The same opinion applies with equal force in regard to General Halleck." Burnside, though, did admit that he lacked the confidence of his principal officers, all of whom were resisting his efforts to make a new offensive. In view of this situation, Burnside concluded that it might be best "to promote the public good" if he retired to private life. He also hinted that it would be in the public interest to do something about Stanton and Halleck.

Lincoln at first was not inclined to fire Burnside or accept his offer to consider resignation. Instead, he decided to send General Halleck to Falmouth to investigate conditions in the army and determine the advisability of an advance. He may also have wanted more time and input to determine a potential successor to Burnside.

Lincoln's purpose in sending Halleck instead of someone else probably also had a specific purpose. Halleck had performed notable service earlier in the war when he helped design the successful Union strategy employed in the western theater of operations. However, he had not performed as well since he came to Washington as general in chief in July 1862. It was no doubt with this in mind that Lincoln ended his 1 January instructions to Halleck with the curt phrase, "If in such a difficulty as this you do not help, you fail me precisely in the point for which I sought your assistance."

Halleck was at once affronted by the tone of Lincoln's statement. Later that same day, he wrote a letter to Secretary Stanton expressing his concern over the "very important difference of opinion in regard to my relations toward generals commanding armies in the field." Halleck continued by admitting "I cannot perform the duties of my present office satisfactorily at the same time to the President and to myself." He felt that he had no choice but to offer his resignation.

Stanton quickly conveyed Halleck's letter to Lincoln, and the president was left in a quandary. Halleck certainly had his shortcomings, but he performed useful duties as the army's head administrator. Lincoln did not like the prospect of possibly making several major command replacements at the same time, so he mended fences with Halleck for the moment. His order for Halleck to proceed to Falmouth was filed with a note in Lincoln's own handwriting that stated, "Withdrawn, because considered harsh by General Halleck."

Within a week Burnside was also attempting to mend fences with Halleck. On 5 January he wrote his general in chief stating that he had determined to attempt another crossing of the river rather than go into winter quarters. Since he did not have the support of his own officers for such a movement, Burnside continued, he especially needed some "general directions" from his superior. Halleck responded two days later with a somewhat conciliatory letter approving an advance. However, he declined to give Burnside any detailed instructions. He also added a reminder that Burnside's primary objective should be the defeat or scattering of Lee's army, not the capture of Richmond.

*The confusion on the Mud March.*

*Major General Ambrose E. Burnside is better remembered for his sideburns than for his generalship.*

Burnside was still painfully aware of his tenuous station as army commander, and on 5 January he again wrote to the president offering to resign. When Lincoln did not press the issue, but instead endorsed an advance if Burnside thought that strategy best, the general began to formulate his plans. Since he had no desire to assault Lee's Fredericksburg lines again, and news had already leaked out on his attempt to cross downstream at Port Royal, he decided he would attempt to cross the Rappahannock upstream from Fredericksburg in an effort to get behind Lee's army. It was not a bad plan, but was definitely a risky one, especially in view of potential problems from the weather—it was, after all, the middle of the winter, even if the weather had been unusually mild since the fight at Fredericksburg in December. But Burnside insisted on pursuing a new campaign, since he desperately needed some sort of success in order to keep his command.

Burnside needed two weeks of preparation for his new advance. The movement finally began on 20 January, but to Burnside's great misfortune a heavy cold rain began that evening and went on for two days. Soon all the roads turned into quagmires and the army was stuck in its tracks.

The Mud March fiasco caused the morale of the troops to sink to a new low. It also brought a new round of criticism of Burnside himself. Burnside was all too aware that his last gamble had failed and that his days as a commander were numbered. He vented his frustrations by preparing orders to relieve those generals who had been most critical of him. His "General Orders No. 8" was dated 23 January 1863, the last day of the Mud March. Its primary target was Major General Joseph Hooker, commander of the entire *Center Grand Division*. Burnside and Hooker had not gotten

# The Mud March

Union army commander Major General Ambrose E. Burnside was desperate for any kind of success in order to retain his command in the dark days following the disaster at Fredericksburg on 13 December 1862. Late in December a crossing of the Rappahannock below Fredericksburg was canceled on orders from Washington. Once news of these plans leaked out to Lee, Burnside felt he could no longer achieve the surprise he needed in that quarter. Since another direct attack on Fredericksburg was totally out of the question—portions of the army might have mutinied if ordered to make any more assaults there—the only choice left to Burnside was to try to cross the Rappahannock at one of the numerous fords west of Fredericksburg, and then try to move against Lee's flank or rear. Such a strategy was not a bad one, and would indeed be the same employed by Joe Hooker the next spring. Rapid movement and proper use of screening forces would be needed to effect the crossing. The key to the matter, though, would be the weather, as Burnside well understood. Any sudden rain or snow storm would render the roads muddy enough to slow a moving army to a crawl. The weather had been relatively mild since the freezing night at the battle of Fredericksburg, and Burnside was willing to stake his career on a gamble it would stay mild long enough for him to run his campaign. The risk was certainly a long shot, since it was the end of January, but Burnside felt he had to take it because he had his back to the wall.

After personal reconnoitering, Burnside decided to make his crossing at Banks' Ford and United States Ford, which were respectively five and eight miles above Fredericksburg. Some 150 artillery pieces would be positioned along the Rappahannock from the army's camps at Falmouth to the crossing points with orders to keep all opposing enemy units pinned down. Franklin's *Left Grand Division* and Hooker's *Center Grand Division* would cross the fords on pontoon bridges while Sumner's *Right Grand Division* made an early morning threat to cross and attack at Fredericksburg. Hopefully Sumner would occupy Lee's attention until Franklin and Hooker finished crossing. He would then lead his troops west to cross the pontoon bridges also. The army's rear area and supply line from Falmouth to Aquia Creek would be guarded by Major General Franz Sigel's newly formed *Reserve Grand Division*.

Burnside scheduled the movement to begin on 18 January 1863, and made all the necessary preparations—the sick were sent to the rear, leaves of absence were canceled, military gear was checked and rechecked, and fresh ammunition was issued to the troops. The Union veterans were well aware that these signs portended the start of a major movement. However, Confederate pickets somehow learned of these preparations and as a result began strengthening their outposts that guarded the river crossings. On the night of 17 January, the eve of the proposed attack, nervous Confederate pockets began launching signal rockets at United States Ford. Their alertness forced Burnside to alter his plans slightly—the crossing was postponed two days to 20 January, and would now be made entirely at Banks' Ford, three miles downstream from United States Ford.

On the morning of the 20th, Burnside's troops packed their gear and cooked three days rations for the campaign. The weather, which had been moderate the day before, became cloudy as a cold northeast wind began to blow. The lead units broke camp and headed for Banks' Ford, where they were to meet the pontoon bridges. Because of the great number of troops involved, the rear units did not begin to move out until midafternoon.

All went well until about 1600, when it started to rain. For a while the precipitation turned to sleet, and then settled to a cold, hard, pouring rain. The roads soon became slippery and then turned into liquid mud. Teams had to be doubled up in order to draw the guns and caissons, and many troops did not reach their assigned camps until midnight. The men were under strict orders not to light any fires, but soon hundreds were burning. One New Jersey soldier wrote, "Pine rails were plenty and they were used freely. The piercing northwest blast chilled one side while the fire heated the other, and the smoke was not minded."

Early on the 21st Brigadier General Daniel Woodbury, commander of the army's engineers, wrote Burnside from Banks' Ford that the movement was behind schedule and the element of surprise had been lost. "Our campfires last night presented the appearance of a large sea of fire. Our smoke today covers the country and reaches far beyond the opposite banks. Before the rain began, we had every prospect of being able to throw three bridges over at daylight. The rain has prevented surprise, and changed our condition entirely. It seems to me to be the part of prudence to abandon the present effort, not only because the enemy must be aware of our intention, but because the roads are everywhere impassable."

Burnside would not change his plans, even though the cold rain continued unabated. The soaked and frozen troops formed up and, as one wag was later put it, "began to wade on to glory." The roads were so mucky and sticky that many men found quicker going in the fields and woods instead. Even so, they had to struggle to cover a mile an hour. The wagons and cannons that stayed on the roads sank in the mud up to their axles, so that twelve horses could not move a small field gun. To make matters even worse, Hooker's command did not receive its promised guide, and early in the morning of the 21st crossed paths with Franklin's corps. The resulting traffic jam took hours to straighten out. Meanwhile, Woodbury's exhausted engineers struggled all day to put a few pontoons in the river. Most of the cumbersome boat wagons were mired in the approach roads. Not even triple horse teams or long ropes pulled by 150 men each could move them.

The rain slowed to a drizzle on the night of the 21st, as the troops sought what shelter and warmth they could find.

By dawn the torrential downpours returned, and the soaked troops could hardly move. The entire *V Corps* was set to work cordoroying roads by chopping down trees and laying them lengthwise across the roadways. Later in the morning some men of the *118th Pennsylvania* and *25th New York* of Barnes' brigade held a tree-cutting contest. This good natured competition soon degenerated into a brawl when some of the troops, fortified by a whiskey ration issued at Burnside's order, took out their frustrations by starting a fight with their comrades. It was not long before the whole brigade was involved in the fracas. The disturbance was not able to be halted until a battery was brought up and two full regiments leveled their guns on the miscreants.

The sight of the soggy Yankees stuck in the mud provided an interesting spectacle to Confederate pickets posted across the river. Numerous signs written in charcoal began to appear on the south side of the Rappahannock: "Burnside Stuck in the Mud", "This way to Richmond," "Shan't we come over and pull you out?."

At noon on the 22nd, Burnside finally admitted that the movement was going nowhere, and directed his men to return to their camps at Falmouth. However, retiring on the muddy roads proved to be just as difficult as advancing. The *4th New York*, which had covered two miles that morning, was strained simply to return to its camp of the previous night. Many horses were so exhausted from overwork and lack of fodder that they could not be pulled out of the mud when they fell into the knee deep muck; they had to be shot on the spot. Colonel Rufus Dawes of the *6th Wisconsin* recounted that his regiment had only one ambulance, which was soon filled with sick and disabled men. "It was a hard decision for our surgeons as to who should ride and who march. As the column was about to move, a man came out of the ranks and declared himself too sick to march. The surgeon could not displace sick men who were already in the overloaded vehicle. The poor fellow succeeded in marching about half the distance to our camp, when he laid down in the mud in a fence corner and died. He had not before been even reported on the sick list."

The weather began to clear on the 23rd, though the roads remained mucky. The next day ironically turned out to be sunny. The exhausted troops began to arrive in their old camps at Falmouth that afternoon. Many would remember the "Mud March" as one of their hardest campaigns, even though they saw no fighting. Some of the army's generals were actually delighted that the bad weather had prevented Burnside from engaging in another battle. Major General George Meade, commander of the *V Corps*, was more compassionate: "I never felt so disappointed and sorry for anyone in my life as I did for Burnside. He really seems to have even the elements against him."

*Scenes from Burnside's infamous "Mud March" of 20-24 January 1863.*

# Ambrose E. Burnside

Ambrose Everett Burnside, ill-starred commander of the *Army of the Potomac* at the disastrous battle of Fredericksburg, was born in Liberty, Indiana, on 23 May 1864. His father had owned slaves in South Carolina before he set them free and moved to Indiana. Young Ambrose was trained to be a tailor, but at age nineteen he decided to seek an appointment to West Point by using his father's political connections. He graduated from the military academy in 1847, ranking in the middle of his class (eighteenth of 38). He was at once sent to Mexico as a brevet second lieutenant, but did not wish glory in battle as did many of his colleagues; most of his service was on garrison duty in Mexico City. After the war he was assigned to the Indian Campaigns in the Southwest. Here he was slightly wounded during a fight with the Apaches in 1849, the only wound he would receive during his military career.

Like many of his fellow officers, Burnside became disenchanted with army life and its limited prospects for advancement. He resigned his commission in 1853, and moved to Bristol, Rhode Island, to manufacture a fifty-four calibre breech loading carbine he had invented while in the army. The weapon, which he patented on 25 March 1856, was the first American gun to use a metallic cartridge. However, it proved to be fragile in use because it had no forestock and used an unperfected tape priming mechanism. Burnside had produced only a few hundred guns when his company, the Bristol Firearms Co., was put out of business during the troubled financial times that followed the Panic of 1857.

By May, 1858, Burnside was desperate for a job, so he wrote to his old army friend and fellow Democrat, George B. McClellan, who was a vice-president with the Illinois Central Railroad. McClellan was able to offer him a post as a cashier, which Burnside readily accepted. McClellan also offered to share his large house in Chicago, and the friendship of the two future generals became even closer.

Burnside's finances recovered enough under McClellan's tutelage to enable him to start a new gun manufacturing establishment, the Burnside Rifle Co. of Providence, Rhode Island. In 1860, he sold about 1500 of his carbines but the troops did not like the lack of a forestock. When Burnside added a wooden forestock in 1862, sales skyrocketted. The gun was particularly popular with cavalrymen. Altogether Burnside's company produced over 55,000 carbines and 22,000,000 cartridges during the war.

Burnside was too ambitious to remain long on the sidelines when the war broke out. In early 1861, he used his military experience and personal connections to win appointment of the 1st Rhode Island Infantry, which was one of the first regiments to reach Washington D.C. He commanded a brigade at First Bull Run, where he was heavily engaged in the piecemeal attacks on Matthews Hill during the early part of the engagement. In spite of his Democratic politics, Burnside somehow became a favorite of President Lincoln, perhaps because they had come to know each other during Burnside's stay in Chicago. He was appointed brigadier general on 6 August 1861, and was soon given command of an amphibious campaign against North Carolina coast. Burnside's capture of Roanoke Island and New Berne in early 1862 increased Northern morale, and won him a promotion to major general as of 18 March 1862.

Some sources claim that Burnside was offered command of the *Army of the Potomac* following McClellan's defeat in the Seven Days' battles at Richmond, but if he was, he declined to supplant his old friend. Later in July, most of Burnside's North Carolina command was organized as the *IX Corps*. He participated in the Second Bull Run campaign but was not present at the battle. He then led his corps at South Mountain, and at Antietam, where he was supposed to lead a wing consisting of Joe Hooker's *I Corps* and his own *IX Corps*. However, as the battle developed, Hooker went into action on the right while Burnside was posted on the left wing. Burnside's delay in locating fords over Antietam Creek and slowness in mounting a final attack once he carried "Burnside's Bridge" enabled Lee to salvage a drawn battle.

Burnside was not actively seeking army command and accepted the post very reluctantly when McClellan was discharged on November 10, 1862. He had proved to be an adequate corps commander, but lacked confidence in his ability to lead the army—a correct feeling, as events would show. Some historians believe that he was persuaded to accept army command only to thwart his main rival, Joe Hooker. During his brief tenure in command Burnside did not enjoy the full support of all his leading officers, a distrust that was deepened by his poor judgement in ordering assault after assault on Marye's Heights at Fredericksburg. Reportedly he was so distraught at the loss of the battle that he wanted to lead his *IX Corps* personally in one last charge on the Confederate lines—a definite death wish. When his "Mud March" ended in utter failure, few men in the army were sad to see him go and be replaced by Hooker on January 26, 1863.

It is quite surprising that Burnside was not retired or assigned a desk job after he was relieved as commander of the *Army of the Potomac*. Exactly two months later, on 25 March 1863, he was named commander of the Department of the Ohio. Here he won attention by arresting copperhead political leader Clement L. Vallandigham, and by directing the successful pursuit and capture of the Confederate cavalryman John Hunt Morgan during a raid into Ohio in July. Burnside also did a good job defending Knoxville, Tennessee, against an attack by Confederate General James Longstreet at the end of 1863.

The spring of 1864 brought Burnside and his *IX Corps* back to the Virginia theater. This brought on an awkward situation because Burnside was senior to George G. Meade, commander of the *Army of the Potomac* since Gettysburg. General Grant resolved the situation by keeping the *IX Corps* separate from

Meade's army and having Burnside report directly to Grant's headquarters. This arrangement worked well enough, and Burnside led his corps in all the battles from the Wilderness to Petersburg. Growing friction with Grant and Burnside finally led to latters replacement as corps commander after he mismanaged the primary attack at the Battle of the Crater on 30 July 1864. Burnside did not resign his commission, though, until 15 April 1865, soon after Lee surrendered.

Burnside enjoyed an active and profitable life in business and government after the war. He became a director of several railroads and corporations, and was elected Governor of Rhode Island three times (1866,1867,1868). In 1874 he was elected to the United States Senate from Rhode Island, and was still serving there when he died on 13 September 1881. The general was buried in Providence.

Burnside is a classic case of a good administrator and competent corps commander who was promoted beyond his ability when he became army commander. He was well aware of his limitations and was reluctant to take or hold supreme command. He did the best he could as army commander, but it is too bad for the thousands of unnecessary casualties at Fredericksburg that Lincoln did not find a better successor to McClellan. General Burnside is best remembered today for the long mutton chop whiskers he wore—now called "sideburns" in his memory.

*Major General Ambrose E. Burnside, beleaguered commander of the* Army of the Potomac *in early 1863.*

along for some time, and their relationship became even move strained when Hooker in his report on the battle of South Mountain glorified his own troops at the expense of Burnside, who had been his superior there. Burnside also felt that Hooker dragged his feet at Fredericksburg and was afterwards too openly critical of his commander for his own personal gain. As a result, Burnside ordered Hooker to be relieved for being "guilty of unjust and unnecessary criticisms of the actions of his superior officers, and of the authorities, and having, by the general tone of his conversation, endeavored to create distrust in the minds of officers who have associated with him, and having, by omissions and otherwise, made reports and statements which were calculated to create inaccurate impressions, and for habitually speaking in disparaging terms of other officers."

It is interesting to note that General U.S. Grant, under whom Hooker served later in the war, shared Burnside's opinion of Hooker. Grant wrote in his *Memoirs*, "I regarded him as a dangerous man. He was not subordinate to his superiors. He was ambitious to the extent of caring nothing for the rights of others. His disposition was, when engaged in battle, to get detached from the main body of the army and exercise a separate command, gathering to his standard all he could of his juniors."

Burnside's order also relieved brigadier generals John Newton and John Cochrane "for going to the President of the United States with criticisms of the plans of their commanding officer." It is clear Burnside had learned the true identities of the two generals who had undermined his attempt to cross the Rappahannock at the end of December. Burnside rightly felt that Newton and Cochrane could not have been acting without the knowledge of their superiors, Major General William B. Franklin of the *IV Corps* and Major General Baldy Smith of the *Center Grand Division*, so he relieved them also. For some reason, he also relieved Smith's assistant adjutant general, Lieutenant Colonel J. S. Taylor. While he was at it, Burnside also chose to relieve another of Smith's division commanders, Brigadier General W. T. H. Brooks, "for complaining of the policy of the government and for using language tending to demoralize his command." Burnside's final dart was thrown at one of the brigadier generals of his beloved *IX Corps*. Edward Ferrero was to be relieved for no offense worse than overstaying a leave of absence.

Burnside was aware of the controversy that would accompany the dismissal of so many officers, so he conditioned the removal of Hooker, Brooks, Cochrane and Newton "subject to the approval of the President." He then prepared to leave for Washington to explain the situation to the president in person.

# CHAPTER II

# Hooker Takes Command

## Late January, 1863

*P*resident Lincoln had not been satisfied with Burnside's performance for several weeks, and so was not surprised when Burnside requested an interview right after the failure of the Mud March. Their meeting at 1000 on 25 January 1863, did not last long. Lincoln properly saw Burnside's General Orders No. 8 as an ultimatum, the only terms by which Burnside would consent to remain in command. The president refused to approve Burnside's orders, and was prepared for the consequences. Burnside promptly offered his resignation, and Lincoln promptly accepted it.

Lincoln now had to choose a successor for Burnside. This was a difficult decision he had been pondering for a number of weeks, for there was no clearcut favorite for the position. If there had been, he would have relieved Burnside much sooner. The leading officers in the *Army of the Potomac* were united in their distrust of Burnside, but most were not otherwise especially friendly to each other; many were still divided into McClellan and anti-McClellan camps, a division that often split along political lines, since McClellan was a Democrat. There were even those in the government who urged McClellan's appointment for a third tenure in command, but Lincoln refused to listen to them. The president might have liked to find a successor from outside the Virginia theater, but the best candidate, W.S. Rosecrans, was having his own problems in Tennessee at the time. Lincoln also recalled how coldly the *Army of the Potomac* had received an outsider, John Pope, as commander the previous summer. As a result, he needed to appoint someone from the *Army of the Potomac* to be its new commander.

There was no clearcut favorite in the army to serve as Burnside's successor. All three of the army's senior officers had well known weaknesses that hindered their candidacies. Major General Edwin V. Sumner, commander of the *Right Grand Division*, was a competent and respected officer, but his age and health did not recommend him for higher command. He was over sixty-five years old, and the pressures of command and field service during the previous year had taken a heavy toll on him physically. Major General William B. Franklin, commander of the *Left Grand Division*, had fought well in the Seven Days Battles and at South Mountain. Burnside's woeful handling of the

*Major General William B. Franklin, leader of the anti-Burnside element, was transferred out west soon after Hooker took command of the* Army of the Potomac.

army at Fredericksburg soured Franklin so much that he became the leader of the movement to dump the commander. On 20 December 1862, Franklin and his crony Baldy Smith had sent a long letter to President Lincoln criticizing Burnside's plans for an overland attack on Richmond; they instead favored another McClellan style movement up the James. A few days later Franklin encouraged brigadier generals Newton and Cochrane to go to Washington to complain about Burnside's leadership, as discussed in the previous chapter. Franklin's machinations were well known and the divisiveness he caused made him a less desireable candidate to lead the army and bring unity to its officer corps. The same criticism was made of Major General Joseph Hooker, commander of the army's *Center Grand Division*. Hooker had been openly critical of Burnside's generalship, and once had even condemned President Lincoln as an incompetent. His attitude did not endear him to his fellow officers and he enjoyed little popularity outside his immediate command. In addition, the president did not much care for Hooker's reputation for drinking and womanizing, and General Halleck and Secretary of War Stanton distrusted his ability to hold independent command.

The faults of the army's three wing commanders forced Lincoln and his advisors to scrutinize the army's other major generals as possible successors to Burnside. Major

General Darius N. Couch, commander of the *II Corps* at Fredericksburg, was a good leader but was found to be too closely allied with the McClellan camp to suit everyone. Major General John F. Reynolds, commander of the *I Corps*, was known as an excellent fighter, and was briefly approached by Secretary Stanton on the question of army command. Reynolds responded that he would not voluntarily undertake command "unless a liberty of action should be guaranteed to him considerably beyond any which he had reason to expect." This blunt response by Reynolds took him out of the running. The third major general under serious consideration was George G. Meade, a division commander in Reynolds' corps. Meade was respected for his fighting ability and had been one of the few Union generals to earn distinction for his handling of his men at Fredericksburg. Meade's candidacy was enhanced by the fact that he had no political goals and was not a member of the McClellan or anti-Burnside camps.

Thus, Major General Meade seemed the best qualified to be Burnside's successor as army commander. However, when the moment to appoint a new commander came on 25 January, some of Lincoln's advisors hesitated to endorse Meade because he was only a division commander. At the last minute Hooker's candidacy was rejuvenated by those who believed he was the least objectionable of the army's three senior commanders. Hooker also found unexpected support from a group of Republican politicians who favored him as a means for helping Secretary of the Treasury Salmon P. Chase win the nomination to succeed Lincoln to the Presidency. It seems that some of Hooker's supporters promised Chase's camp that their man would support Chase's aspirations in return for Chase's support of Hooker's candidacy for army command. Soon Chase and Hooker were informed of the arrangements and gave their approval.

Chase's support proved to be decisive for Hooker. President Lincoln was anxious to keep the Republican party as unified as possible, and also greatly needed Chase's help with some problems he was having in trying to finance the war. Since no one was forcefully backing Meade or any other candidate for Burnside's job, Lincoln at last gave his consent to the appointment of Chase's favored candidate, Hooker. Hooker's appointment put Secretary of War Stanton in an awkward situation, since he distrusted the new army commander and had spoken out strongly against him. Stanton's first inclination was to offer his resignation. Later, though, he decided to remain loyal to the president and support Hooker in hopes that he would lead the army better than Burnside had done.

Later on 25 January the president issued General Orders Number 20, announcing that Burnside was relieved at his own request and was to be replaced by Hooker. Significantly, the directive also relieved two other generals from duty with the army—major generals E. V. Sumner and W. B. Franklin. Sumner was relieved at his own request because he was getting too old for field service. At 65, he was one of the oldest field generals in the Union army. He was reassigned to duty in the Department of Missouri but died two months later before reaching his post. Clearly, Franklin was relieved for his leading role in stirring up the army's officer corps against Burnside. He was reassigned to duty in the western theater, where he was wounded at the battle of Sabine Crossroads while commanding the *XIX Corps*. Lincoln's decision to relieve Sumner and Franklin was a wise one as it removed two of Hooker's principal rivals from the army, so giving the new commander the opportunity to develop a more harmonious and unified command. Franklin's departure in particular signalled to Smith and other Burnside critics to be more supportive of their head commander. It

*Major General "Fighting Joe" Hooker did not live up to his reputation at Chancellorsville.*

is also significant that Burnside, Sumner and Franklin were the last remaining leaders who had held high rank under McClellan. Their leaving marked the end of McClellan's influence with the army and the beginning of what Lincoln hoped would be a more aggressive and winning leadership team.

The next day President Lincoln penned a personal letter to the new army commander promising his support but urging him to take counsel of his actions. The letter, quoted here in full, is remarkable for its bluntness. The president was well aware of Hooker's military skill and lack of political aspirations, but was also concerned about Hooker's character and decisiveness:

EXECUTIVE MANSION,
Washington, D.C., January 26, 1863.
Major-General Hooker:
General: I have placed you at the head of the Army of the Potomac. Of course I have done this upon what appears to me to be sufficient reasons, and yet I think it best for you to know that there are some things in regard to which I am not quite satisfied with you. I believe you to be a brave and skillful soldier, which, of course, I like. I also believe you do not mix politics with your profession, in which you are right. You have confidence in yourself, which is a valuable, if not an indispensable, quality. You are

ambitious, which, within reasonable bounds, does good rather than harm; but I think that during General Burnside's command of the army you have taken counsel of your ambition, and thwarted him as much as you could, in which you did a great wrong to the country and to a most meritorious and honorable brother officer. I have heard, in such a way as to believe it, of your recently saying that both the Army and the Government needed a dictator. Of course, it was not for this, but in spite of it, that I have given you the command. Only those generals who gain successes can set up dictators. What I now ask of you is military success, and I will risk the dictatorship. The Government will support you to the utmost of its ability, which is neither more nor less than it has done and will do for all commanders. I much fear that the spirit which you have aided to infuse into the army, of criticizing their commander and withholding confidence from him will now turn upon you. I shall assist you as far as I can to put it down. Neither you nor Napoleon, if he were alive again, could get any good out of an army while such a spirit prevails in it. And now beware of rashness. Beware of rashness, but with energy and sleepless vigilance go forward and give us victories.

Yours, very truly

A. LINCOLN

Noah Brooks, one of Lincoln's close friends, happened to be in Hooker's camp when the general received Lincoln's letter. Brooks later recorded that Hooker "finished reading it almost with tears in his eyes; and as he folded it and put it back in

*Major General E. V. Sumner was considered too old to hold army command.*

# Joseph Hooker

"Fighting Joe" Hooker was born in Hadley, Massachusetts, on 13 November 1814. His grandfather served as a captain during the Revolution. Young Joseph decided to continue this military tradition and entered West Point in 1833; he graduated four years later ranking twenty-ninth in a class of fifty. His service was commendable the next few years as he saw duty in Florida (Second Seminole War), along the Canadian border, and as adjutant at West Point. He then performed notably in the Mexican War, where he served with Generals Zachary Taylor and Winfield Scott and won battlefield promotions at Monterrey, National Bridge, and Chapultepec. At war's end he held the rank of brevet lieutenant colonel, but he had also incurred the wrath of General Scott by supporting Gideon Pillow in a quarrel between the two generals.

Like so many of his fellow officers, Hooker found postwar army life dull after the excitement of combat in Mexico. He served in California as assistant adjutant general of the Pacific Division from 1849-1851, and then went on an extended leave of absence. He finally resigned in 1853 to become a farmer in Sonoma, California. When this effort proved unprofitable, he became county road overseer, and then moved to Oregon to become superintendent of military roads there.

Hooker was certainly restless at his lack of success in civilian life. The coming of the war in 1861 rekindled his enthusiasm for active military service. At the time he was a Colonel of militia in California, but he was certain that he could win a higher appointment in Washington D.C. The biggest immediate problem was that he was so broke he had to borrow money from his friends in order to be able to pay for his trip east. Once in the capital, he met another obstacle—his application for command was rejected by the government, perhaps because of the grudge held by General in

*Major General "Fighting Joe" Hooker.*

Chief Scott over the Pillow affair in Mexico.

Thus Hooker witnessed the battle of First Bull Run as a civilian bystander. Soon after he pushed his personal cause by obtaining an interview with the President. His response at being incorrectly introduced as Captain Hooker was typical of his brashness: "Mr. President, I am not 'Captain' Hooker, but was one Lieutenant-Colonel Hooker of the regular army. I was lately a farmer in California, but since the Rebellion broke out I have been here trying to get into the service, and I find that I'm not wanted. I am about to return home, but before going I was anxious to pay my respects to you, and to express my wishes for your personal welfare and success in quelling the Rebellion. And I want to say a word more. I was at Bull Run the other day, Mr. President, and it is no vanity in me to say that I am a dammed sight better general than any you had on that field."

Hooker's boldness was rewarded with an appointment as brigadier general, dated retroactively to 17 May 1861. He liked to point out later that his commission was two numbers higher than that of an obscure Illinois general named U.S. Grant.

Hooker was at first assigned to the defense of Washington. As the army grew, he rose to command a division that was eventually assigned as the *Second Division* of Heintzelman's *III Corps*. During the Peninsula Campaign and the Seven Days Battles he was often in the thick of the fighting and won attention for his leadership. At the battle of Williamsburg he had a horse shot from under him, and soon wore the nickname "Fighting Joe." He later led his division at Second Bull Run, and was promoted to command of the *I Corps* during the Antietam Campaign. He handled his men well at the battle of South Mountain, where he fought as part of the army wing led by Ambrose E. Burnside. Hooker did not much care for Burnside, and at the battle of Antietam found himself fighting on the army's right wing while Burnside

---

the breast of his coat, he said, 'That is just such a letter as a father might write to a son. It is a beautiful letter, and although I think he was harder on me than I deserved, I will say that I love the man who wrote it'." Brooks' account, though, does not seem totally compatible with what we know of Hooker's character. It may have been reshaped for the purpose of magnifying Lincoln's stature. Another version of Hooker's response to the letter has him saying, "He [the president] talks to me like a father. I shall not answer his letter until I have won him a great victory." This seems to be more in line with what Hooker actually may have said.

The army's change of command took place on the 26th. Before leaving his post, Burnside issued his last General Orders, in which he regretted his lack of success and

commanded the army's far left. About 0900 he was hit in the foot by a Confederate sharpshooter and had to leave the battlefield. He would be on sick leave for seven weeks recovering.

Upon his return to the army in November, Hooker was appointed commander of the newly formed *Center Grand Division* (*III* and *V Corps*) by new army commander Ambrose Burnside. During the battle of Fredericksburg on 13 December, Hooker was ordered to conduct charge after charge against the strong Confederate position on Marye's Heights. The heavy casualties and senseless slaughter confirmed Hooker's belief that Burnside was unfit to command the army. He did not hesitate to criticize his superior after the battle, and was at the center of much of the controversey attending Burnside's removal from command after the Mud March fiasco, as discussed in the text. President Lincoln was aware of Hooker's character and personal short comings (he was a heavy drinker and a womanizer), and was not eager to appoint him as Burnside's successor. Eventually, though, he was persuaded to accept Hooker by several key cabinet officials who backed "Fighting Joe" for their own personal reasons.

Hooker's reorganization of the army and restoration of its morale was a key contribution to the Union war effort. At the battle of Chancellorsville he gained an initial advantage over Lee through his well planned flanking maneuver, but then allowed himself to be outgeneraled. It should be pointed out that he was

stunned by a cannon ball on the evening of 2 May, and was not thinking clearly afterwards. (Detractors have accused him of being drunk during the battle).

Hooker remained in command of the army after Chancellorsville, but did not have Lincoln's full confidence. During the Gettysburg campaign he quarreled with army chief Henry W. Halleck over use of the garrison at Harper's Ferry, and submitted his resignation when the garrison was not put under his control. Lincoln accepted and replaced Hooker with Major General George G. Meade on 28 June 1863, just three days before the battle of Gettysburg would begin.

Hooker did not retire from the army as he could have, but lobbied for another field command. His wish was granted, and in September 1863 he was sent west to command the combined *XI* and *XII Corps*, which were being sent from the *Army of the Potomac* to reinforce Grant at Chattanooga. Hooker led these troops to victory at the "Battle Above the Clouds" at Lookout Mountain on 24 November, for which he was promoted to brevet major general in the Regular Army.

In April 1864 Hooker's former command was reorganized as a new *XX Corps*, still under Hooker's command. "Fighting Joe" regained much of his former reputation by his skillful handling of his corps during the campaign from Chattanooga to Atlanta. When General James B. McPherson, commander of the *Army of the Tennesee*, was killed at Atlanta on 22 July, Hooker felt he should receive McPherson's command. Sherman instead

appointed Oliver O. Howard, whom Hooker outranked. Hooker soon asked to be relieved because he could not serve in "an army in which rank and service are ignored." Sherman complied, and Hooker's war service was over. A friend who saw him later in the year "was much disappointed with his appearance: red-faced, with a lack-lustre eye and an uncertainty of gait and carriage that suggested a used-up man."

Hooker still did not resign from the army, as it was the only successful career he knew. He became an administrator and commanded the Northern Department (Michigan, Ohio, Indiana and Illinois) from October 1864 to June 1865. He was serving as Commander of the Department of the Lakes when he suffered a stroke in 1868 and was forced to retire on 15 October 1868. He lived out his last days in Garden City, New York, where he died on 31 October 1879. He lies buried in Cincinnati, his wife's home town.

Hooker was by all accounts handsome and very soldierly in bearing. He was six feet tall, and had sandy hair and steel-blue eyes. Critics said he had a weak chin, and there is no doubt his rosy complexion became more intense when he was drinking, which he did all too often. He was also known for his womanizing. In fact, the slang term "hooker" originated as a term for the type of women who used to hang aroung his headquarters—which were said to be a place to which "no gentleman cared to go and no lady could go."

---

wished the army well in the future. The document is notably restrained in its mention of Hooker, and significantly does not express good wishes to the next commander specifically.

GENERAL ORDERS HDQRS. Army of the Potomac,
No. 9. Camp near Falmouth, Va., January 26, 1863.
By direction of the President of the United States, the commanding general this day transfers the command of this army to Maj. Gen. Joseph Hooker.
The short time that he has directed your movements has not been fruitful of victory, or any considerable advancement of our lines, but it has again demonstrated an amount of courage, patience, and endurance that under more favorable circumstances

would have accomplished great results. Continue to exercise these virtues; be true in your devotion to your country and the principles you have sworn to maintain; give to the brave and skillful general who has so long been identified with your organization, and who is now to command you, your full and cordial support and co-operation, and you will deserve success.

In taking an affectionate leave of the entire army, from which he separates with so much regret, he may be pardoned if he bids an especial farewell to his long-tried associates of the *IX Corps.*

His prayers are that God may be with you, and grant you continual success until the rebellion is crushed.

By command of Major-General Burnside.
LEWIS RICHMOND,
Assistant Adjutant-General.

Hooker's first General Orders, issued the same day, were also carefully worded. He kindly wished Burnside success in the future, but did not thank him for his past services:

*Major General George G. Meade, commander of the Union V Corps, was totally disgusted with Hooker's handling of the army at Chancellorsville. He would succeed Hooker on 28 June 1863.*

GENERAL ORDERS,HDQRS. Army of the Potomac,
No. 1Camp near Falmouth, Va., January 26, 1863.

By direction of the President of the United States, the undersigned assumes command of the Army of the Potomac. He enters upon the discharge of the duties imposed by this trust with a just appreciation of their responsibility. Since the formation of this army he has been identified with its history. He has shared with you its glories and reverses with no other desire than that these relations might remain unchanged until its destiny should be accomplished. In the record of your achievements there is much to be proud of, and, with the blessing of God, we will contribute something to the renown of our arms and the success of our cause. To secure these ends, your commander will require the cheerful and zealous co-operation of every officer and soldier in this army.

In equipment, intelligence, and valor the enemy is our inferior; let us never hesitate to give him battle wherever we can find him.

The undersigned only gives expression to the feelings of this army when he conveys to our late commander, Major-General Burnside, the most cordial good wishes for his future.

My staff will be announced as soon as organized.
JOSEPH HOOKER,
Major-General, Commanding Army of the Potomac.


Hooker's next duty was to proceed to Washington for a meeting with the president and Secretary of War Stanton. The meeting took place on the morning of 27 January, and covered a number of topics. Stanton began by asking Hooker his opinion about Major General Samuel Heintzelman's request to detach the troops in the defenses of Washington from the responsibility of the commander of the *Army of the Potomac*. Hooker agreed to the request, since he wanted to concentrate his energy totally on leading his field army. As a result of this conversation, the Department of Washington was created on 2 February. The main topic of the meeting turned out to be Hooker's bad feelings about Henry Halleck, his immediate superior as general in chief of all the Union armies. Hooker was concerned that Halleck had not endorsed his appointment and so might not give him as much support as he might need, especially in light of Halleck's bias in favor of the western armies over those in Virginia. Hooker's suggestion was that he should bypass Halleck and report directly to the president, who would then keep Halleck informed on the army's activity. The proposal was a sound one, for Hooker was well aware that previous army commanders had experienced difficulty answering to three different bosses in Washington—the president, the general in chief, and the secretary of war. Hooker was in essence asking to report only to the president, which would make both his and Lincoln's jobs easier. The president's response to the request is not recorded. Since no official changes were ordered, we can only surmise that Lincoln left the chain of command as it was. Later correspondence from Washington, particularly from Halleck, however, strongly suggests that Lincoln personally requested everyone to give Hooker all the support they could. The North needed victories desperately and Hooker, despite his faults and the circumstances of his appointment, was Lincoln's choice to lead the *Army of the Potomac* to success.

*Yankees of the* 110th Pennsylvania. *These Yankees served in the* III Corps *and were heavily engaged in the battle of Chancellorsville.*

# CHAPTER III

# Reorganization

## February - March, 1863

One of Hooker's first jobs as newly appointed commander of the *Army of the Potomac* was to create his staff. He chose to retain several competent specialists who had served under McClellan and Burnside, most notably Brigadier General Seth Williams as assistant adjutant general, Brigadier General Henry J. Hunt as chief of artillery, Brigadier General Marsena R. Patrick as provost marshall general, and Colonel Rufes Ingalls as chief quartermaster. In addition, Brigadier General James A. Hardie, assistant adjutant general under McClellan and Burnside, was appointed judge advocate general. The most important staff position was that of chief of staff, whose job it was to work closely with the commander and help coordinate the army's preparations and movements. Hooker's choice for this key position was Brigadier General Charles P. Stone, a fellow Bay Stater with whom Hooker had served briefly in California after the Mexican War. Stone was a West Point graduate (1845) and was named one of the army's senior brigadiers in 1861. That fall he had the bad luck to be appointed commander of a division posted along the Potomac above Washington. On 21 October he sent part of his force across the Potomac near Leesburg, where it was routed and Colonel Edward Baker, a close friend of the president's, was killed. Stone soon became the scapegoat for the disaster, though most of the blame lay on other shoulders. He was even arrested in early 1862, and was incarcerated for 189 days without charges before being released. He was still waiting reassignment and so was very much available when Hooker selected him to be his chief of staff.

Secretary of War Stanton, however, objected strongly to Stone's appointment because of the unresolved charges against him. (For various reasons Stanton remained so hostile to Stone that he ended up driving him out of the army in 1864.) Stanton's opposition forced Hooker to drop Stone and appoint his second choice, Major General Daniel Butterfield, to be his chief of staff. Butterfield, the commander of the *V Corps*, had never attended West Point, but had been a successful businessman before the war. He was not known for his fighting abilities as much as for the excellent parties he gave. His addition to Hooker's headquarters staff would give the group a definite flavor not of Lincoln's liking.

# How "Fighting Joe" Hooker Got His Name

Major General Joe Hooker acquired his popular nickname "Fighting Joe" through a mistake made by an unknown typesetter in a New York newspaper office during the 1862 Peninsula Campaign. The following account was written by Sidney V. Howell of Brooklyn, who was working at the time as a proofreader for the New York *Courier and Enquirer*.

It was three o'clock in the morning...McClellan had come to grips with the Confederate forces, and was pressing them back upon Richmond. Every two or three hours through the night had come from the Associated Press Reporters' Agency sheets of manifold, that is, tissue paper upon which a dozen sheets (by the use of carbon sheets interleaved) could be written at once—one for each newspaper. These sheets told of desperate fighting all along McClellan's line. Among his Corps Commanders was General Hooker, whose command had been perhaps too gravely engaged.

Just as the forms—indeed the last form, was being locked, that is, the type firmly held together in a great frame that the impression might be taken for printing, came another dispatch from the reporters with the Union army. It was a continuation of the report of the fighting in which General Hooker's Corps had been so gravely involved. At the top was written "Fighting—Joe Hooker." I knew that this was so written to indicate that it should be added to what we had had before. The compositor (typesetter) who had set it up set it up as a heading, "FIGHTING JOE HOOKER."

I rapidly considered what to do; as if it were yesterday I can remember the responsibility I felt and how the thing struck me. Well, I said to myself, it makes a good heading—let it go. I fully realized that if a few other proof-readers beside myself acted as I did it would mean that Hooker would thenceforth live and die as "Fighting Joe Hooker." Some did and some did not, but enough did as I did to do the business.

The nickname "Fighting Joe" caught on fast and helped make Hooker more popular with his troops and the general public. In spite of this, Hooker did not care much for the nickname. "It sounds to me like 'Fighting Fool'. People will think I am a highwayman or a bandit."

---

Butterfield's new job, Hooker's promotion, and the departure of Sumner and Franklin left several important command posts to be filled. Franklin's job as commander of the *Left Grand Division* was filled by his crony Baldy Smith, former commander of the *VI Corps*; Smith's position as corps commander was filled by his senior division commander, John Newton. Sumner's job as commander of the *Right Grand Division* went to Major General Darius Couch, former commander of the *II Corps*; Couch's position as corps commander went to his senior division commander, Brigadier General Oliver O. Howard. Hooker assigned his old slot as commander of the *Center Grand Division* to Major General George G. Meade, former commander of the *Pennsylvania Reserves*. Butterfield's post as commander of the *V Corps* was filled by the corps' senior division commander, Major General George Sykes of the *Regulars Division*.

All these command changes left only one of Burnside's four grand division commanders at his old job. This was Major General Franz Sigel, commander of the *Reserve Grand Division*, which had not been present at Fredericksburg. In addition, only two of his eight corps commanders were veterans in their office—John Reynolds of the *I Corps* and Henry Slocum of the *XII Corps*. Besides all the changes noted above, two other corps received new commanders in January. Burnside's *IX Corps* had been led for some time by Brigadier General Orlando B. Willcox, who had often filled in for Burnside. The men of the corps would have liked to see Willcox continue in command, but he was replaced before Hooker's appointment by a more senior officer, Major General John Sedgwick. Sedgwick was an excellent officer who had been wounded while heading the *Second Division* of the *II Corps* at Antietam, but he was resented by the men of the *IX Corps* as an outsider. The *III Corps*, which had been led at Fredericksburg by Brigadier General George Stoneman, also had a new commander. Stoneman was in the process of being reassigned, so acting corps command was assigned to his senior divisional commander, Brigadier General Daniel E. Sickles. This appointment annoyed a number of generals in the army who outranked Sickles.

All these newly appointed grand division and corps commanders had held their posts only a week when Hooker decided to do away with the grand divisions and return to the corps as his largest operational group. His decision was sound on administrative and personal terms. There was certainly no doubt that time was lost by having to issue commands to the corps through the grand division commanders, rather than by issuing orders directly to the corps. The grand division arrangement had proved awkward at Fredericksburg when infantry divisions were sent into action several times without orders going through the entire chain of command. Another major consideration for terminating the grand divisions was the fact that the grand division commanders would have noticeably more power and influence than the numerous corps commanders. Hooker was all too aware from his own experience as a grand division commander how an ambitious general could use his post to undermine the commanding general.

Hooker's decision to dissolve the grand divisions was not a sound one tactically. His army contained eight infantry corps averaging 17,000 men each, whereas Lee's much smaller army had only two corps averaging 34,000 each. It was clearly much easier for Lee to communicate with his two corps commanders than it was for the Union army commander to reach and coordinate the actions of eight corps. In addition, it can be debated whether the *Army of the Potomac* actually contained eight capable leaders competent enough to lead corps well. This problem was intensified when viewed at the division level, where the Confederates had eight divisions and the Yankees three times as many. Confederate infantry divisions tended to have over twice as many men as their Union counterparts. This strength differential and the more streamlined Confederate command structure often gave Lee's troops tactical advantages during battle. What the Union army really needed was someone to decrease the number of corps and increase the strength of its divisions, as U.S. Grant finally did in the spring of 1864. Hooker was definitely not ready for such a step. His men were too attached to their unit assignments, and no one was prepared to deal with the amount of complaining that would arise from all the generals who would be displaced by extensive consolidation of the army's corps and divisions.

Hooker officially ended the army's grand division structure with his General Orders Number 6, dated 5 February 1863. His stated reasons for the move were a little awkward—that the grand divisions were too cumbersome on the march, and they were "impeding rather than facilitating the dispatch of its current business." By terms of the order, three of the grand division commanders were returned to the Corps they had previously led: Couch to the *II Corps* (returning Howard to division command), Meade to the *V Corps* (returning Sykes to division command), and Sigel to the *XI Corps* (returning Stahel to division command). The *I Corps* (Reynolds), *III Corps* (Sickles), and *XII Corps* (Slocum) retained their previous commanders.

The most awkward situation in this reorganization involved the *VI Corps*. Baldy Smith, commander of the old *Left Grand Division*, had formerly led the *VI Corps* and should have been returned to this post. However, Hooker did not totally trust Smith because of the way he and Sumner had worked to undermine Burnside. He decided it would be desireable to have Smith transferred, and had an excellent opportunity at

*Major General Oliver O. Howard, newly appointed commander of the XI Corps, would have a major effect on the course of the coming battle.*

hand for accomplishing this. It had recently been decided in Washington that Burnside's old command, the *IX Corps*, should be transferred from the *Army of the Potomac* for service elsewhere. All Hooker had to do was to assign Smith to command the *IX Corps* and both would be removed from his command. He drew up the appropriate orders on 4 February. The next day Hooker assigned Major General John Sedgwick, who had been acting commander of the *IX Corps*, to Smith's old command, the *VI Corps* (returning John Newton to division command).

Couch and Meade, two of the former grand division commanders, did not object to their return to corps command since they had served for only a few days in the higher position. Major General Franz Sigel, former commander of the *Reserve Grand Division*, felt quite differently about his demotion to command of the *XI Corps*. He was one of the army's senior major generals (senior even to Hooker), and felt quite at home as a grand division commander. He felt his reassignment to the *XI Corps*, which he had led during most of 1862, was an affront because it was by far the smallest of the army's eight corps. He argued with Hooker that he should be assigned to one of the larger corps led by a "less experienced" general. He may have had his sights set on the army's largest corps, the *VI*, which had recently been assigned to John Sedgwick, or the *III Corps*, whose commander, Daniel Sickles, had experienced difficulty getting his commission as major general approved by Congress.

Sigel's attempt to get a different corps command from Hooker proved fruitless, so the disgruntled major general sent his commander a letter on 12 February asking to be relieved, citing ill health as the reason. Hooker reluctantly complied, with a note that "This officer is my senior, and feels that he should have the largest corps to command. In breaking up the grand divisions, I preserved the corps organizations, for in that seemed to be strength. The officers knew the men, and the men their officers." Sigel would be inactive for the next year, until he was appointed Commander of the Department of West Virginia in March 1864.

Sigel's departure disturbed many of the troops of the *XI Corps*, particularly the "German" regiments that had enlisted "to fights mit Sigel," as the popular marching song went. These troops were all the more upset when Hooker chose to appoint Major General Oliver O. Howard, a division commander from the *II Corps*, as Sigel's replacement. Howard had become annoyed because he outranked Dan Sickles, new commander of the *III Corps*, so he was also pressing Hooker for a larger command. Though Howard was a good officer, Sigel's men did not know him at all. They would much have preferred to have one of their division commanders, Major General Carl Schurz or Brigadier General Julius Stahel, as Sigel's replacement. Howard's unfamiliarity with the officers and men of his new command, and their dissatisfaction at serving under him, would play an important role in the coming campaign.

Hooker's General Order of 5 February contained two other directives that changed the face of the army. One clause directed all the cavalry to be consolidated into one corps. Previously the cavalry had been assigned piecemeal by regiment and brigades as adjuncts to various infantry divisions, corps and grand divisions. All too many good cavalry regiments had spent the entire war serving as headquarters escorts or guarding supply trains. The few units committed to useful roles of scouting, screening and fighting enemy cavalry found themselves constantly outfought and outgeneraled by the Confederate horsesoldiers. All this accumulated ineffective use of the Union cavalry had greatly weakened their morale. Hooker's consolidation of his cavalry units into one corps would not guarantee superiority or even parity with the more experienced and better led Confederate cavalry, but it was certainly a step in the right direction.

What Hooker now needed most was a dynamic officer to lead the army's new cavalry corps. Unfortunately, no one was available to match or even come near the skill, experience and daring of Jeb Stuart and his brigade commanders in Lee's army. All of the better Union cavalry commanders at that time were in the western theater and were unavailable or unknown to Hooker. One of the best prospects in the eastern theater had been Brigadier General George Bayard, who was mortally wounded at Fredericksburg. After much searching, Hooker's choice for the post was Brigadier General George Stoneman, commander of the *III Corps* at Fredericksburg. Stoneman had been a veteran cavalryman before the war, and served as McClellan's chief of cavalry during the Peninsula campaign before transferring to the infantry. Stoneman's inexperience at handling so large a body of cavalry would have a key role in the upcoming campaign.

Hooker's final organizational change ordered on February 5 was less constructive than his creation of the *Cavalry Corps*. He directed that "hereafter the corps will be considered as a unit for the organization of the artillery, and no transfers of batteries will be made from one corps or division except for purposes of equalization." This order was intended to strengthen the artillery support rendered to each corps in the field, but would fail to achieve this goal for two major reasons. Firstly, Hooker promoted or reassigned so many experienced artillery field officers that there were not enough left to lead the corps artillery commands adequately. Secondly, Hooker's directive clipped the wings of Brigadier General Henry J. Hunt, the army's dynamic artillery chief. Hunt was always transferring units from one assignment to another in order to achieve his goals, and had found particular success by forming impromptu mass batteries at Malvern Hill, Antietam and Fredericksburg. Hooker's announced philosophy was to place tactical control of the artillery in the hands of the less skilled corps artillery officers, so reducing Hunt's job to solely an administrative one. In fact, Hunt was specifically directed not to give any orders to field units unless specifically authorized to do so, and all such authority would "expire with occasion." As a result, Hunt would spend the entire coming campaign north of the Rappahannock River, far from the front lines. His tactical expertise would be sorely missed.

Another of Hooker's less effective reforms was to direct that pack mules be used instead of wagons for transporting ammunition and baggage. This charge, announced on 19 March was intended to help the army move faster, both in good weather and under adverse conditions such as had been met in the recent Mud March. In practice, however, the use of pack mules did not achieve Hooker's desired effect for a number of reasons. A line of mules occupied more road space than the wagons they replaced, and the cargo they carried was transported much less effectively in smaller packs than in the large wagons. In fact, use of the pack mules was much more labor intensive than the cargo wagons because of the number of drivers needed and the amount of time needed to unpack and repack the mule's burdens at each overnight stop. Another problem was that pack mules liked to keep moving at their own steady pace while on the march; they often became difficult to manage during the frequent stops and starts that usually characterized an army on the march. Lastly, pack mules had the unfortunate habit of rubbing against trees or even each other in order to loosen their packs. This caused much extra work for the packers, as well as injury to the animals themselves. Noted historian John Bigelow observed that "The abolition of the grand

*Union army in winter quarters near Fredericksburg, January 1863.*

*Brigadier General Henry J. Hunt, Hooker's able artillery chief, was not permitted to go near the battlefield during the campaign.*

divisions was unfortunate, but perhaps necessary. The introduction of the pack trains was unfortunate and unnecessary, or ill advised."

A much more positive change was Hooker's creation of the Military Information Bureau. It seems that the *Army of the Potomac* had not previously made any effort to use scouts or spies to report on enemy movements. General McClellan had relied almost exclusively on a Secret Service organization set up by detective Allan Pinkerton to get information on the enemy. Pinkerton in turn got most of his information from enemy newspapers and runaway slaves, with the result that he constantly overestimated the strength of the Confederate units facing McClellan. This system proved to be ineffective and even downright misleading. The Confederates, on the other hand, had a very useful system of dedicated scouts and spies that operated even in Washington D.C. and points farther north.

Union ineffectiveness at gathering intelligence led Hooker in late March to appoint Colonel George H. Sharpe of the *120th New York* as deputy provost marshall with great freedom to create and run the new Military Information Bureau as he thought best. Sharpe set up a three faceted organization that included carefully

# Corps Badges

At the beginning of the Civil War units did not have distinctive badges or patches, such as every military division and specialized unit has today. Individual regiments and batteries sometimes had distinctive uniforms or hats, but most units, especially after the first year of the war, had uniforms similar or identical to the other commands they served with. One of the few units to have its own special means of identification was the noted Washington artillery of New Orleans, whose members wore strips of red flannel on their left arms at the battle of First Bull Run. They did this for their own safety, since the artillerymen were wearing blue uniforms and feared being mistaken for Yankees and being shot by their own troops.

The first widespread use of unit insignias was in June, 1862, when Major General Philip Kearny, commander of the *First Division* of the Federal *III Corps*, issued two-inch square patches of red flannel for his men to wear on their hats. Officers were to wear theirs on the left side of their caps, and enlisted men were directed to wear theirs on the crown. Kearny's purpose in issuing the patches was to be able to identify his men when they straggled or became separated from their units during battle. Reportedly Kearny had created a scene in an earlier battle by reprimanding officers from someone else's command; identifying patches would prevent such a mistake from occurring again. In a bit of effective propaganda, Kearny announced to his men that the patches would increase their reputation and morale: "Now you are marked men. The enemy will quail when he sees that scarlet patch, and well he may!" The harangue worked, and Kearny's men wore their "Kearny patches" with pride, even more so after Kearny was killed in the battle of Chantilly on September 1, 1862.

Popular as the Kearny Patches were, no other commander or unit chose to emulate them later in 1862. Major General Hooker became aware of their positive effect on morale during the Fredericksburg Campaign, when he led the *Center Grand Division* that included Kearny's old division. After he became commander of the *Army of the Potomac*, Hooker decided to institute an army wide system of badges in order to increase efficiency and sagging unit morale. His plan was to assign a specific emblem to each corps, with the color of the emblem to vary by division: First Division, red; Second Division, white; Third Division, blue; Fourth Division, green; Fifth Division, orange.

Hooker directed his chief of staff, Major General Dan Butterfield, to devise the shapes to be used for each corps. A square patch, later worn as a lozenge or diamond, was assigned to the *III Corps* out of respect for the similar Kearny Patch already being worn by Kearny's old division. The *II Corps* was assigned a trefoil or cloverleaf (a four leaf shamrock), because it contained so many Irish troops. The *I Corps* was given a disc (or full moon) as "the first thing thought of." Other patterns devised were *V Corps*—Maltese Cross; *VI Corps*—Greek Cross; *XI Corps*—crescent moon; and *XII Corps*—five pointed star.

The corps badge system was officially instituted by the following General Order dated March 21, 1863: "For the purpose of ready recognition of corps and divisions in this army, and to prevent injustice by reports of straggling and misconduct through mistake as to its organization, the chief quarter master will furnish without delay the following badges, to be worn by the officers and enlisted men of all the regiments of the various corps mentioned. They will be securely fastened upon the center of the top of the cap. Inspecting officers will at all inspections see that these badges are worn as designated." The badges as issued were made of flannel and were about one and a half inches across. They apparently were not continually issued or replaced after their first distribution, and soldiers had to cut and make their own or buy them from the quartermasters. It should be noted that the corps emblems were also painted on ambulances, wagons and other equipment. In addition, each division and corps commander had a flag with the proper badge and color.

The idea of wearing corps badges caught on quickly and it is estimated that two thirds of the fighting infantry in the *Army of the Potomac* were wearing badges in 1864. Besides the cloth badges worn as prescribed on their hats, many of the men also wore tin or enamel pins on their lapels or jackets. Sometimes they would inscribe their name or regiment number on the pin or badge. Wealthier soldiers often wore specially designed embroidered badges or gold or silver badges made by Tiffany's in New York. Many men became so attached to their badges that they refused to change them when their units were reassigned. This posed a particular problem in early 1864 when Grant dissolved the *I Corps* and *III Corps* and transferred their regiments to the *V Corps* and *VI Corps*.

The wearing of corps badges did not catch on in the western Union armies until late 1863, when the *XII Corps* with its star badges was transferred from Virginia to Tennessee. Supposedly one veteran of the *XV Corps*, which had no badge, saw some *XII Corps* men with the star badges and asked if they were all generals. When the reason for the stars was explained, the *XV Corps* man was asked where his badge was. He slapped his cartridge box and responded "This is my corps badge." Unwittingly he had created the badge for his corps—a cartridge box with the words "40 rounds."

Eventually all the Union corps but two, the *XIII* and *XXI*, had their own badge symbols. In addition, several cavalry commands and specialized units also devised distinctive badges. The idea of wearing unit badges never caught on in the Confederate army for some reason.

The corps symbols as adapted by the Union army were as follows:

*I*—Disk
*II*—Trefoil
*III*—Lozenge
*IV*—Triangle
*V*—Maltese Cross
*VI*—St. Andrew's (Greek) Cross
*VII*—Crescent and Star

*VIII*—Six-pointed star
*IX*—Shield with crossed anchor and
cannon
*X*—Square Bastion
*XI*—Crescent
*XII* (later Twentieth)—Five-Pointed

*XIII*—none
*XIV*—acorn
*XV*—Cartridge Box
*XVI*—Crossed Cannon
*XVII*—Arrow
*XVIII*—Trefoil Cross
*XIX*—Modified Maltese Cross
*XX*—Star (see *XII Corps*)
*XXI*—none
*XXII*—Pentagon Cross
*XXIII*—Shield
*XXIV*—Heart
*XXV*—Lozenge on a Square

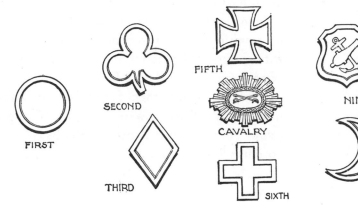

*Corps badges of the* Army of the Potomac *under Hooker.*

selected military scouts, civilian spies, and a system of signalmen posted on observation towers. All information gathered was sent promptly to Sharpe at headquarters, where the data was analyzed and reported to General Hooker. Sharpe's organization would grow continually throughout the remainder of the war, and can rightly be called the father of today's army intelligence system.

By far the most effective of Hooker's reforms were those directed at restoring the army's morale and efficiency. In the period after Fredericksburg, desertions and cases of "French leave" had become epidemic as weary soldiers left for home in droves without permission or simply disappeared. At the height of the problem the army was wasting away at the rate of 200 per day because of lax discipline and ineffective deterrents. (One of the problems here was President Lincoln himself, who would usually pardon any soldier condemned to death for desertion if he were approached by the soldier's mother or wife or sister.) Hooker ordered a study of the absentee problem made as soon as he took command, and on 15 February reported to Washington that 85,123 of his men were absent from the army—approximately half of his command. Out right desertions varied from 43 per thousand in the *XI Corps* to 136 per thousand in the *XII Corps*, with an average about 100 per 1000.

Hooker began to take measures to restore the army's strength less than a week after he assumed command. On 30 January he notified General Halleck that leaves of absence would no longer be granted in the field. On the same day, he issued a detailed General Order (No.3) to the army that limited and defined the rules concerning furloughs. Since absenteeism was especially critical among the officers, Hooker ordered that only one brigade commander per corps and one field officer and two line officers per regiment could be granted leave at the same time. Furloughs for the enlisted men would be limited to two per cent of any regiment or battery at one time. This last provision may seem harsh, but was actually productive. Hooker wanted his men to understand that legitimate furloughs were available on a rotating basis in each company. Those who waited for their turn would be granted a ten day leave (fifteen days if they lived in Maine or the Ohio Valley), so there would be no need to desert or go AWOL.

Hooker nevertheless increased the army's security measures in order to crack down on desertions. The provost marshall was given control of all mail coming to the army, with specific orders to intercept all shipment of civilian clothing to the front. All too often a soldier would send for his civilian clothes from home, and when they arrived he would substitute them for his uniform and simply walk out of camp. In another measure, army pickets were strengthened to prevent unauthorized men from leaving camp. There was even a special order issued on 1 February that the commander of the Potomac River flotilla should make an extra effort to catch all deserters who tried to cross the river in small boats.

Another method Hooker devised to cut down on desertions was to assign a system of corps and division badges to his regiments. The purpose of the badges was to make it possible to identify the command of any straggler or deserter, and so be able to

*Camp of the* 12th Massachusetts *Infantry near Falmouth.*

return them more promptly to the proper authorities. The use of the corps badges was widely accepted by the troops and had the added benefit of developing and increasing unit identity and morale. Less effective was Hooker's directive that each corps headquarters should carry a standardized blue swallow tail flag bearing a white Maltese cross with the corps number. The purpose of the flags was to make it easier for the men to locate their corps commanders. However, the head generals did not care much for the flags for some reason, and not everyone used them.

In order to keep better track of unit strengths and absentee rates, Hooker appointed a new inspector general of the army, Colonel E. Schriver, as well as new and more efficient inspectors for brigades. Frequent unit inspections were held, and regular reports had to be filed and scrutinized. As a result of these, Hooker announced on 3 March that thirty-six regiments and batteries were not operating up to expectations and would receive no more furloughs, while twenty-five regiments and batteries were operating especially well and would be entitled to more and longer furloughs.

This same report noted that the *II* and *I Corps* had by far the best level of instruction and discipline, while the *VI, III* and *V Corps* needed improvement, and the *XI Corps* was the most undisciplined.

Hooker's drive to cut down on desertions was supported by President Lincoln, who issued a proclamation on 10 March offering amnesty to all absent soldiers who would rejoin their units by 1 April. Lincoln also promised to stop reviewing court martial decisions. From then on soldiers and their families would have no appeal from court martial findings. As John Bigelow succinctly put it, "Deserters were arrested, and promptly tried, sentenced and punished accordingly. The spectacle of a few of them shot to death in the presence of the troops produced a most salutary effect."

Hooker was well aware that all the arrangements just described dealt only with the symptoms of the army's low morale, not the causes. The real reason so many soldiers were improperly leaving camp in droves was not their lack of patriotism or even their disgust at losing so many battles. The simple fact was that the Union Camps near Falmouth in the winter of 1862-63 were damp and unhealthful, spawning all kinds of disease and discomfort. In addition, many troops were becoming sick because of unappetizing and unhealthy rations.

Immediate steps were taken under Hooker's orders to improve physical conditions in the camps. Many of the troops were living in log and canvas huts built over small pits excavated in the ground. As the winter progressed, most of these huts became damp, muddy and full of germs, no better than pigsties. Hooker directed the worst of the camps to be relocated, and the others to be cleaned and aired out. Troops had to carpet the floors of their huts with boughs or other material so they would no have to sleep directly on the ground. Bedding had to be aired daily, and everyone was to dig an eighteen inch deep drainage ditch around their huts in order to keep water out. Kitchen garbage was to be buried properly each day, and latrines were to be better located and maintained. In addition, "the men should be required to wear their hair cut short, to bathe twice a week, and put on clean underclothing at least once a week."

Hooker also took prompt steps to improve the army's food supply and the quality of rations issued to the men. He knew that plenty of food was available at the depots, yet the camps were full of dysentry, scurvy and related diseases. Too many of the men were living on an unhealthy diet composed almost entirely of hardtack (large thick crackers) and salt pork. Clearly, most of the fresh and even dried vegetables procured by the army were not reaching the men, while other fresh items (primarily potatoes) were not being picked up by the corps commissaries.

To ensure that the troops received fresher rations, Hooker decided that bread should be issued more often in place of hardtack, and that now vegetables of all types should be made available. On 7 February, he directed that "Flour or soft bread will be issued at the depots to commissaries for at least four issues per week to the troops. Fresh potatoes or onions, if practicable, for two issues per week. Desiccated mixed vegetables or potatoes for one issue per week."

The second part of 7 February order established much stricter guidelines for making sure that the commissaries actually issued the food they received from the government. Since ration issues often exceeded what the soldiers could eat, or at least what they wanted to eat, it had become the custom for commissaries to sell off surplus food and put the money into regimental funds. All too often, commissaries kept the money for themselves, or worse yet, sold off food (particularly fresh vegetables) before it even reached the troops. Thus many soldiers at the front would be suffering from poor diet while their commissaries, and sometimes even their officers, grew fat from eating the best foods or selling it illegally.

Another move to improve the soldiers' diet was made by a Congressional law passed on 3 March. The government was finally ready to recognize that many troops did not eat well simply because they did not know how to cook or did not have proper cooking utensils. The new law directed that medical and line officers should supervise food preparation. Soldiers who knew how to cook could be specifically detailed for that work, and each company could enlist "two under-cooks of African descent" to help with the cooking chores. The same law also directed that the pepper ration be increased to four ounces per hundred rations, since pepper was thought to be healthful for the diet.

Hooker's efforts to improve the health and living conditions of his men met with considerable success at improving their morale and readiness to fight. In March Medical Director Dr. Jonathan Letterman was pleased to report that "All the more serious diseases to which troops in camp are liable, and especially those which depend upon neglect of sanitary precautions and bad diet have decreased in a marked degree during the month of February...This favorable state of health of the army, and the decrease in the severity of the cases of disease, is in a great measure to be attributed to the improvement in the diet of the men, commenced about the 1st of February by the issue of fresh bread and fresh vegetables; to the increased attention to sanitary regulations both in camp and hospitals" and to improved cooking practices.

The men in the ranks were well aware of Hooker's changes, and thankful for them. One soldier from New Hampshire wrote, "From the commissary came less whisky for the officers and better rations, including vegetables, for the men. Hospitals were renovated, new ones built, drunken surgeons discharged, sanitary supplies furnished, and the sick no longer left to suffer and die without proper care and attention. Officers and men who from incompetence or disability could be of no further use to the service were allowed to resign or were discharged, and those who were playing sick in the hospitals were sent to their regiments for duty."

| Corps | Deserters per 1,000, February | Sick per 1,000, 28 March | Rating of Instruction and Discipline (worst to best) | Composite Figures of Efficiency (worst to best) |
|---|---|---|---|---|
| Eleventh | 43 | 69 | 105 | 32.94 |
| Fifth | 91 | 61 | 96 | 16.23 |
| Sixth | 122 | 46 | 93 | 15.70 |
| Third | 119 | 76 | 94 | 9.60 |
| Twelfth | 136 | 53 | 61 | 9.01 |
| First | 108 | 90 | 14 | 1.32 |
| Second | 90 | 85 | 1 | 0.12 |

From Bigelow, *The Campaign of Chancellorsville*, pp. 36, 491, 493.

*Soldier's graves at Falmouth. The Federal camps were quite un-healthy until Hooker cleaned them up in February 1863.*

# CHAPTER IV

# The Army of Northern Virginia

### December, 1862 - March, 1863

*T*he months after the battle of Fredericksburg provided a much needed breathing space for General Robert E. Lee and his Army of Northern Virginia. In a little over six months since he had taken command on 1 July 1861. Lee had fought four major campaigns that had kept his army almost continuously on the move. His victories at the Seven Days' Battles, Second Bull Run, and Fredericksburg, and even the draw at Antietam had earned him the undying respect of his men and increased their morale to new heights at the expense of their opponents. What his command now needed most was a chance to rest, an opportunity to recruit its strength and let its wounded men heal and return to the ranks.

The structure of Lee's army was streamlined and battle tested, with talented and experienced commanders at almost every key position. As discussed in the previous chapter, Lee's division of his army into two infantry corps of four divisions each was a much more streamlined and efficient organization than Hooker's army of seven infantry corps. Equally significant was the fact that Lee was secure in his position due to his age, extreme competence, his recent battle successes, and the trust of his president and subordinates. His presence gave a stability and confidence to his army that was sorely lacked in the *Army of the Potomac*, whose commanders were fired after every defeat. This also meant that Lee's principal subordinates were not competing with each other or undercutting each other for personal or political reasons in order to replace their commander, as was constantly occurring in the Federal armies.

Lee was extremely fortunate to have two talented and experienced corps commanders to serve as his principal lieutenants, men whose abilities supported Lee and complemented each other. Lieutenant General James Longstreet held command of the I Corps and was a master of defensive tactics. Longstreet could be slow and stubborn at times, but was always reliable and could mount smashing offensives when needed. A native of South Carolina, Longstreet was the highest ranking non-Virgin-

# General Lee's Health During the War

At the beginning of the war General Robert E. Lee was in excellent health. He was fifty-four years old, five feet ten and a half inches tall, and a trim one hundred seventy pounds. Except for a slight wound suffered in the Mexican War and a bout with malaria while building a fort near Baltimore in 1849, he had been in good health all his life, and even seemed to thrive on the rigors of military campaigning.

Lee was never wounded during the war, though he did come under enemy fire a few times. The most memorable instances were during the battles of the Wilderness and Spotsylvania in May 1864, when he twice attempted to lead counterattacks personally in order to turn the tide of battle. Each time he was lovingly turned back by his troops and staff officers for fear he would be hurt.

Though he was not wounded in battle, he did suffer one significant service related injury. It occurred on 31 August 1862, the day after the successful conclusion of the battle of Second Bull Run. Lee was at Stewart's Farm, near Centreville, directing the operations against Pope's retiring army that would culminate the next day in the Battle of Chantilly. Because of bad weather he was wearing rubber overalls and a rubber poncho. He was standing next to Traveler, his favorite horse, when the sudden cry "Yankee cavalry" was heard. Traveller started forward at the commotion, and Lee grabbed his bridle to keep him from running off. As he did so, Lee tripped in his long overalls and fell forward. He used his hands to stop his fall and got up at once, but it was clear he was hurt. A doctor was immediately called, as the enemy cavalry scare proved to be a false alarm. Dr.N.S. Walker of the 48th Georgia arrived and determined that the general had broken a small bone in one hand, while the other hand was painfully twisted and strained. Both hands were put in splints, and Lee was given a linament to relieve the pain. As a result of the injury, Lee could not hold the reins of his horse or use his binoculars to view enemy positions. Consequently he had to ride in an ambulance during the invasion that led north to Sharpsburg. It can only be conjectured how much the pain and inconvenience of these injuries affected his performance during the Antietam campaign.

General Lee's first decline in physical health came seven months later on the eve of the great battle of Chancellorsville. On 27 March 1863, he came down with a bad sore throat, and then complained of sharp stabbing pains in his chest, back and arm. His doctors thought his condition was serious enough to move him from his field headquarters to a private home. The sharp pains continued for another ten day from what the doctors believed to be pericarditis, an inflammation of the heart sac. Lee did not wish to alarm his wife, and wrote her that he had only a bad cold and annoying rheumatism. Little did he and his doctors understand that his heart had been permanently damaged by this illness.

Thus, Lee was in weakened physical condition when he planned and fought his greatest battle at Chancellorsville. Clearly, his constitution was still strong to fight his illness and still enable him to make the clear decisions necessary to direct the battle. However, the tension of the battle and Stonewall Jackson's subsequent death did put more strain on him. The general was observed to be "thinner and a little pale" at a conference in Richmond on 14 May, during which plans for a second invasion of the North were discussed and approved.

Lee entered the Gettysburg campaign in confident spirits and no signs of the ailments that had struck him earlier. However, during the climactic battle itself he was observed to be weak and walking in pain. One staff officer was aware that Lee was suffering "a good deal from an attack of diarrhea" on 2 July. General Longstreet believed that his commander was suffering from sciatica, a painful condition of the central spinal nerve. More recent analysts suggest he may have been suffering a recurrence of the malaria he contracted in 1849. Edwin Coddington, author of a recent monumental study of the campaign, believes that Lee was not physically weakened during the battle, though he was probably suffering from anxiety due to he loss of Stonewall Jackson and the unknown whereabouts of Jebs Stuart. Whatever were the causes, it seems clear that Lee was not at his physical and mental best during the three days of the battle of Gettysburg.

Concern over the defeat at Gettysburg brought Lee to submit his resignation on 8 August 1863. One of his primary reasons for wishing to resign was his declining health. The general wrote "I sensibly feel the growing failure of my bodily strength. I have not yet recovered from the attack I experienced the past spring. I am more and more incapable of exertion and am thus prevented from making the personal examinations and giving the personal supervision to the operations in the field which I feel to be necessary."

Lee's resignation was refused by President Davis, and Lee would remain in command with ever increasing responsibilities until the end of the war. The strains of command and field service would continue to take a physical toll on him. In late September he had an attack of severe back problems that were attributed to sciatica, lumbago, or rheumatism. For several days he was unable to ride his horse or direct the army personally. He even became so uncomfortable that he lost his temper several times, with the result that his loving staff officers learned to avoid him "when he was sick and rendered irritable by inability to move about." Modern medicine interprets that he was suffering from angina pectoris, pains caused by decreased blood supply to the heart muscle.

Lee's condition was stable over the winter of 1863-64, and he did not fall sick again until late May 1864, after the bloody battles of The Wilderness and Spotsylvania. On 24 May while the armies were near the North Anna River, Lee had a violent attack of diarrhea that prostrated him for six days, and did not subside until a week after that. In spite of his discomfort, he remained in active command of his army. He attributed his illness to "bad food and long hours," but the nature and length of the sickness strongly suggest it was not a common camp disease. Instead, it was probably a primary intestinal infection, most likely amebiasis or bacillary dysentery.

Lee would suffer no additional major health problems in the last months of the war. His mind remained keen and his body stayed surprisingly fit, considering his age, heart condition, and the rigors of field service. However, the strain of command caused his hair to turn entirely gray, and his face showed the weariness and cares he had to endure. He also continued to suffer the pains of sciatica and rheumatism. In actuality, the pressures of the war had aged Lee prematurely, and the attack of pericarditis suffered on the eve of Chancellorsville would be the underlying cause of his death seven years later.

*General Robert E. Lee astride his favorite mount, Traveller.*

ian in Lee's army, and was sometimes sensitive to the preponderance of Virginians in high command. He was also yearning for a chance to manage an independent command, perhaps out of repressed jealousy of Jackson's success in the spring 1862 Shenandoah Valley campaign. The spring of 1863 would offer him such an opportunity, with results that were much less than desired.

Lee's Second Corps commander, Lieutenant General Thomas J. "Stonewall" Jackson was an aggressive leader who nicely balanced Longstreet's strengths. Jackson's successes in the Valley Campaign and the maneuvers against Pope in August won him popularity and recognition throughout the South. Even so, he was considered junior to Longstreet by most officers, though this did not bother him at all. Jackson was intensely religious, and did his duty solely to serve his God and his nation. He was without question a military genius in many respects, but he was certainly not without his faults. He tended to be overly harsh in maintaining discipline and at times expected too much physically of himself and of his men. He was also too secretive in forming his plans, a trait that at times made his subordinates hesitant in action. Jackson's personal eccentricities are well-known today, but they must have made him an awkward man to work with.

Six of Lee's eight infantry division commanders were veterans in their positions, well known to their men. All four of Longstreet's division commanders had led their units at Fredericksburg. The senior officer Major General Richard H. Anderson of South Carolina, had led his division since Second Bull Run, while Major General Lafayette McLaws of Georgia had been appointed to his division command just before the Antietam campaign. George E. Pickett of Virginia and John B. Hood, former commander of the Texas brigade, had been appointed major generals in the month after Antietam. Three of the eight rose to corps command later in the war, and one, Hood, would eventually command an army.

Jackson's Second Corps had two veteran division commanders and two newcomers. All were from Virginia. Major General A.P. Hill had been heading his Light Division since May 1862 and was the army's senior division commander. Major General Jubal A. Early had taken command of his division during the battle of Antietam and then led it at Fredericksburg. Jackson's two new division commanders were brigadier generals Robert E. Rodes and Raleigh E. Colston. Rodes was a veteran brigade commander who took over Major General D. H. Hill's division when "the other Hill" was sent to command the Department of North Carolina. Harvey Hill, who happened to be Stonewall Jackson's brother-in-law, was an excellent fighter but was often ornery and difficult to get along with. Lee felt he would do better in an independent command, so he transferred him out of Virginia. Jackson's first choice to succeed Hill was Brigadier General Ed "Allegheny" Johnson, who had fought briefly under Stonewall in the Valley campaign. However, Johnson was not sufficiently recovered from a foot wound he had received at the battle of McDowell on 8 May 1862, so he could not accept the command. Command of Hill's division then fell by default to Rodes as senior brigadier general.

Jackson's other divisional commander change came about through much more complex circumstances. It seems that Jackson did not much care for Brigadier General William B. Taliaferro, commander of Jackson's old division. Taliaferro was senior brigade commander when division leader Brigadier General Charles Winder was killed at Cedar Mountain in August 1862, so he succeeded to the office over Jackson's

*Brigadier General William N. Pendleton, Lee's chief of artillery, was also an ordained minister. He was thought to be much like General Lee in appearance.*

*Brigadier General Raliegh Colston was a relative unknown when Jackson assigned him to division command.*

# How "Stonewall" Jackson Got His Nickname

There is no question that Thomas J. Jackson was one of the South's most popular generals in the war, and that his nickname "Stonewall" was one of the most noted to emerge from the war. His nickname was bestowed during the battle of First Bull Run, fought on 21 July 1861. At the beginning of the day, Jackson was posted in a reserve position on the right of the Confederate army along with the brigades of generals Bee and Bartow. The battle opened soon after dawn with a strong Union flank attack on the Confederate left. Bee and Bartow were hurried to the far left at Matthews Hill, and met heavy fighting and many casualties. Eventually enemy forces in their front became too numerous to hold back, and the troops on Matthews Hill were forced to withdraw across Young's Branch. Jackson had arrived on Henry House Hill sometime after 1100, and declined to commit his men right away to the confused fracas raging on Matthews Hill. Instead, he placed some cannons in the center of Henry House Hill, three-quarters of a mile to the south, and formed the regiments of his brigade behind the hill's crest in support of the cannons. This hill appeared to be the key to the battlefield, and Jackson wanted to make sure he could hold it until more troops arrived.

At about noon Brigadier General Barnard E. Bee rode back from his hardpressed men to seek help from the troops on Henry House Hill. He located Jackson and reported, "General, they are beating us back." To this Jackson replied, "Sir, we'll give them the bayonet." Bee took this as an order, and rode north to form up his men. In all the smoke and confusion the only troops he could find in formation were part of his 4th Alabama. He then gave the men a brief pep talk before counter-attacking. Reportedly his concluding words were, "There

is Jackson standing like a stone wall. Let us determine to die here, and we will conquer. Follow me." Bee's exact words are not known for certain, and were reported in several variants. The version

*Thomas J. "Stonewall" Jackson earned his famous nickname at the battle of First Bull Run.*

quoted here is the best known one, as quoted by the Richmond correspondent of the *Charleston Mercury* on the front page of the 25 July 1861 issue. All the versions include the phrase mentioning Jackson and the Stonewall. No one was able to ask Bee what he had said because he was mortally wounded later in the fighting and died that afternoon.

Bee's comment concerning Jackson was soon reported in newspapers throughout the South, and in short time the nickname "Stonewall" was being applied to both Jackson and his brigade. Almost everyone meant the nickname as a compliment, one praising the steadfastness of the troops at the height of the

battle. In fact, General Joseph E. Johnston later on 21 July, independently used the term to describe the stand made by Jackson's 4th Virginia.

Several more recent historians, however, have questioned whether Bee meant to praise Jackson when he called him a "Stonewall." At the time he made the comment, Bee was forming what was left of his brigade for a desperate counterattack. Jackson's men were not withstanding any heavy enemy combat or fire at that moment. Instead, they were some distance to Bee's rear, holding the reverse slope of Henry House Hill, under occasional Union artillery fire. It is very possible that Bee did not call Jackson a stonewall as a compliment, but as a criticism, since Jackson was holding a relatively safe position and was not coming to Bee's aid.

This interpretation of the incident is supported by J.C. Haskell, of the 1st South Carolina artillery. Haskell later wrote in his memoirs that he had spoken with a Major Rhett of Johnston's staff, who was with Bee after the general was mortally wounded. Rhett, according to Haskell, felt that Bee was angry at Jackson for not coming to the aid of his hard pressed brigade and for "standing like a stonewall and allowing them to be sacrificed." Haskell also claimed to have heard James Hill, Bee's brother-in-law and aide de camp, say that Bee was very angry at Jackson for not bringing his troops forward to help him. It must be noted, however, that Haskell's accounts may be prejudiced, as he did not care much for Jackson for reasons of his own.

Thus we can never know exactly what General Bernard Bee meant when he compared Jackson to Stonewall. Jackson himself took the nickname as a compliment, and definitely much more positive than the nickname "Fool Tom" his V.M.I. cadets had once given him.

objections. Taliaferro was wounded at Groveton later that month, but recovered and returned to command of the division after Antietam because of the units heavy officer losses. Jackson, however, refused to have Taliaferro appointed to permanent command and was looking for a replacement. Taliaferro was deeply offended at this, and threatened to request a transfer if he were not given permanent plan. Matters came to a head when Taliaferro became engaged in a petty quarrel with Brigadier General Frank Paxton, leader of the Stonewall brigade, and had Paxton arrested for being disrespectful. Jackson in return refused to support Taliaferro's pending promotion to major general. Taliaferro thereupon submitted his transfer request, and left in early February for South Carolina (where he would command Battery Wagner when it was attacked by Colonel Robert Shaw and the *54th Massachusetts* on 11 July 1863). Jackson replaced Taliaferro with a relative unknown, Brigadier General Raleigh E. Colston, who had been a friend and fellow professor of Jackson's at Virginia Military Institute.

During the winter, Lee decided to improve the organization of his artillery batteries in order to make it easier to group them in mass batteries in the field. Previously most of the batteries were assigned to the various divisions, with the rest assigned to reserve status. Many of the division batteries were so closely attached to their unit or even to specific brigades that they were reluctant to go on detached service to help out a different command. As a result, it had become the practice to call on reserve batteries for help at critical times, even if divisional batteries of another unit were closer and unengaged. Another problem with the army's artillery structure was an administrative one. The divisional artillery commands did not have proper support staffs, and the division commanders were usually too busy or too untrained to see that their batteries were being maintained properly.

Lee directed his artillery chief Brigadier General William N. Pendleton, to review the army's batteries, battalions and artillery officers and make a recommendation for a more efficient organization of the artillery. Pendleton responded on 11 February with a thorough and detailed report that was implemented almost in its entirety. The nucleus of Pendleton's recommendation was to form the army's batteries into formal battalions averaging four batteries each. One battalion would be attached to each division, and each corps would have two reserve battalions, with an additional two battalions held as an army reserve. Each battalion commander would be directed to form a support staff consisting of ordnance officers, surgeons, and supply officers, so that the guns, men and horses would be better supplied and cared for.

Pendleton's plan was a model of classic simplicity. The battalion staffs greatly increased the efficiency of the batteries, while the new battalion organizations provided support to the brigades while still making it possible, via the battalion officer, to loan batteries from one command to another when needed. The creation of a two-tiered reserve system seems redundant on the surface, but was actually an efficient way of providing additional support at the division level while still leaving spare batteries available in the general reserve. This new artillery organization would be an advantage in the coming battle, and is especially significant when compared with Hooker's ineffective, even counter-productive, efforts to improve his artillery organization.

Lee's organization of his artillery also created a positive side effect. The creation of the new battalions formally created a need for artillery field officers, and made it

*Inside a winter hut.*

possible to promote a whole group of talented artillerists who had shown their skill in earlier battles. Promotion in the artillery was exceptionally slow, since batteries could be commanded only by a captain, whereas promotion in the infantry was much faster because of heavier battle losses and the greater number of openings available. As a result of this situation, promising artillery officers (especially in the Union army) would become frustrated with lack of promotion, and requested transfer to the cavalry or infantry. Pendleton did a careful analysis of the staffing of the new battalions, and his recommendations for promotion included such veterans as J. J. Garnett, E. Porter Alexander, Thomas H. Carter, W. T. Poague, R. S. Andrews, W. N. Nelson, William Pegram, and David McIntosh.

It is interesting to note that Longstreet accepted the artillery reorganization without complaint, but Jackson found fault with several of the promotions that Pendleton recommended. Specifically, he did not support a promotion for Major H. P. Jones, on the principal that promotion should be solely for "meritorious services," otherwise promotion would be cheapened. He also objected to the assignment of Captain Barnwell to his command, since he had never met him, and was displeased that promotions were not offered to Captain David McIntosh or Captain R. P. Chew.

Lee, with his usual conciliatory nature, did his best to answer Jackson's complaints in general terms: "I think the interest of the service as well as justice to individuals,

*Butchering cattle for the troops.*

requires the selection of the best men to fill vacant positions....I do not think it right, however, at any time to pass over worthy men who have done good service, unless you can get better." Jackson, however, was not satisfied that his preferences for artillery and infantry promotions were being heard, and replied to Lee in words that sound disrespectful: "I have had much trouble resulting from incompetent officers having been assigned to duty with me regardless of my wishes. Those who assigned them have never taken the responsibility of incurring the odium which results from such incompetency." The tone of Jackson's letter succeeded at catching Lee's attention, and when the artillery reorganization was completed and announced on 16 April, Stonewall got everything he asked for except for two points (H. P. Jones was promoted and R. P. Chew was not).

Lee's greatest problem as he prepared for the next campaign was the fact that the *Army of the Potomac* was much larger and better supplied than his force. Thanks to battlefield captures and pickups, the infantry had sufficient weapons and equipment. Clothing was a different matter. Government issued apparel was scarce and not always the best quality. All too often the men had to rely on care packages sent from home for socks and underwear, and even shirts, pants and coats. In addition, there were not enough blankets to go around, a shortage that became all the more severe when the weather turned sharply colder at the end of January.

The army's inferiority in artillery had been alleviated a great deal by battlefield captures and by the melting down of most of the iron six-pounders after the battle of Antietam. Nevertheless, the army did not contain the quantity and quality of good cannons, particularly rifled pieces, that Hooker's army had. Lee's artillery was also affected by a shortage in equipment, particularly harnesses. Both the artillery and the cavalry were short on horses, and forage became so scarce that Lee had to send his artillery battalions to camps much farther from Fredericksburg than he really desired.

Lee was also experiencing difficulty getting enough food for his men. On 26 January, he wrote Secretary of War James A. Seddon that the army had only a weeks supply of rations, and less than a week's supply of fresh meat and salt meat. His men were already living on reduced rations, and it was not possible to glean much more from the countryside about Fredericksburg, which had been occupied for a number of months. Lee pleaded with Seddon to do what he could to supply the army, since he did not want to have to resort to impressing food from local farmers, a move that would be unpopular and dangerous to the health of the civilian population.

The greatest weakness of Lee's army was its strength, which was only half of his opponent's force. The Army of Northern Virginia reported 64,799 present for duty on 31 March 1863, compared to 136,724 in Hooker's army. This number did not include 5,050 men on special duty, 6,308 present but sick, and 1,222 under arrest or in confinement. Not included were 6,251 men on detached duty, 16,136 absent sick, 4,140 absent with leave, and 5,953 absent without leave. This last figure was fully three times the number absent without leave in Hooker's army. This is a reflection of two major factors—Hooker's successful attempt to cut down on desertion and unauthorized leaves through a more liberal furlough system, and the Confederate practice of looking the other way when men (almost exclusively Virginians) went to see their families or spend a good part of the winter at home. These men were expected to return to their units in time for the spring campaign, and most did.

Lee's numerical disadvantage was exacerbated in mid-February, when he became concerned about the departure of the Federal *IX Corps* to Norfolk and decided to send

# The Stonewall Brigade

The Stonewall Brigade was probably the single most famous unit in the Confederate army, being the only brigade to have its nickname sanctioned by the Confederate Congress, (30 May 1863). It consisted of five Virginia infantry regiments (the 2nd, 4th, 5th, 27th, and 33rd) that were raised in the eighteen counties which lay in the Shenandoah Valley; the Rockbridge Artillery was also a part of the brigade until October 1862. When first organized in the spring of 1861, the brigade seemed to offer no more promise than any of the others being created at the time. The brigade's morale may have been helped by the fact that all its men came from the same district of Virginia, but what really forged the brigade's unity was the long and hard training it received from Jackson both before and after First Bull Run. Jackson took command of the brigade in May of 1861, and immediately asserted his control by limiting passes for the men to see their families and installing guards to keep the soldiers in camp. Then constant drill and strict discipline shaped the men into the efficient fighting machine that Jackson wanted and demanded.

Jackson and his brigade arrived at Manassas, Virginia, with Joe Johnston's army just in time to help Beauregard's army defeat Irvin McDowell's attacking Union force. At the opening of the battle of First Bull Run, Jackson was stationed on the Confederate right wing, but he was shifted to the left in order to meet McDowell's flank attack.

When Jackson arrived on Henry House Hill, things were not going well for the Confederates. Several brigades had been crushed on Matthews' Hill, and the remaining men were streaming back over Jackson's position. Undaunted, Jackson, who had suffered a slight hand wound, held his men in line in a woods on the edge of the hill. Though this was the first battle for most of his men, Jackson was able to hold them until just the right moment. Confederate Brigadier General Barnard E. Bee saw this, and gave Jackson and his brigade their immortal nickname by shouting, "Look at Jackson's Brigade, it stands like a stone wall! Rally behind the Virginians!"

Jackson had such regard for the brigade that he requested it be transferred to him when he was given command of the Valley district on 5 November. The brigade served him well as it marched up and down the Valley and fought desperately whenever called upon, particularly at Kernstown and Port Republic. After the Valley Campaign, the brigade continued to be one of Lee's crack units, ranking at the top, along with Hood's Texas Brigade. At Gaines' Mill (27 June 1862), the Stonewall Brigade helped break the Union line in bloody frontal attacks. At Groveton (28 August 1862) it fought the Yankees' best outfit, the *Iron Brigade*, to a stand-still. Perhaps the Stonewall Brigade's sternest test was at Antietam (17 September 1862), where it was worn to a frazzle while helping to hold Lee's left wing at the West Woods. The brigade was engaged at Fredericksburg, and fought with distinction at Chancellorsville 2-3 May 1863. Another successful flank attack came at Stephenson's Depot (15 June 1863), where the brigade captured six enemy regiments. The unit did well at Gettysburg, but was positioned on Culp's Hill, away from the main action of the battle. The next spring it fought at the Wilderness and met disaster at Spotsylvania, where most of Ed Johnson's division was captured at the Bloody Angle. After this catastrophe only 200 men were left in the brigade, and it had to be consolidated into one regiment. As such it took part in Early's Valley campaign, Monocacy, and the attack on Washington. It then went to the Petersburg trenches. Only 210 men remained in the once proud Stonewall Brigade at the time of Lee's surrender at Appomattox.

The Stonewall Brigade enjoyed its success partly because of its series of distinguished commanders. Stonewall Jackson, who took command on May 1861, was succeeded by Dick Garnett on 14 November 1861. Garnett, who was a strict disciplinarian, was at first received coldly by his men. Though he soon earned their respect, he never seemed to be able to satisfy Jackson. Garnett was relieved of command by Jackson on April 1862 for withdrawing the brigade without orders at Kernstown.

Charles Winder, Garnett's successor, was transferred to the brigade from the 6th South Carolina. He was one of the war's best brigade commanders until he was killed by an artillery shell at Cedar Mountain on 9 August 1862.

Colonel W. H. S. Baylor of the 5th Virginia was acting commander of the Stonewall Brigade until his death at Second Bull Run, after which the brigade was led by Liutenant Colonel Andrew J. Grigsby at Antietam. Due to heavy losses Grigsby was commanding Jackson's division at the end of the battle and Major H.J. Williams of the 5th Virginia led the Stonewall Brigade.

For some reason Jackson did not like Grigsby, and had Colonel Elisha F. Paxton of the 27th Virginia put in command of the brigade. Paxton served until he was killed at Chancellorsville on 2 May 1863, the same day that Jackson was mortally wounded. Paxton's successor was Colonel James A. Walker of the 4th Virginia. Walker was a stern disciplinarian who did not enjoy immediate popularity with his men. He led the brigade for almost a year, until he was wounded and captured at Spotsylvania, the battle that destroyed the brigade.

Jackson was justifiably proud of his brigade, though he did not often reveal his feelings to its men, beyond his congratulatory orders after battles. His true sentiments were expressed when he was in his sick bed after his wound at Chancellorsville. Upon hearing that Jeb Stuart, his temporary replacement as *II Corps* commander, had urged his troops forward with the cry "Remember Stonewall Jackson!" Jackson said, "The men of the Brigade will be, some day, proud to say to their children, 'I was one of the Stonewall Brigade'. The name 'Stonewall' ought to be attached wholly to the men of the Brigade, and not to me; for it was their steadfast heroism which earned it at First Manassas."

Lieutenant General James Longstreet with two of his divisions (Hood's and Pickett's) to that theater. Longstreet was to coordinate his movements with those of D. H. Hill in neighboring North Carolina in order to monitor enemy movements and also gather what supplies they could. Longstreet was supposed to be ready to return to Lee on a moment's notice, but his campaign would develop on different lines than anticipated. His extended absence from Lee's command with 13,000 of his veterans would further increase the long odds that Lee would have to face in the pending campaign against Hooker.

*Weighing rations preparatory to a contemplated movement.*

# Jackson's Ancestry and Early Life

Thomas Jonathan Jackson was born on 21 January 1824 in Clarksburg in western Virginia. His lineage was Scotch-Irish, the predominant stock of the early settlers of the Shenandoah Valley region. In 1748 the 23 year-old John Jackson, Stonewall's great-grandfather, had left London for America. Aboard ship he met and fell in love with an attractive six-foot-tall blonde named Elizabeth Cummins. Elizabeth was indentured to a family from Calvert County, Maryland, whom she had promised to work for in exchange for the cost of her boat ticket. John Jackson settled in Baltimore and waited patiently for her term of service to pass. The couple were married about two years after their arrival, and moved to western Virginia to get a start on life. They settled first at Moorfields in Hardy County, later going farther west to a village on the Buckhannon River called Jackson's Fort, now Buckhannon. The area was wild and populated by hostile Indians, but the Jacksons stayed and prospered.

John Jackson and several of his sons served in the American army during the Revolution. In their later years, John and Elizabeth lived in Clarksburg, Virginia (now West Virginia). There John died at 86. Elizabeth, who was physically and intellectually the backbone of the clan, passed away in 1825, at the extraordinary age of 105.

John and Elizabeth began a closeknit family that achieved a fair level of distinction in western Virginia. John's eldest and most notable son was Colonel George Jackson of Clarksburg. George won his rank as colonel during the Revolution, and later served in the Virginia legislature and U.S. Congress. While in Washington, he had the opportunity to meet Senator Andrew Jackson of Tennessee, the future President, and the two discovered that their families had come from the same parish near Londonderry, so that they were probably distant cousins.

George Jackson's son, John G. Jackson, was also a man of note, being a congressman and federal judge. His first wife was Polly Payne, sister of Dolley Madison, the wife of President James Madison; after Polly's death in 1807, John G. married the only daughter of Governor Meiggs of Ohio. John G. Jackson died in 1825 at the comparatively young age of 48. One of John G.'s sons, George Washington Jackson, was the father of Colonel Alfred H. Jackson, who was mortally wounded at Cedar Mountain while serving on Stonewall's staff.

Stonewall was descended from John Jackson's second son, Edward. Edward's line was less distinguished than that of his older brother George. This was perhaps because of the great size of Edward's family. Edward, who was a surveyor in Lewis County, had no fewer than fifteen children, six by a first marriage and nine by a second. One of this brood was Jonathan, the father of Stonewall. Jonathan studied law under his more prosperous cousin, Judge John G. Jackson, and then became a lawyer in Clarksburg.

In Clarksburg, Jonathan Jackson married Julia Beckwith Neale, daughter of a merchant from Parkersburg. Her family had also been settlers of western Virginia. One source describes her before Stonewall's birth as "rather a brunette, with dark brown hair, dark gray eyes, handsome face, and when at maturity, of medium height and symmetrical form." Her husband, Stonewall's father Jonathan, was "a man of short stature, with an open, pleasing face, blue eyes, and a handsome mouth."

Jonathan and Julia Jackson had four children in their cottage at Clarksburg. Jonathan did well as a lawyer, but did not handle his income wisely. When he died in 1826, from a fever that also took his eldest child Elizabeth, his family was left in poverty. Young Thomas Jonathan was only three at the time, so he had no recollection of his father or the poverty his widowed mother lived in. For several years the small family lived in a one-room house loaned by the Freemasons, a society to which Jonathan had belonged. In the summers Julia took her three children to her father's home in the mountains in order to escape the heat.

In 1830, three years after Jonathan

died, Julia remarried. Her second husband, Captain Blake B. Woodson of Cumberland County, was a lawyer of good social standing, but he was an elderly widower without much money. In fact, Julia's Jackson kin advised her against the marriage on the grounds that Woodson would not have the means to support Julia's three children. That is exactly what happened. Julia kept her youngest child, Laura, with her, but had to send her two sons to live with her relations. Warren was sent to live with an aunt, Mrs. Isaac Brake, and Thomas Jonathan with an uncle.

Julia died a year later. After giving birth to a son, Wirt, she weakened and passed away in the fall of 1831 at age thirty-three. The whole situation—separation from his mother at age six and then her death when he was seven—made a lifelong impression on young Thomas Jonathan; he always spoke of his mother with tenderness, and named his only child, Julia, after her. In 1855 Stonewall sought her grave in Ansted, Fayette County, for the purpose of marking it. He wrote an aunt, Mrs. Neale of Parkersburg, describing the visit: "I stopped to see the Hawk's Nest, and the gentleman with whom I was put up was at my mother's burial, and accompanied me to the cemetery for the purpose of pointing out her grave to me; but I am not certain that he found it. There was no stone to mark the spot. Another gentleman, who had the kindness to go with us, stated that a wooden head or foot board with her name on it had been put up, but it was no longer there. A depression in the earth only marked her resting place. When standing by her grave, I experienced feelings to which I was until then a stranger." Jackson did not mark his mother's grave then because he was uncertain of its exact location and because he had no money after losing his wallet. Nor did he have the opportunity to return later. The grave of Julia Neale Jackson Woodson was finally marked after the war by one of Stonewall's former soldiers, Captain Thomas D. Ransom of Staunton.

After their mother died, Laura and

Thomas lived for awhile with an aunt, Mrs. White, and then with their step-grandmother, Mrs. Jackson. She treated them kindly until she died. Laura was sent to live with her Neale relations. She later married Jonathan Arnold of Beverly, Virginia and had two sons, Thomas Jackson Arnold and Stark W. Arnold, Stonewall's only nephews.

Following the death of his Grandmother Jackson, Thomas J. stayed at her house, which passed to his uncle, Cummins Jackson. Cummins was a large, big-hearted man, and was about the only relative to show any great interest in Thomas' upbringing. Cummins also took an interest in Thomas' brother Warren, after Warren at age nine or ten ran away from the Brake family, who had taken him in. Cummins treated the boys as his own

sons, and particularly favored Thomas. Thomas thrived, working hard at school and at the violin, one of the few things he attempted but could not master. Warren, however, proved to be restless, and left his foster home in 1836 at age fourteen. The sad thing was that he persuaded Thomas, age twelve, to come with him. The two spent the summer kicking around Ohio, spending some of their time with relatives and the rest on their own. Finally things got so bad that they returned east, aided by a kind boat captain who gave them passage. Thomas was accepted by Uncle Cummins as a prodigal son. Warren, though, was too proud and went to live with the Brakes again. There he began withering from ill health, and died of consumption at age nineteen.

Thomas thrived under his uncle's tu-

telage, attending school when he could and helping to administer the farm. It was a happy time for him, but he was all too aware that he had little means or formal education to earn a good career. At age eighteen his uncle won him appointment as constable of Lewis County. Thomas did not enjoy the job, which included collecting debts. Consequently he sought and earned an appointment to West Point in order to better himself. In 1842 he left Uncle Cummins to live on his own. Uncle Cummins a few years later was caught up in the fever of the California gold rush and went west by wagon train, even though he was fifty years old. He survived in California only a few months. Thus Thomas lost his foster father and best supporter soon after he applied to West Point.

*Stonewall Jackson's grave in Lexington, Virginia.*

*A day in camp after Hooker's re-forms.*

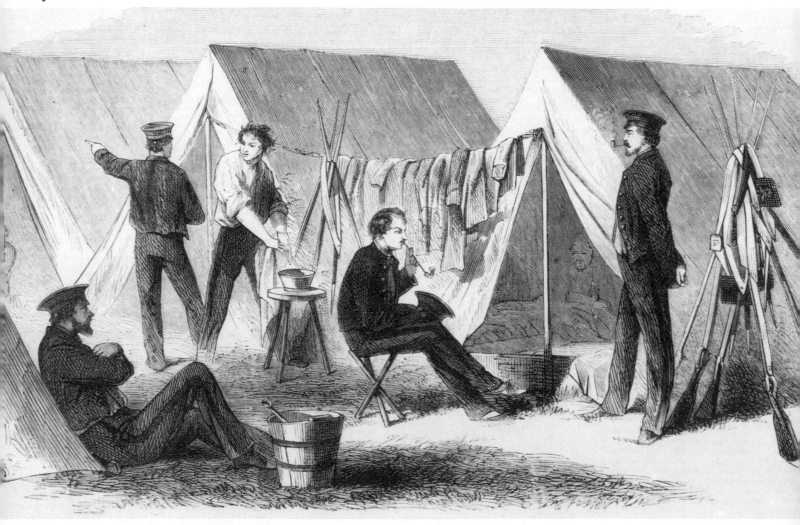

# CHAPTER V

# Cavalry Stroke and Counter Stroke

## February - March, 1863

On 31 January 1863, Major General Joseph Hooker, newly appointed commander of the *Army of the Potomac*, received formal operating orders from his immediate superior, Major General Henry W. Halleck, general in chief of the Union armies. Halleck reminded Hooker that Brigadier General Benjamin F. Kelley, commander at Harper's Ferry, and Major General Samuel Heintzelman, commander of the newly created Department of Washington, would operate independently of the *Army of the Potomac*, as previously agreed. However, they were both ordered to cooperate with Hooker as much as they could, and Hooker was in return directed to always keep those two posts covered. Other than this restriction, Hooker was free to lead his army against the enemy in his front "whenever circumstances will permit." Halleck then hinted it might be best to advance across the Rappahannock above Fredericksburg. Hooker, though, had no intentions of beginning a new campaign in the dead of winter. The aftertaste of the "Mud March" was still in everyone's mouth, and there was too much work to do to reorganize the army and build up its morale. He would wait a couple of months until spring came to decide the best way to attack Lee's army.

Both sides, then, remained inactive by their own choice for the rest of the winter and early spring. Their positions were essentially the same as they occupied after the battle of Fredericksburg in December 1862. Lee kept his headquarters at Lee's Hill near Fredericksburg, and kept a few brigades of Longstreet's Corps in the strong entrenchments that had defeated Burnside's attacks. Other brigades from Longstreet's command were assigned to watch the Rappahannock above Fredericksburg as far as U.S. Ford, which was about eight miles from Lee's headquarters. The rest of Longstreet's men and most of his artillery were in various camps behind Fredericksburg, some as far as Massapanox Court House, six miles south of Fredericksburg. They had to be scattered farther apart than Lee would have liked because of the scarcity of forage and provisions. Jackson's Corps was encamped ten miles below Fredericksburg in the area of Moss Neck, where it had been sent to block any potential Federal crossing on the lower Rappahannock. Both corps were in easy supporting distance of each other, and the army was astride its supply line, the Fredericksburg and Richmond Railroad. Lee at the time had only three brigades of cavalry with the army. Rooney Lee was stationed on the far right at Port Royal, six miles below Moss Neck, while Fitz Lee and Wade Hampton were guarding the Rapidan River line on the army's far left. Lee clearly had no intentions of mounting any offensive, and was only awaiting Hooker's first move, which he did not expect until spring.

Most of Hooker's army at this time had taken up winter camps between Falmouth (located on the Rappahannock a mile above Fredericksburg) and Stafford Court House, six miles to the northeast. Hooker established his headquarters at White Oak Church, five miles east of Fredericksburg, and other divisions were encamped at nearby Belle Plain or the army's supply base at Aquia Creek Landing on the Potomac River. Only one division was posted opposite the imposing Confederate works at Fredericksburg. Around all the army's camp ran an infantry picket line that ran from Dumfries (forty-five miles north of Fredericksburg) to Falmouth, along the Rappahannock to Moss Neck, and then north again to the Potomac east of Belle Plain, a total of about thirty miles.

Hooker's first orders for his newly constituted cavalry corps were to screen the infantry picket line from the Rapidan to Dumfries, and then connect up with the

*Confederate defenses south of the Rappahannock near Falmouth.*

troops of the Washington defenses near Fairfax. This was a wasteful assignment that dispersed the 12,000 man *Cavalry Corps* into a plethora of outposts scattered over one hundred miles of wooded Virginia terrain. Eventually Hooker realized his mistake and allowed the cavalry to operate in more traditional probing and screening assignments closer to the main army.

Hooker's first probe was ordered on 5 February, the day the *Cavalry Corps* was formed. Three cavalry regiments, a battery, and a full division of infantry, altogether some 16,000 men, were ordered forward to Falmouth and to strike at the Rappahannock Bridge, about twenty-two miles to the east. The purpose of the expedition was to test Confederate defenses in the area and explore the condition of the local roads since Rappahannock Bridge was an important but not critical railroad crossing. It had been damaged the previous summer, but was now repaired, and was not strongly guarded against enemy raids.

The raid began in terrible weather conditions that rivaled those encountered during the infamous Mud March. Snow, hail, and rain fell from the sky for a day and a half. At length the cavalry section reached its goal, only to find Wade Hampton's Confederate cavalry brigade formed on the other side of the river. The bridge could not be destroyed without driving Hampton away, a task the Union cavalry was too weak to accomplish. Some Yankee troopers tried to set fire to the eastern end of the bridge, but found its wooden timbers were too rainsoaked to catch fire. Since the Yankees had not brought along combustibles or incendiary material, they had to give up and return home without having accomplished anything of importance.

In the second week of February, Lee became concerned when he heard that the Union *IX Corps* was on its way to Newport News and southeastern Virginia. What particularly concerned him was that the Federals might attempt a large scale invasion of North Carolina or another attack on Richmond from the east, as McClellan had attempted before. At mid-month Lee sent Longstreet with Hood's and Pickett's divisions to watch the *IX Corps*, but he was still anxious to determine if any additional troops had left Hooker's army for Newport News. For this reason he ordered Brigadier General Fitzhugh Lee to take his cavalry brigade and break through the Union picket line near Falmouth, with the goal of determining the size of the Federal camps in the area.

Fitz Lee accordingly gathered a picked force of 400 men at Culpeper Court House on the morning of 24 February. The fact that the ground was covered by fifteen inches of snow helped him travel a great distance before being detected by the enemy. He crossed the Rappahannock at Kelly's Ford, and ran into a few Union scouts about noon. That night he encamped near Morrisville. As Lee approached Hartwood Church the next morning, the local Union commander, Lieutenant Colonel Edward S. Jones of the *3rd Pennsylvania Cavalry* expressed concern to his division commander, W. W. Averell, that he would soon be attacked. Averell simply replied "If the enemy attack, whip him."

Lee's advance reached Jones' pickets near Hartwood Church at about 0930 on the 25th, and the two sides began exchanging shots. According to doctrine, Jones sent a detachment of twenty-two men from second line to assist the pickets. They had the misfortune of running into Lee's 4th Virginia cavalry, and were all captured. Lee then continued on to Hartwood Church itself. Union vedettes seemed confused by the captured blue overcoats that some of Lee's skirmishers were wearing, and more Yankees were captured.

*Union cavalry breaks for the rear.*

*Brigadier General Fitz Lee, nephew of the commander of the Army of Northern Virginia was an excellent cavalry leader.*

As confusion grew in the Union lines, Lee came upon another bit of good fortune. It was now approaching noon, and was time for the Yankee pickets to be relieved. Jones' command was already scattered and not putting up much opposition. His relieving force that day happened to be two squadrons of the *16th Pennsylvania*, a green regiment that had never been under fire, and two squadrons of the *4th New York*, which was not known for its fighting stamina. The 600 men of this command should have been able to check Lee, but quite the opposite occurred. The men of the *4th New York* "with the greatest alacrity broke by individuals to run for the rear." The green men of the *16th Pennsylvania* became unnerved and "after firing a few shots from their carbines, instead of obeying Lieutenant Colonel Thompson's order to charge, followed the example of the departed squadron, and, considering the condition of the roads, made very good time to the rear."

Lee followed up his success, and began to encounter infantry pickets of the Union *III Corps* located behind the line of cavalry pickets. It was by now clear that Hooker's infantry were still strongly posted in the area. Lee became concerned that he might be trapped or cut off, so he began to return the way he came.

Meanwhile, the news of Lee's bold attack spread rapidly through the Union camps. Soon rumors were spreading that three Confederate brigades were at Hartwood Church and were headed towards Stafford Court House or Dumfries. George Stoneman, commander of the Union cavalry, ordered W. W. Averell to take his whole division to Hartwood Church, and Alfred Pleasanton was directed to have his *First Cavalry Division* ready to march at dawn the next day. Joe Hooker directed a *Second Corps* infantry brigade to march on Hartwood Church, and requested Major General Samuel Heintzelman to send down troops from Fairfax to intercept Lee.

Hooker's effort to catch Lee was a clear case of too much coming too late. Lee's cavalry rode back to Morrisville with 150 Yankee prisoners, and camped that night unmolested on the Union side of the Rappahannock. While the bluecoats fumbled about looking for him the next morning, Lee marched back to Culpeper. Meanwhile Union Colonel Sir Percy Wyndham was leading 2000 cavalrymen in a mad dash south from Fairfax in a vain attempt to cut off Lee's retreat. His exhausted command covered ninety miles and reached Hartwood Church on the morning of the 28th, two full days after Lee left the area.

Fitz Lee's raid on Hartwood Church accomplished more than it set out to do by embarrassing the Union Cavalry so thoroughly. Lee also aggravated Averell personally by leaving him a taunting note. It seems that Lee and Averell had been good friends at West Point, and Lee could not resist the opportunity to rib his buddy: "I wish you would put up your sword, leave my state, and go home. You ride a good horse, I ride a better. Yours can beat mine running [away]. If you won't go home, return my visit, and bring me a sack of coffee."

Averell took Fitz Lee's challenge to heart, and soon sought permission to make a dash across the Rappahannock and surprise Lee in his camps. Hooker readily granted Averell's request, not so much out of desire for revenge as for the purpose of taking some of the aggressiveness out of the Confederate cavalry. Hooker rightly reasoned that the enemy would continue to harass his pickets until they were given legitimate reason to hold back and respect the Union cavalry. Averell's projected raid would be ideal for accomplishing this purpose.

*Brigadier General W. W. Averell performed much better at Kelly's Ford than he did during the Chancellorsville campaign.*

It was during Hooker's discussions with Averell that Hooker used the phrase, "Who ever saw a dead cavalryman?" What Hooker probably meant was that the Union cavalry seldom fought hard engagements or suffered casualties of note; he no doubt wanted to stir up Averell to fight hard and fast and not worry about his losses. The cavalry needed to become engaged in order to get battle experience so that it could put up a still better showing against the enemy in the future. Hooker's phrase, though, was taken by many as a severe criticism of the cavalry, and it soon became a standing joke with the army, particularly the infantry.

Averell's attack was authorized by an order Hooker issued in the second week of March, directing the cavalryman to take 3000 horsemen and six cannons and rout or destroy "the cavalry forces of the enemy reported to be in the vicinity of Culpeper Court House." Averell promptly issued four days rations to the two brigades of his *Second Cavalry Division* and to Brigadier General John Buford's *Reserve Brigade*, which would accompany him. He told his men to expect a fight, and to emphasize the point he ordered them to sharpen their sabers.

Stoneman's column broke camp at 0800 on 15 March and headed for Morrisville, a major road junction in the no man's land between the two armies. As he camped there that night he heard rumors of a strong enemy cavalry force at Brentsville, twenty miles to the north. For fear of being attacked from the rear or being cut off once he crossed the Rappahannock, he decided to leave 900 men of the *1st Massachusetts* and *4th Pennsylvania* behind to guard the river fords he might need to use during his return from the raid. This move proved to be an unnecessary one, as there was no Confederate cavalry column bearing down on him from the north. More importantly, the move significantly weakened his force on the eve of what would be the largest cavalry engagement yet fought in the Virginia theater.

Averell's approach was no secret to Brigadier General Fitzhugh Lee, who commanded the cavalry brigade that pocketed the river above Fredericksburg. Late in the morning of the 16th Lee received a telegram from army headquarters advising him that "a large body of cavalry had left the Federal army, and was marching up the Rappahannock." Lee located Averell's column at Morrisville that evening, but was uncertain whether Averell intended to force a crossing of the Rappahannock or was heading towards Warrenton. All he could do was reinforce his alerted pickets at the fords and wait until morning. He was well aware that the approaching Yankees outnumbered his command of 1,100 by odds of two to one or more.

Averell had his men up before dawn on 17 March and headed them out on the direct road to Kelly's Ford. His advance guard consisted of about 100 men, for some strange reason selected mostly from the same *4th New York Cavalry* that had performed so badly at Hartwood Church. The advance squadron reached Kelly's Ford about 0600 and found the approaches on both banks blocked by abatis (encumbrances made of sharpened stakes and tree trunks). The river at this point was one hundred feet wide, and four feet deep, with a fast current.

Averell had hoped to achieve tactical surprise by dashing across the ford, and was disturbed to find the abatis in his way. He had no choice but to send out skirmishers to put down a covering fire while a force of twenty men with axes attacked the abatis. Meanwhile the rest of his command waited on the road in columns of fours for the obstruction to be cleared. The Confederate defenders on the other bank had only 130 men, and could not hope to hold on indefinitely against Averell's 2,100. They defended their ground well until overwhelmed by a charge made by part of the 1st Island. In the sharp melee that followed, twenty-five of the Confederate cavalry men were captured and the rest were put to flight.

Though the Confederate resistance at the ford was ended, it still took Averell over two hours to get his men across the river and reformed. The long delay was caused by

*Kelly's Ford, scene of the cavalry engagement on 17 March 1863.*

# The Gallant Pelham

Major John Pelham was a young, noted Confederate officer whose premature death at the fight at Kelly's Ford made him a martyr for the lost cause. He was born in Alabama in 1838, and entered West Point as part of a new five year program in 1856. He had a knack for the artillery and learned his lessons well under Major Henry J. Hunt, future chief of artillery for the *Army of the Potomac*. After the Civil War broke out, Pelham resigned in April 1861, just a few weeks before his graduation, and became a lieutenant of ordinance. He at once won attention for his superb job as drillmaster shaping Alburtis Virginia battery into a crack unit.

Pelham's genius for handling artillery became more apparent at the war's first big land battle, First Bull Run. He led his men calmly and effectively all day on Henry House Hill, with the result that army commander Joseph E. Johnston recommended him for a promotion to Captain. Even more significantly, his skill brought him an appointment to command a newly organized eight gun battery of horse artillery raised specifically to serve with Brigadier General Jeb Stuart's cavalry. He proved to be a master at developing the technique called "flying artillery," whereby he would move guns quickly to the front, fire, and then limber up and dash somewhere else to fire again. In this manner he could escape enemy counter battery fire, and also give illusion of having more guns in position than there actually were.

Pelham accompanied Stuart on his raids and fought in all the major battles from Williamsburg to Fredericksburg. His greatest moments came at Antietam, where his guns raked the Union night flank, and at Fredericksburg, where two of his guns moved about so much they looked like two batteries, and held up the Federal advance for two hours. His skill earned the nickname "Gallant Pelham" from both Stuart and Robert E. Lee. Due to his good looks and young age, he became a popular member of Stuart's colorful camp.

Spring 1863 found Pelham a major in command of Stuart's battalion of horse artillery. His untimely death from a wound received at Kelly's Ford on 17 March, 1863, was all the more tragic because he was at the battle only as a spectator. As described in the text, Pelham and Jeb Stuart were on court-martial duty in Culpeper when news came of the Federal attack on Kelly's Ford. Both rushed to the front, and Pelham for a time directed the fire of Breathed's battery. During the height of the fighting he got carried away and drew his saber to join a cavalry charge. As he advanced, he turned to the cavalrymen following him and shouted "Forward, Let's get 'em!" Just then an artillery shell struck a nearby stone fence, and a piece of metal the size of a cherry entered the back of his head. He went down and never regained consciousness. His grief stricken friends car-

ried him from the battlefield to the Culpeper home of his fiancée, Bessie Shackleford. The young officer lasted only a few hours and died early the next morning. He was only twenty-four and one-half years old.

Pelham's death was lamented by almost everyone in the Confederate army. His remains were laid out in the capital at Richmond beneath George Washington's statue, where thousands came to pay their last respects. Jeb Stuart ordered the men of the horse artillery to wear mourning badges for a month, and then honored his fallen comrade naming his nextborn daughter Virginia Pelham Stuart. Pelham's image was almost sanctified after the war by the writings of his one-time tentmate John Ester Cooke, who also wrote a laudatory biography of Stonewall Jackson. General Robert E. Lee was more objective when he wrote the following note to President Jefferson Davis concerning Pelham's posthumous promotion to Lieutenant Colonel: "I mourn the loss of Major Pelham. I had hoped that a long career of usefulness and honor was still before him. He has been strucken down in the midst of both, and before he could receive the promotion he had richly won. I hope there will be no impropriety in presenting his name to the Senate that his comrades may see that his services have been appreciated, and may be inclined to emulate them."

---

the need to remove all the abatis and the necessity of carrying artillery ammunition across by hand in order to keep it dry. Once across, Averell headed for a clearing his scouts had found three-quarters of a mile from the river. Here he formed up behind a long stone wall near Wheatleyville and waited for the Confederate troops to arrive. He hoped to give them a hot reception if they came rushing up to relieve the troops that had been defending the ford.

Fitz Lee was not long in coming. He had heard of the Federal crossing at 0730 and immediately led his force of about 1,000 eastward from Culpeper. He reached the area of Kelly's Ford in the forenoon, and formed up for battle. The engagement began in earnest about noon when Lee sent the 3rd Virginia in a charge against the Federal left.

# The Cavalry

The Confederate cavalry was very well led and organized at the time of the Chancellorsville campaign and may have been at its peak efficiency for the war. It consisted of confident, veteran regiments and experienced commanders who through their superior ability and aptitude had bested their Union counterparts at almost every encounter. The Union cavalry, however, was newly reorganized and strengthened, and was fully ready to challenge the acknowledged Confederate superiority. Federal superiority in numbers and equipment had previously been dissipated by fragmenting regiments and assigning cavalry brigades and detachments to infantry commanders. Now that Hooker concentrated all the cavalry into one corps under the command of Major General George Stoneman, the stage was set for a critical confrontation with Lee's horse soldiers.

Lee's cavalry was organized into a division of four brigades of four to seven regiments each. The brigade commanders were accustomed to work together or go on separate assignments, and the division had a veteran battalion of four horse artillery batteries that usually campaigned with specific brigades. The greatest weakness of the Confederate cavalry was its strength, which totaled about 7,000 at the end of March. This was well below Union cavalry strength of about 11,000, a difference great enough to make a significant difference if the two commands met head on. Fortunately for the Confederates, an all out cavalry confrontation did not arise during the campaign.

Major General J. E. B. Stuart, Commander of Lee's cavalry division, was at the peak of his efficiency and fame, and would contribute significantly to the Confederate victory at Chancellorsville, both as a cavalry and an infantry commander. His four brigade commanders were all experienced brigadier generals. Two happened to be relatives of the army's commander, General Robert E. Lee. William Henry Fitzburgh Lee (called "Rooney") was the commander's second eldest son, but did not owe his rank to any nepotism. Rooney, who was born in 1837, graduated from Harvard and served as a Lieutenant in the U.S. Regular Army before the war. In 1861 he was named a major of Confederate cavalry and served as chief of cavalry during W. W. Loring's operations in West Virginia in 1861-1862. He then became Colonel of the 9th Virginia Cavalry, and was appointed brigadier general in September 1862. Rooney was badly wounded at the great cavalry battle of Brandy Station on 9 June 1863, and went to his wife's family home to recover. He was captured there by a Union cavalry raid on 26 June, and held prisoner until exchanged nine months later; in the meanwhile his wife died in December 1863. Rooney was promoted to major general in April 1864, the youngest Confederate officer to hold that rank. He fought well in the war's last year, leading the cavalry corps for a time. In the army's final retreat to Appomattox, he was in effect serving as the army's second-in-command. After the war he served in the Virginia legislature and U.S. Congress. He died in 1891 and is buried in the Lee family mausoleum on the campus of Washington and Lee University in Lexington, Virginia.

Rooney Lee was a solid officer but not as outgoing as his younger cousin Fitzhugh Lee. Fitz Lee was born in 1835, and graduated from West Point in 1856. He served as Colonel of the 1st Virginia Cavalry before being named a brigadier general in July 1862. He was a hard fighter, and rose to major general after Gettysburg. By war's end Fitz was the army's senior cavalry commander. He rode away from Appommatox but was forced to surrender two days later at Farmville. Lee had an active life after the war, serving as Democratic Governor of Virginia and a major general commanding the U.S. VII Corps during the Cuban War. He died in 1905, well respected by his former opponents.

Stuart's senior Brigadier was Wade Hampton (1808-1902), a wealthy planter from South Carolina. Hampton was strong and brave and personally popular with his men. At the start of the war he raised his own command, the Hampton Legion, and rose in rank from colonel to lieutenant general commanding the cavalry corps. Hampton was always in the thick of the fighting, and was wounded three times, at First Bull Run, Seven Pines, and Gettysburg. After the war he served as Governor of South Carolina and U.S. Senator.

Stuart's fourth brigade commander was more eccentric than Hampton. William E. Jones was a veteran Indian fighter who bore the colorful nickname "Grumble." He was born in Virginia and graduated from West Point in 1848. In 1852 his young bride died in a shipwreck, and he was not the same again. In 1861 he succeeded J.E.B. Stuart as Colonel of the 1st Virginia Cavalry, but the two for some reason could not get along, so Jones transferred to the 7th Virginia Cavalry. Jones then won the favor of Stonewall Jackson by his hard fighting, and rose to the rank of brigadier general in command of the famed Laurel Brigade. His feud with Stuart, however, flared up again, and Jones was eventually court-martialled for insulting his superior. He was transferred to West Virginia, where he continued to do good service until he was killed in action at the battle of Piedmont on 7 June 1864, less than nine months after his nemesis, Stuart, was mortally wounded at Yellow Tavern.

The Union cavalry commanders during the Chancellorsville campaign were not as colorful as their Confederate counterparts. Major General George Stoneman (1822-1894), commander of the newly formed *Cavalry Corps*, was a West Point graduate (1842) who served in the Mexican and Indian Wars. In 1861 he was named brigadier general of cavalry and was the army's senior commander in that branch until he transferred to the infantry in July 1862. He performed well enough in the field and even led McClellan's cavalry division on the Peninsula, but may have been seeking faster advancement in the infantry. There he quickly rose to major general, and led the *III Corps* at Fredericksburg. His performance as *Cavalry Corps* commander was so disappointing that he was relieved and made cavalry chief of the Department of Washington D.C. Later he was sent west, where he briefly led the *XXIII Infantry Corps* before taking command of one of Sherman's cavalry divisions. Here he had the misfortune of being captured during a raid in Georgia in July 1864. After being released he returned to duty, and was named commander of the Department of the Ohio. He must have had some important connections to keep receiving such high appointments in the face of his inconsistent command record. After the war, he was Democratic Governor of California from 1883-1887. He died in 1894.

Stoneman's *Cavalry Corps* consisted of seven brigades of three to five regiments each. His three division commanders were the best the theater had to offer, but were still a mixed lot. The most respected of the group was Brigadier General David McMurtrie Gregg (1833-1916) of the *Second Division*. Gregg, who was a cousin of Governor Andrew Curtin of Pennsylvania, saw service against the Indians after graduating from West Point in 1855. He was original colonel of the *8th Pennsylvania Cavalry*, and was promoted to brigadier general for his excellent service on the Peninsula in 1862. He fought in almost every major cavalry engagement of the Virginia theater and rose to the rank of major general, even commanding the corps for several periods in 1864. His distinguished career came to a sudden close in February 1865 when he unexpectedly resigned from the army for reasons that are still not understood today. He lived a nondescript post war life in Reading, Pennsylvania, with the exception of a tour as U.S. Consul in Prague in 1874.

Brigadier General Alfred Pleasonton (1824-1897) was the competent but uninspired leader of Stoneman's *First Division*. He was an 1844 graduate of West Point, and, like so many of his fellow officers, had experience fighting in the Mexican and Indian Wars. He led the *2nd U.S. Cavalry* in 1861-62 before being named a brigadier general in July 1862. He was then appointed com-

mander of the army's cavalry during the Antietam and Fredericksburg campaigns, but was passed over in favor of Stoneman when Hooker created the *Cavalry Corps* in early 1863. Even so, Pleasonton played a major role in helping to organize the new corps. He then became Stoneman's replacement as corps commander, and

*Major General Jeb Stuart, commander of Lee's cavalry, led Jackson's infantry corps on 3 May*

led the Union cavalry to success in its resurgence at Brandy Station and Gettysburg. In the spring of 1864 Pleasonton was a victim of reorganization when U.S. Grant became army commander and brought in Phil Sheridan as new cavalry commander. Pleasonton found himself reassigned to be cavalry chief in the Department of Missouri, where he played a key role in repulsing Stirling Price's October 1864 invasion. He wanted to remain in the army after the war, but became embittered because he was not promoted as fast as Grant's lieutenants, so he resigned in 1868.

William Woods Averell (1832-1900), commander of Stoneman's *Second Division*, showed much promise early in the war but never progressed beyond division command. An 1855 graduate of West Point, he led the *3rd Pennsylvania Cavalry* in 1861. He won much attention for his work during the Seven Days battles and was promoted to brigadier general in the fall of 1862. He did not have the opportunity to use his troops actively again until the skirmish at Kelly's Ford in March 1863, where he inflicted the first battlefield loss on Stuart's Cavalry. On 3 May, General Hooker requested Averell to scout the army's right flank during the height of the battle of Chancellorsville. Averell responded that the area was too rough for cavalry operations, and found himself promptly relieved of command. He was reassigned to the mountains of West Virginia, where he fought well enough to be recalled to command a division under Phil Sheridan in late 1864. At the battle of Fisher's Hill in September he failed to pursue the defeated Confederates rigorously enough, and found himself relieved once again. His later career was much more successful than his military service had been. He was U.S. consul general of Canada from 1866-69, and then became wealthy as an inventor and manufacturer of steel, asphalt, and electrical machinery.

The cavalry forces of both armies would probably have been evenly matched if they were to meet head on in the coming campaign. The Confederates were weaker in strength, but had superiority in leadership, experience and confidence. In addition, the Union

commanders and new corps structure were not yet fully tested in action. Such a confrontation, however, was not destined to take place during this campaign. Union inactivity in the early spring persuaded Lee to detach half of his cavalry from his army. Hampton was sent with his brigade to recruit and gather horses south of the James River, while Grumble Jones was sent on a raid into Western Virginia in mid-April. This left only two brigades of less than 3000 men for duty in the main army—Fitz Lee was based at Culpeper to watch the upper fords of the Rappahannock, on the left of the army, while Rooney Lee was based at Port Royal, seventeen miles below Fredericksburg, to guard the lower Rappahannock.

Hooker did not choose to exploit Lee's scattered disposition of his cavalry, probably because he was not aware of the total situation. Instead he had new plans all his own—to draw Lee's attention away from Fredericksburg by sending most of Stoneman's cavalry on a grand raid toward Richmond. Stoneman would leave only one brigade, Colonel Thomas C. Devin's of the *First Division*, with the main army. This would prove to be a grave mistake on Hooker's part, for

Stoneman would accomplish nothing of importance on his raid, and Devin's small command would not be sufficient to scout and screen for the whole army during its movement to Chancellorsville.

Lee did not overreact to the threat posed by Stoneman's raid, but sent only one brigade, Rooney Lee's, to keep an eye on the raiders. Lee kept what was probably his best unit, Fitz Lee's Virginia brigade, with the army, and it proved to be more than a match to Devin's brigade. Fitz Lee did a commendable job at reporting Hooker's movements once the campaign began, and then played a key role at discovering Hooker's exposed right flank and the route to reach it on 2 May. Devin's brigade ended up being underused and then misused, especially when the *8th Pennsylvania Cavalry* conducted a mad attack through the woods on Confederate infantry. Thus Hooker wasted his cavalry and lost what otherwise would have been a distinct advantage for his operation.

*Three Union cavalry commanders—Brigadier Generals Alfred Pleasonton and George Bayard, and Colonel Percy Wyndham.*

The regiment was formed in columns of fours and did not expect heavy enemy resistance. Instead they ran into a withering fire from dismounted Federal troopers armed with carbines. The 3rd Virginia then veered to the left and ran across the front of the entire Union line. They received heavy fire and were not able to reply effectively with their pistols.

It was at this point of the battle that Major John Pelham, promising young leader of Stuart's Horse artillery, was killed by Union fire. Pelham and his commander, Jeb Stuart, had been attending a court-martial at Culpeper when word came of Averell's foray. Neither could resist the prospect of a good fight, so they both accompanied Lee's command to the front. Pelham went much too close to the firing to see how the battle was going, and was mortally wounded.

*Major General George Stoneman left much to be desired as the commander of Hooker's cavalry.*

Lee now formed up most of his brigade to make a massive mounted attack. He was most surprised to see the scrappy Yankees counterattack with a stronger force armed with better weapons than those available to the Confederates. Lee had no choice but to turn and fall back. losing a number of captured in the process. He reformed them a mile to the north behind a stream called Carter's Run, and awaited Averell's advance. In due time the Yankees came up and once again drove Lee back, this time to a new position one-half a mile to the north, near Providence Meeting House.

By this time Lee's regiments were exhausted and scattered, with his one four piece battery providing the only organized resistance. Lee simply did not expect the Yankees to fight so well or with such ferocity at Hartwood Church since in other recent engagements the Union cavalry had seldom held their ground very long. Now the tables were completely turned. One more attack by the bluecoat troopers would surely destroy Lee's command. However, instead of attacking, Averell chose to recall his men and withdraw. Apparently he had never experienced such success on the battlefield before, and did not know how to exploit his gains. He went back the way he had come, having caused about 150 enemy casualties while losing 100 of his own. Before withdrawing, Averell was careful to send the following note to his one-time friend Fitz Lee: "Here's your coffee. How's your visit. How do you like it? How's that horse?"

The engagement at Kelly's Ford might well be called a draw. The Yankees had fought better and inflicted more casualties, but it was the Confederates who held the field at the end of the day's fighting. The most significant outcome of the battle was the death of young Major Pelham. The battle was also important for serving notice to the Confederates that the Union cavalry could and would be more aggressive fighters in the coming campaigns. The days of Confederate cavalry superiority in Virginia were beginning to come to an end. Averell's success increased the confidence and morale of the Union cavalrymen, and earned the following praise from Secretary of War Stanton: "I congratulate you upon the success of General Averell's expedition. It is good for the first lick. You have drawn the first blood, and I hope now soon to see the boys up and at them."

*Union cavalry crossing the Rapidan River on 30 April.*

# CHAPTER VI

# Stoneman's Raid

## 29 April - 6 May, 1863

*H*ooker was pleased with the newfound aggressiveness shown by his cavalry at Kelly's Ford on 17 March, though he was annoyed with Brigadier General W. W. Averell for breaking off the successful action prematurely. In the next couple weeks he decided to expand the cavalry's role in his plan of operations and give it a major role in the coming campaign. As soon as the roads became dry enough, he would send Major General George Stoneman with most of the army's cavalry on a bold strike against Lee's supply bases and communication lines, specifically the Virginia Central Railroad and its facilities at Hanover Junction. Hooker believed that Stoneman's thrust would force Lee to withdraw towards Richmond, thereby giving the *Army of the Potomac* the chance to strike and defeat the Confederates away from their prepared defenses at Fredericksburg. This was a bold plan, worthy of the great Union cavalry raids conducted later in the war. Yet Stoneman was no Wilson or Grierson, and the movement would depend totally on his ability to meet objectives and hold to timetables. Hooker also failed to consider what the effects would be of stripping most of his cavalry away from the army's front for an extended period. Without question, the execution of this raid would have a significant effect on the outcome of the coming campaign.

Hooker's strategy called for the grand cavalry raid to begin two full weeks before the infantry moved out against Lee. Stoneman was to take all his cavalry and horse artillery with him except one brigade, Colonel Thomas Devin's *Second Brigade* of the *First Division*. The raiding force was directed to cross the Rappahannock at Rappahannock Bridge, thirty miles upstream from Fredericksburg. Hooker anticipated the force would be engaged near Culpeper, but felt it was strong enough to prevail and continue on its way, since intelligence told home that Fitz Lee's brigade of 2,000 men was the only Confederate cavalry in the area. From Culpeper the raid would divide into two columns, W. W. Averell would lead his division to Louisa Court House in order to cut the Virginia Central Railroad, while Stoneman himself would take the larger part of the corps through Gordonsville to Hanover Junction, where Lee's

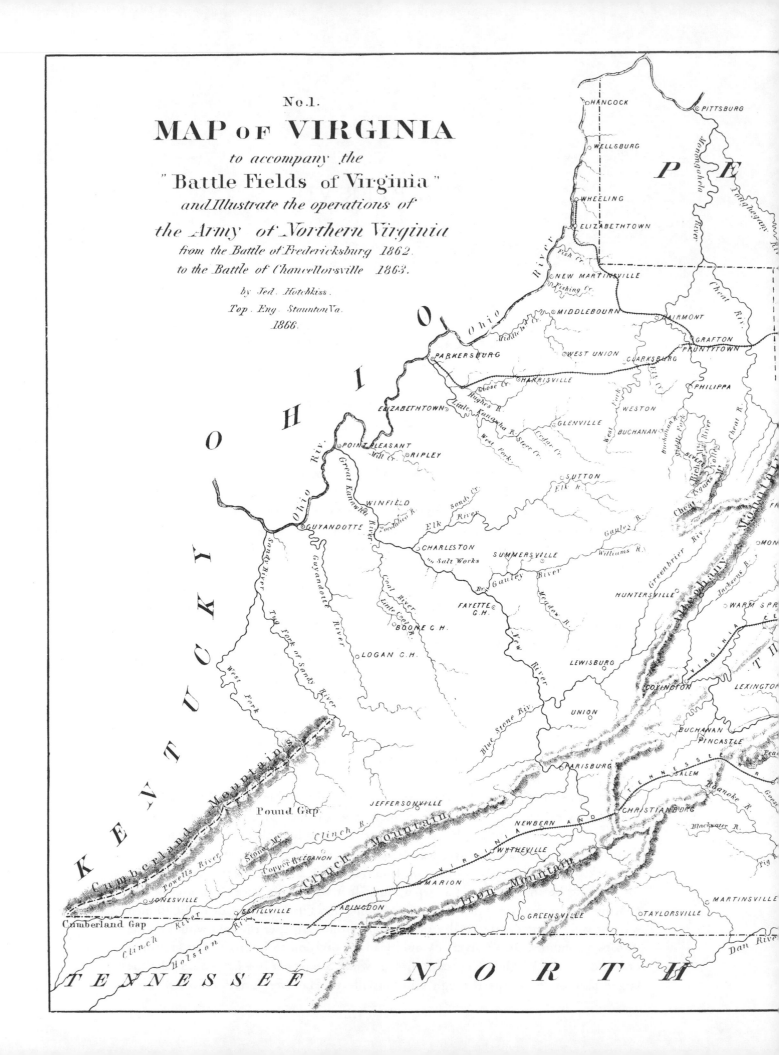

# No. 1.
# MAP OF VIRGINIA
*to accompany the*
## "Battle Fields of Virginia"
*and Illustrate the operations of*
### the Army of Northern Virginia
*from the Battle of Fredericksburg 1862.*
*to the Battle of Chancellorsville 1863.*

by Jed. Hotchkiss.

Top. Eng. Staunton Va.

1866.

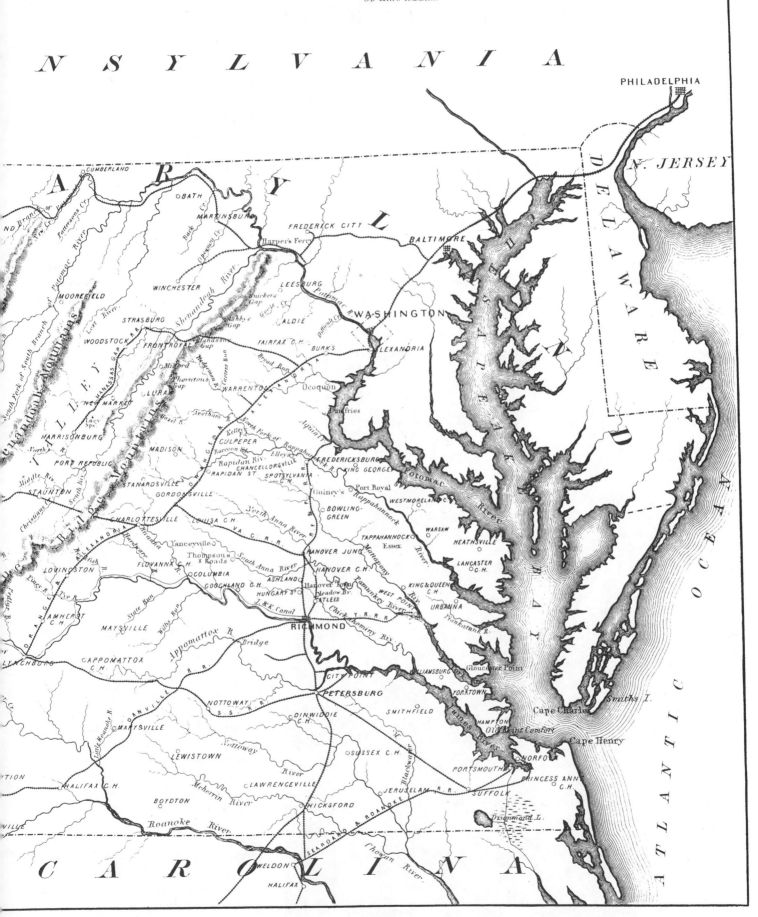

# The Suffolk Campaign

One of the most important events of the Chancellorsville campaign did not occur on the battlefield, but happened almost one hundred miles to the south at Suffolk in southeastern Virginia. Soon after Hooker took command of the *Army of the Potomac* in late January, the *IX Corps* was transferred from Fredericksburg to Fortress Monroe. Lee was anxious about the purpose of the move, whether it was intended to threaten Richmond from the east or it meant that an invasion of North Carolina was imminent. For this reason he sent his trusted second in command, James Longstreet, with two of his veteran divisions (Hood's and Pickett's) to keep an eye on the developing situation there.

Longstreet had been chafing for the chance to have an independent command, and was delighted to be given the opportunity at last.

Longstreet's troops reached the Suffolk area in mid-February, and would remain there about three months. Longstreet himself was given overall command of three departments—the Department of Richmond under Major General Arnold Elzey, the Department of southern Virginia under Major General Samuel French, and the Department of North Carolina under Major General D. H. Hill. From 13-15 March Longstreet conducted an unsuccessful expedition to recapture New Bern, North Carolina. He

then set about attempting to drive out Major General J. J. Peck's 40,000 man army from Suffolk. At first, Longstreet thought that Suffolk could be captured in a few days, but then "he sat down before it and commenced an investment according to the most improved principles of military science." When the "Siege of Suffolk" did not progress favorably, Longstreet turned his attentions to gathering supplies from nearby Virginia and North Carolina farms. The siege itself ended up being spectacularly unsuccessful, as Longstreet did not achieve his military goal, and lost 900 casualties in various attacks while inflicting only 260 on the enemy.

More notably, the Suffolk campaign kept Longstreet and his two divisions away from Lee's army at Fredericksburg and Chancellorsville just at the time when Lee was straining every resource to meet Hooker's army that outnumbered his over two-to-one. Lee in fact had been concerned about this disparity for some time. As early as 17 March he had ordered Longstreet to return to Lee with his two absent divisions, before Hooker began his spring campaign. Longstreet managed to persuade Lee to change his mind. The two worked out an apparent compromise later in the month after Lee learned that the *IX Corps* had been transferred out of Virginia. Longstreet was supposed to keep Hood and Pickett close to a railroad so that they could be transferred to Lee quickly when needed. Longstreet, though, became too involved in his own operation and did not keep up his end of the bargain. On 29 April, at the start of Hooker's flank march, Lee sent Longstreet a request via Richmond to return Hood and Pickett. Longstreet did not respond quickly enough, and as a result his troops did not reach Lee until 9 May, long after the fighting was over. It is difficult today to judge how the campaign might have gone differently had Longstreet and his divisions been with Lee. It is certain, however, that Lee would have put them to better use than they were at Suffolk.

supply depot was believed to be located. He would then intercept all supplies being sent north, and make every effort to prevent Lee from reaching Richmond.

When all preparations were completed, the jump off time was set for late on Monday, 13 April. Orders were carefully issued to all supporting commands, and Hooker even took the precaution of ordering the army's outgoing mail stopped for twenty-four hours in order to mislead the Confederates if they did learn of Stoneman's advance. Hooker let a false rumor leak out that the Union cavalry was being sent to oppose Grumble Jones' Confederate brigade in the Shenandoah Valley.

Stoneman formed up his command of 10,000 men on the morning of 13 April and began moving his men towards the Rappahannock. Colonel Grimes Davis was directed to take his brigade to Freeman's Ford, five miles above Rappahannock bridge, and cross before dawn on the 14th. He would then move south to clear away any Confederate forces in the area. As soon as he reached Beverly Ford, two miles above Rappahannock Bridge, Averell and Gregg would cross there with their divisions. Brigadier General John Buford would then lead his *Reserve Brigade* across at Rappahannock Bridge.

The night of 13 April was a bitter one with a frost. Since the men were ordered to light no fires in order to preserve secrecy, most got little rest as they stayed awake trying to keep warm. Davis crossed the river as directed and began working his way south towards Beverly Ford. He was an ideal choice for the assignment, for he was an opportunistic leader who had refused to surrender when he was trapped with his command in Harpers Ferry by Stonewall Jackson in September 1862. Davis bravely led his men across the Potomac in a bold night march and escaped Jackson's trap, even capturing a portion of Longstreet's supply train during his dash to safety. Grimes' promising career would be cut short by his death in action at Brandy Station on 9 June.

Davis reached Beverly Ford in good order on the 14th, but Stoneman chose not to send his troops across until the next morning. Some sources believe he was having difficulty getting his 275 supply wagons to their starting positions. The delay proved to be a disastrous one. About 0200 on the 15th it started to rain, and by dawn the river was swollen and dangerous to ford. The various units were drawn up at their designated crossing points, only to be told to stand in the heavy rain and await "further orders." Eventually they returned to their camps. Davis now had to return to the other side of the river before he became stranded on the Confederate side. His last men had to swim their horses across, and some twenty-five members of his rearguard were captured by a Confederate probe.

Hooker was overeager on the 15th, and telegraphed President Lincoln that Stoneman was well on his way. When he discovered later in the day that the raid was completely stalled, he directed Stoneman to proceed even if he had to leave his artillery stuck in the mud. Stoneman instead chose to do nothing and waited for the rain to stop. Lincoln saw through Hooker's boastful messages and correctly surmised the situation in this telegram sent at 2215:

> The rain and the mud were, of course, to be calculated upon. General S. is not moving rapidly enough to make the expedition come to anything. He has now been out three days, two of which were unusually fair weather, and all three without hindrance from the enemy, and yet he is not 25 miles from where he started. To reach this point [Richmond] he still has 60 miles to go, another river (the Rapidan) to cross, and will be hindered by the enemy. By arithmetic, how many days will it take him to do it? I do not know that any better can be done, but I greatly fear it is another failure already.

Hooker still expected Stoneman to cross and begin the raid, but the cavalry commander was in no mood to do so. Instead, he wrote Hooker that the rivers were "swimming," and noted that he was lucky not to be trapped on the other side of the Rappahannock by the swollen torrents! To make matters worse, he had established no supply base, and his men would soon be out of food, since they had started out with only six days' rations. Hooker reluctantly responded by ordering Stoneman to resupply his men and then cross at the first opportunity. Instead of keeping his men in readiness at the river, though, Stoneman chose to withdraw most of them thirteen miles to the northeast to Warrenton Junction. Here he was so discouraged by the muddy roads and still swollen river that he did not make any movements for almost two weeks. He tried to keep some of his men busy with daily scouting parties, but most became edgy and lost the sharpness they had possessed when the campaign first started.

Stoneman's long delay in getting started altered Hooker's strategy for the campaign. Since he could not count on the cavalry to get behind Lee in time to force him to retreat from his Fredericksburg lines, Hooker decided to make a broad flank move with a large part of his infantry command. The cavalry raid would now be a supporting role, even a side show, designed to disturb Lee's communications and hopefully draw off some of his strength. Hooker's decision to continue his orders for the raid has been universally criticized. He was removing most of the cavalry from the immediate theater of operations just when he needed their services most to screen his infantry flanking movement. Even more importantly, he was setting up his own flanks to be unprotected, a situation that Lee and Jackson would not hesitate to exploit.

The long delayed raid finally got underway on 29 April. Ironically, the cavalry did not lead the way for Hooker's infantry, but actually moved in the rear of the advance wing of infantry. Stoneman crossed the Rappahannock at Kelly's Ford and camped four miles to the south at Madden. The next day he split his command in half, sending Averell with his division and Davis' brigade west towards Culpeper. Stoneman continued southward with the other half of his force, Gregg's Division and Buford's Brigade.

Averell's command was the first to meet serious Confederate opposition. Lee only had two cavalry brigades available for service, since Grumble Jones was absent on a raid in Western Virginia and Hampton was off gathering supplies south of the James River. Fitz Lee's brigade of about 1,500 men had been picketing the Rapidan line for some time, but was too spread out to offer serious resistance at any one point. Rooney Lee's brigade of equal size was at Brandy Station, which it had occupied after being transferred from the army's far right flank to meet the threat posed by Stoneman's aborted crossing earlier in the month.

Averell outnumbered the two small Confederate brigades, but was unable to bring his force to bear on them. The two sides skirmished at various points, whereupon the Confederates withdrew. Fitz Lee moved to the east, where he would perform superb service for his father's army during the battle of Chancellorsville that was just beginning. Rooney Lee chose to withdraw south along the line of the Orange and Alexandria railroad.

To his misfortune, Averell chose to pursue Rooney Lee. He followed the Confederate force south through Culpeper to Rapidan Station, where he crossed the Rapidan River. He there found himself in an awkward position when some of Lee's men set fire

to the Rapidan bridge. Averell falsely assumed the bridge was destroyed, and did not ascertain its damage—it actually had been too wet to burn and was still useable. He then became concerned about being outnumbered, for captured dispatches seemed to indicate that Stonewall Jackson and all the Confederate cavalry were at Gordonsville. As a result, he took up a defensive posture at Rappahannock Station instead of continuing on to Gordonsville as ordered. When Stoneman found this out he became angry and sent a series of confusing orders to Averell, who interpreted them to direct him to stay put and keep an eye on Rooney Lee. Lee for his part was also satisfied to sit still, since he was successfully neutralizing Averell's much larger force.

This impasse between Averell and Rooney Lee at Rapidan Station continued for two critical days as the great battle of Chancellorsville flared up only twenty miles to the east. When Hooker finally learned of Averell's inactivity on 2 May, he tried to put Averell to more constructive work by directing him to return to the main army. It took two direct orders to get Averell to move. Even then, he marched his command only as far as Ely's Ford, five miles from the battlefield, and went into camp. When Hooker directed him to scout the terrain on the army's right the next day, Averell made a reconnaissance and reported that the country was impracticable for cavalry work. What was clouding his judgement that week we do not know. His indecisiveness completely wasted the services of forty percent of the army's cavalry at the culmination of a critical campaign. Hooker was in no mood to hear Averell's excuses and fired him early on 4 May, replacing him with Brigadier General Alfred Pleasonton.

While Averell was trapped in a state of lethargy, Stoneman continued on his raid as ordered. After leaving Averell's command on 30 April, Stoneman headed south to cross the Rapidan at Raccoon Springs. The weather again turned rainy, and the men once again spent a restless night with no campfires permitted. Some units were ordered to stand at the ready all night. One soldier in the *6th Pennsylvania Cavalry* wrote: "Hungry, wet and fatigued, we were illy prepared to spend a night standing to horse, but such were our orders, and without unsaddling, the regiment was drawn up in close column of companies, the men dismounted, and ordered to stand at their horses' heads all night. It became very cold, and our clothing being wet, we suffered greatly before morning."

Stoneman's weary men got off to a late start on 1 May because of heavy ground fog. At Verdiersville they were pleased to see fresh manure and other indications that Fitz Lee had withdrawn to the east. This meant that their march would be unopposed for the moment. Stoneman took advantage of the situation to rest Buford's brigade near Orange Springs, while Gregg was sent on to take Louisa Court House. Gregg reached his destination before dawn on 2 May, and sent his men flying into town in a wild charge designed to surprise and overwhelm the Confederate garrison. The Yankees were quite disappointed to find no enemies in town.

Gregg now set to work tearing up the Virginia Central Railroad, which was demolished for a stretch of five miles. When Stoneman arrived later in the day, he cleverly put one of his telegraph operators to work in the town telegraph office. This enabled him to receive uncoded messages from Richmond for over an hour until the operators on the other end finally caught on to what was happening.

After sending raiding parties even farther up the railroad line, Stoneman marched onto Thompson's Station. Here he heard cannon fire on the morning of 3 May from the fighting at Chancellorsville, thirty-five miles to the northeast. At Thompson's, Stoneman boldly divided his force into five smaller raiding parties, each directed to a specific goal. Their commanders were directed to head next towards Richmond, and if they ran into trouble, they should head for the safety of Union lines at Williamsburg on the Peninsula. Surprisingly, nobody was directed to hit Lee's supply depot at Hanover Junction, which was supposed to have been one of the main objects of the expedition. Stoneman decided to stay at Thompson's with a small covering force to await any of the detachments that could return in that direction. His purpose in dividing up his command into so many parts was to cause as much destruction as he could "like a shell bursting in every direction" and thus "magnify our small force into overwhelming numbers." One source suggests that Stoneman stayed behind with the cavalry force rather than accompany one of the raiding detachments because he was suffering from a bad case of hemorrhoids that was aggravated by riding.

The first of Stoneman's five columns was a two regiment force under colorful Sir Percy Wyndham, an English soldier of fortune with large muttonchop whiskers. Wyndham's orders were to take the town of Columbia on the James River and destroy an important nearby aqueduct on the nearby James River Canal. Wyndham promptly led his *1st Maryland* and *1st New Jersey* regiments to Columbia and burned a large amount of supplies there. He also destroyed a number of canal boats, some loaded with supplies. The canal aqueduct over the Rivanna River proved to be much harder to destroy. Its heavy stonework on concrete abutments looked too solid, and the

*Colonel Percy Wyndham at the head of the* 1st New Jersey Cavalry.

*Union cavalry under Colonel Percy Wyndham destroying boats on the James and Kanawha Canal at Columbia on 3 May.*

# Grumble Jones' Raid

In March 1863 Brigadier General John Imboden, commander of a brigade of irregular cavalry in the western part of Virginia, wrote a letter to General Lee proposing a raid against the Baltimore and Ohio Railroad line in northern West Virginia. The railroad was a lifeline for Washington D.C. carrying tons of supplies each day from the western states to the federal capital. A raid of under one hundred miles from established Confederate bases in the Shenandoah Valley could put the railroad out of commission for months and so aid the Confederate cause significantly. In addition, the raiding party might be able to destroy scattered Union garrisons in West Virginia and open up these new grounds to Confederate recruiting officers. Lee did not need much persuasion to accept Imboden's plan. He readily approved it and hoped also that the raid would gather much needed supplies and horses for the main army at Fredericksburg.

Plans were firmed up in early April, calling for a joint incursion to be made by Imboden and Brigadier General William E. "Grumble" Jones, whom Lee would detach for the mission. Many of the men of Jones' command were natives of the western Virginia mountains and so could better deal with the rough terrain and other difficulties there. Union inactivity across the Rappahannock at Fredericksburg persuaded Lee that Jones could be loaned for the expedition and still return before Hooker began his spring campaign.

Lee's gamble could have been a poor one for the Confederate cause. The two brigadiers had to wait for muddy roads to begin to dry up. As a result, Imboden did not leave Staunton to begin the campaign until 20 April. Once in motion his command was reinforced to over 3,000 men in a combined infantry, cavalry and artillery command. The march began well but soon turned into a nightmare because of snow, sleet, swollen mountain streams, and slippery, rock covered roads; Imboden called the weather "the most gloomy and inclement I ever saw." At length the column reached the Union

post at Beverly, which was surprised and driven off after a sharp fight. The capture of over $100,000 worth of Federal supplies greatly heartened the cold and hungry Confederates.

The sudden loss of Beverly greatly disturbed the Union district commander Brigadier General Benjamin Roberts, who had only recently taken up headquarters at Buckhannon, twenty miles northwest of Beverly. Roberts panicked and began marching his force to the railroad at Clarksburg, twenty miles to the north on the Menongahela River. Imboden did not respond in much better fashion. He sent a tentative prove towards Buckhannon, but withdrew to Beverly when he heard a false report of an enemy advance from Philippi. Once he received correct intelligence on the true situation, he advanced again and occupied Buckhannon on the 29th. He then settled down to await news of Grumble Jones' whereabouts.

Grumble Jones advanced on a route east of Imboden's and had more success than his partner at reaching their goal, the railroad line. He and his force of about 3,000 men began marching northwest from Lacey Spring, near Harrisonburg, on 21 April. He also encountered bad weather that included a heavy rainfall and dense fog. His greatest obstacle came up on the 25th, when the South Branch of the Potomac proved uncrossable. At length, he located a ford ten miles upstream near Petersburg. Even so, it was so deep that only the cavalry could cross. Jones reluctantly sent his infantry and artillery back to the Shenandoah Valley. He then proceeded on to Moorefield, which he found abandoned by the Yankees.

On 25 April, Jones headed northwest towards his immediate goal, the railroad bridge over the Youghiogheny River at Oakland in extreme western Maryland. At Greenland Gap, fifteen miles northwest of Moorefield, he found his path blocked by a force of only eighty-five Yankees who holed up in log church that had easily been converted into a fort. Jones no longer had his artillery with

him, and was unable to take the fort by direct attack. He attempted several ruses and then tried in vain to blow up the pesky fort with barrels of gun powder. Several brave volunteers tried to set the fort on fire only to be shot down. At length one plucky cavalry man managed to set the roof on fire, and the stubborn Yankees were compelled to surrender. Their gallant resistance cost Jones one hundred casualties and a half day's delay.

Jones now divided his force into several detachments in order to cause as much damage as he could on the rail line, which was less than twenty miles away. He himself led three regiments to destroy the grand and expensive railroad bridge over the Cheat River at Rowlesburg. When he arrived there, he found the span guarded by a force of 250 Yankees in a prepared position. A poorly organized attack was launched on the 26th and failed to get near the bridge.

Jones was frustrated at this goal, and decided to go after bigger game, the 615 foot suspension over the Menongahela at Fairmont, the longest and most expensive on the railroad. His men crossed the Menongahela at Morgantown, just a few miles from the Pennsylvania border, and approached Fairmount from the north. He scattered several militia units and at length reached his goal. On 29 April he blasted the iron bridge apart, an engineering marvel that had taken two years to build. The splash that the collapsing bridge made in the river was a sight to remember. Meanwhile Jones' other columns were also meeting success as they tore up stretches of the railroad and commandeered supplies, horses and forage.

Jones' successes brought near panic to Wheeling and the towns of southwestern Pennsylvania. Several banks shipped their currency to Pittsburgh, which was also in a state of confusion, and millworkers in Wheeling were transformed into homeguards. Governor Curtin of Pennsylvania demanded that action be taken to stop the raiders, while the Union forces at Clarksburg mainly attempted to locate the Confederate column. Officials in Washington refused to overreact; they realized that the Confederates would be gone before any substantial Union reinforcements could reach the area. President Lincoln felt the raid was an attempt to draw off forces from Hooker's army at Falmouth, and would not give in to the supposed muse. Lee's actual plan, however, as already discussed, was less serious, and had as its goal the interruption of the railroad and the gathering of supplies and recruits.

Having achieved his principal goal, Jones headed south towards Clarksburg in an attempt to locate Imboden, who had failed to link up with him on the railroad line. He wisely avoided the Union stronghold at Clarksburg, and moved on to destroy more railroad property at nearby Bridgeport. He then moved on to Philippi, where he learned that Imboden had been at Buckhannon for the past five days. The two forces finally linked up on 2 May.

The two generals gave their exhausted troops a rest, and began to plan the next phase of their campaign; the raid had been reasonably successful so far, and they saw no reason to return home as yet. At first they planned to assault the Yankee base at Clarksburg, but this attack had to be scrapped when the enemy post was reinforced. They then devised a more grandiose plan—Jones would attack the railroad line west of Clarksburg all the way to the Ohio River, while Imboden would take all the captured animals and supplies south to Summerville.

The two forces parted on 6 May. Jones' march of destruction met as much success as earlier—he burned two bridges and captured one hundred Yankees at West Union, and then burned three more bridges and damaged a railroad tunnel at Cairo. On 9 May he reached the oil fields at Oil Town, located less than twenty miles east of Parkersburg and about the same distance southeast of Marietta, Ohio. Jones ordered all the wells and machinery to be set afire, including over 150,000 barrels of oil. The resulting blaze was truly spectacular, as the burning oil spread and made the nearly Little Kanawha River appear to be on fire. One soldier noted that "Great pillars of flame, resembling pyramids of fire, rose to a prodigious height in the air from the burning wells, lighting the surrounding country for miles."

Jones rightly felt that there was little more he could do for an encore, so he turned back to meet Imboden at Summerville, some sixty miles distant. He arrived there on 14 May to find that Imboden had experienced a tough march south from Buckhannon. Bad roads, bad weather, and the number of captured wagons and animals reduced his advance so much that at one point he only covered fourteen miles in three days. The two commands then rested before heading back to the Shenandoah Valley by separate routes. They arrived at the end of May, three weeks after the battle of Chancellorsville was over.

The Jones-Imboden Campaign just described was one of the most successful but little known raids of the war. This Confederate force of less then 6,000 men successfully dodged 25,000 Union soldiers and caused over 1,000 casualties at a loss of less than one hundred men. Over 5,000 cattle and 1,200 horses were gathered in to support Lee's army, and about 400 new recruits were taken in. The raid was not a total success, as it failed to destroy the bridge at Rowlesburg and did not overthrow the Unionist government of Western Virginia, as some hoped. The railroad was so damaged that goods had to be transshipped by wagon at several stretches for a long while, but repairs were eventually made and replacement bridges erected. The most lasting effect of the raid was the weeding out of inept Union commanders such as Benjamin Roberts, and the establishment of additional fortified posts on the railroad line and in western Virginia, held by larger and more alert garrisons. More immediately, the raid had little effect on the Chancellorsville campaign other than the absence of Jones' brigade from the immediate theater of operations. Nevertheless, the management of the raid and its accomplishments shine all the brighter when compared with the failures of Stoneman's great Union raid conducted at the same time.

---

Yankees spent quite awhile trying to decide how to bring it down. By the time the right spots for powder kegs were determined, part of Rooney Lee's Confederate cavalry appeared and forced the would be bridge blasters to retreat. In the face of this opposition, Wyndham had to abandon his other goals and returned to Thompson's Crossroads. He had done a full day's work, covering fifty miles in sixteen hours.

Wyndham's raid was much more successful than the columns led by General Gregg and Captain Wesley Merritt. Merritt had only a small detachment and managed to burn only one bridge on the South Anna before returning to base. Gregg had a larger force of two regiments, and burned several bridges before turning aside to tear up some track in the Gordonsville and Richmond Railroad. Then he, too, returned to Stoneman's base at Thompson's Crossroads.

By 5 May three of Stoneman's five detachments had returned to their starting point. Wyndham, Merritt and Gregg were resting their men and horses at Thompson's Crossroads, while Kilpatrick and Davis were nowhere in sight, presumably on their way to Williamsburg. Stoneman decided to head back north on the night of 5 May, marching under cover of darkness in order to evade Rooney Lee's men and any other Confederate troops in the area. It was a difficult march, as one soldier later recalled: "The night was very dark, and much of the way led us through dense woods, intensifying the darkness; and for several hours it was utterly impossible to see the person riding immediately in advance, or even the head of the animal upon which he was himself mounted."

Stoneman's weary column finally reached Kelly's Ford on the Rappahannock late on 7 May, and arrived within the safety of their own lines the next day. Here the men were dismayed to learn that Hooker's army had been defeated at Chancellorsville several days before. One Massachusetts soldier wrote on hearing the news that he felt "sick of the war, of the army, almost of life."

Stoneman's two absent detachments, led by Colonel Judson Kilpatrick and Lieutenant Colonel Hasbruck Davis, endured much more exciting adventures. Davis followed the South Anna River and struck the Fredericksburg and Potomac Railroad at Ashland Station, fifteen miles north of Richmond. His sudden appearance totally surprised the Confederates there, and he managed to capture a train and two locomotives and cause a great deal of destruction. He then headed for Hanover Station on the Virginia Central, where he enjoyed similar success on the evening of 3 May. That night he encamped within seven miles of the Confederate capital, much to the apprehension of its residents. Davis prudently did not challenge Richmond's defenses, but instead headed for the Richmond and York River Railroad. He struck the

*Stoneman's cavalry burning Confederate warehouses north of Richmond on 3 May.*

*Kilpatrick's cavalry charging a Confederate battery near Richmond on 3 May.*

line near Tunstall Station, only to be repelled by a trainload of armed soldiers. Davis now headed up the James Peninsula for Williamsburg, over thirty miles away. His command arrived exhausted at Gloucester Point near Yorktown on 6 May, having covered over 120 miles in a week of constant riding and wrecking.

Colonel Judson Kilpatrick also made a bold march that took him even closer to Richmond than Davis. Twenty-seven year old Kilpatrick was noted for his boldness, a trait that brought him his nickname of "Kil-cavalry." By hard marching he reached the Fredericksburg and Richmond Railroad near Hungary Station on 4 May. After destroying several miles of track, he brashly advanced within sight of Richmond, where he heard church bells tolling the alarm and saw militia rushing to arms. He took a few prisoners and rode on to try to destroy Meadow Bridge on the Chickahominy, but soon found himself on the verge of being surrounded by militia. He managed to escape by riding northeast to the Pamunkey River, which he crossed on flatboats near Hanovertown. His orgy of destruction was still not over as he continued to burn wagons and military supplies on his ride towards Williamsburg. He finally reached the safety of the Union lines at Gloucester Point in the forenoon of 7 May, being glad to find safety and rest under "our grand old flag." Kilpatrick and Davis rested at Gloucester Point until the end of the month, when they marched back to Falmouth via Urbanna on the Rappahannock. They did not reach Hooker's army until early June, just when the next campaign was beginning.

As soon as he returned to the army's main lines, Stoneman wrote a report exalting his accomplishments on the raid. He had indeed done a fair amount of damage to Confederate railroads, bridges, and supply lines, but he failed to achieve his primary objective and did not cause anywhere near the amount of damage he could have. No part of his force struck at the key point of Hanover Junction, not did anyone threaten Guiney's Station, where Lee was keeping most of his transport under a very slight guard. The damage Stoneman's men did cause was all repaired within a few days. Indeed, much of the little success Stoneman met came about because he was virtually unopposed, as Lee properly judged the raiders only to be a passing annoyance not worth the trouble of pursuing. Stoneman's accomplishments would have been much more significant had he been able to keep Averell's column with him, an error that rests solely on his shoulders. He also would have been of much greater help to the army at Chancellorsville had he sent even part of his command in Lee's rear rather than trying to make splashy headlines by throwing a scare into Richmond.

Stoneman certainly bears responsibility for mismanaging the raid, for which he was properly dismissed by Hooker on 22 May. Yet the ultimate responsibility for the strategic failure of the campaign has to be placed on Hooker's own shoulders. The very concept of the raid was not a good one, as it removed too much of the army's cavalry from the immediate campaign area. Once the original jump off date was postponed, Hooker failed to adjust the cavalry's role to his revised strategic plan for the campaign. Thus he lost the service of most of his "eyes and ears" and made his army vulnerable to flank actions that Lee chose to exploit. In the last analysis, the Stoneman raid must be considered a total waste of manpower, as it removed 10,000 quality troopers from Hooker's control during a critical battle, and wore out hundreds of them as well as over 2,000 horses for no appreciable purpose.

# CHAPTER VII

# Hooker Steals a March

## 5 - 29 April, 1863

*A*s winter 1863 was turning into spring, Lee was becoming more and more concerned about growing Union cavalry activity and what connection they might have with Hooker's campaign plans. The boldness of the enemy attack at Kelly's Ford on 17 March seemed to prove Hooker's army was preparing for a general advance, so Lee at once ordered Longstreet to return Pickett's and Hood's divisions from Suffolk. Longstreet, however, did not want to release the two divisions and told Lee they were necessary for his operations. When the Federal cavalry withdrew to its lines and Hooker's army did not move, Lee gave in and permitted Longstreet to keep his two divisions, provided they stayed near the railroad line so they could be transferred immediately to Fredericksburg if needed. Longstreet did not take this proviso seriously enough, as coming events would show.

Lee understood well that Hooker would begin his campaign as soon as the roads began to dry out. In preparation for the coming battle, he gave orders on 6 April to his artillery chief, Brigadier General William N. Pendleton, to bring his batteries out of their scattered winter camps and concentrate them near Guiney's Station, a point at equal distance from the three most likely places that Hooker might cross—Port Royal, Fredericksburg and U.S. Ford.

Part of Lee's genius was that he prepared for all potentialities. Because there was a slight chance that Hooker might delay his offensive or even not move out at all, he formed a campaign plan of his own. On 9 April he wrote to Secretary of War Seddon, "Should General Hooker's army assume the defensive, the readiest method of relieving the pressure upon General Johnston and General Beauregard would be for this army to cross into Maryland." In anticipation of such a move, he ordered Captain Jed Hotchkiss, chief topographical officer in Jackson's Corps, to prepare a detailed map of Maryland and southern Pennsylvania as far as Harrisburg. Lee would not have occasion to use the map in the coming campaign, but it would prove most valuable in the next campaign afterwards.

As already discussed, Hooker was in no hurry to begin the next campaign until he finished reorganizing the army and the weather grew better. He fully intended to take the offensive, being confident in his superior members and perhaps overconfident in his own abilities. He knew he could not delay too long to start because of pressure from Washington and because of the fact that a fairly large number of his troops (those who had enlisted for two years service in the spring of 1861) would soon see their enlistments expire and go home.

Hooker's most important decision was where to make his attack. Hitting Lee's center at Fredericksburg was impractical because of the increased strength of the enemy fortifications there, and because of the army's bad memories of what had happened there the previous December. Hooker appears to have seriously considered crossing the Rappahannock below Fredericksburg, one of the moves planned by Burnside before his demise as army commander. The details of his plan are not known, since they were kept secret and never released. He probably planned a crossing near Moss Neck, supported by feints at Fredericksburg and upstream as far as Banks' Ford. To gain success, the troops destined for the main crossing would have to arrive secretly at their jump off points. Upon more consideration, Hooker discarded the plan because he did not believe sufficient surprise could be attained. There were not enough good roads to the projected crossing area, and the river's width (1000 feet at Port Royal) would make it very difficult to set up the needed pontoon bridges. He also would have experienced difficulty at this crossing because Stonewall Jackson's corps was encamped and waiting on the opposite shore.

Hooker's revised plans called for an attack against the Confederate left flank, a movement that General Halleck had been urging for several months. There were a number of good roads in that direction, and there were enough good fords on the

*Headquarters of the* Army of the Potomac, *early spring 1863.*

*President Lincoln reviewing the Union army at Hooker's side in early April.*

Rappahannock and Rapidan to make those two rivers less important as military obstacles. An attack on the Confederate left had the additional advantage of striking exactly that part of their line that had been weakened by the departure of Pickett's and Hood's divisions. There is no evidence to show, however, that Hooker was aware of exactly how weak Lee's left flank was at this time.

Hooker discussed his campaign plans with the president when Lincoln came to visit the army in the camps for several days beginning 5 April. Lincoln turned the excursion into a rather large outing as he brought along Mrs. Lincoln, his youngest son Tad, Attorney General Edward Bates, and several friends. The president left in a snowstorm, and then landed at Aquia Creek to meet an escort of 200 mounted officers. There followed a series of conferences, inspections and parades, culminating in a review of half the army on 8 April. Lincoln was impressed with what he saw, but at times seemed pale and morose at the prospect of all the casualties who would fall in the coming campaign.

Hooker conveyed his final plans for the campaign in a letter he wrote to Lincoln on 11 April, just after the president returned to Washington:

> I have concluded that I will have more chance of inflicting a heavier blow upon the enemy by turning his position to my right, and, if practicable, to sever his communications with Richmond with my dragoon force. I am apprehensive he will retire from before me the moment I should succeed in crossing the river. I hope that when the cavalry have established themselves on the line between him and Richmond they will be able to hold him and check his retreat until I can fall on his rear...while the cavalry are moving I shall threaten the passage of the river at various points and after they have passed well to the enemy's rear, shall endeavor to effect the crossing.

*The Grand Review held for President Lincoln near Falmouth on 8 April.*

Lincoln wired approval of Hooker's operational plan as soon as he returned to Washington. Hooker immediately gave orders for Stoneman to move his cavalry out on 13 April. The infantry had already been told to pack their wall tents and personal gear in preparation for the campaign that everyone knew was now imminent. As discussed in the previous chapter, Hooker intended his infantry to move out two weeks after Stoneman's cavalry left camp. When bad weather delayed Stoneman too long to suit Hooker, the army commander revised his campaign plan to have the infantry lead the movement around Lee's left flank, with the cavalry assigned a less critical role than in the plans announced two weeks earlier.

In order to draw attention away from the planned crossing upstream from Fredericksburg, Hooker ordered a series of demonstrations to be made below the town. None were particularly effective at achieving their goal. One such demonstration began on the afternoon of 22 April. Two regiments, *24th Michigan* and *84th New York*, were directed to construct canvas boats and cross the Rappahannock at Port Royal. The crossing was excessively delayed when the men experienced difficulty building their boats. A heavy rain further complicated their effort. Finally the Yankees managed to get thirteen boats across the river. They captured some Confederate wagons, took a few prisoners, and quickly recrossed the river. Their raid did not deceive Lee at all, and the Confederate general properly interpreted all evidence to show a movement against his left. The only question was whether Hooker would attempt to cross close by, at Banks' or U.S. Ford, or farther upstream, even as far as Rappahannock Station. Since he did not have enough men to maintain his present lines and also guard the upper Rappahannock line closely, he would simply have to sit and await developments.

*Federal troops abandoning the winter camp at Falmouth.*

Hooker's final plans were laid out on 26 April. As Chief of Staff Daniel Butterfield later explained, Hooker's goal was to crush and destroy Lee's army rather than simply defeat him and drive him back towards Richmond. To accomplish this goal, Hooker would divide his 130,000 man army into two wings, each approximately equal to the size of Lee's army. The right wing would consist of four infantry corps. Major General Henry Slocum would lead the *XI* and *XII Corps* on a forced march to Kelly's Ford in the Rappahannock and then would turn southeast to cross the Rapidan at Germanna Ford or Ely's Ford. Major General George Meade would follow Slocum with his *V Corps*. The *II Corps*, minus one division left at Fredericksburg, would move to U.S. Ford and wait for the rest of the right wing to arrive on the opposite bank. It would then cross the Rappahannock, and the four corps, now joined by Hooker, would march together to Chancellorsville and then to clearer terrain to the southeast. Meanwhile, Major General John Sedgwick would hold the army's left wing (*I*, *III* and *VI Corps*, plus one division of the *II*) opposite Fredericksburg with orders to cross over and tie down as many of Lee's troops as possible. The two wings of the army could then smash Lee between them, while Stoneman's cavalry cut off his retreat to Richmond.

Hooker issued marching orders to his corps commanders on the night of 26-27 April, with orders to move to their starting points at the river crossing on the 27th.

*Pontoon wagons on their way
from Aquia Creek to the Rappahannock. Hooker's engineers performed most admirably
throughout the entire campaign.*

Meade, Slocum, and Howard were to move as quietly as possible in order to protect the secrecy of their march. Couch, on the other hand, was encouraged to make as big a show as he could of forming his troops at Banks' Ford, in order to convince Lee that the principal crossing would be conducted there. Ambulances, wagons, and extra artillery batteries (including all *XII* and *XI Corps*) were sent in secrecy to U.S. Ford.

The march was a difficult one for the troops, who were stiff from their long months in winter camp and unused to such exertion. The men had been instructed to leave all excess personal gear behind, but most everyone brought along more than they needed. Each man was supposed to limit his pack to forty-five pounds of clothing and effects, but most brought along extra clothing and personal items to bring the total up to sixty pounds. Their load was further increased by eight days' worth of rations they were required to carry; they usually carried just three days' worth in their haversacks. Stories abound of how many men soon grew tired of their weight in their packs and began to discard winter overcoats, extra ponchos and other heavy gear, which littered the roadside as the army marched by. The men who tossed their warm garments soon regretted their rashness as the weather turned rainy and cold.

A key element of Hooker's plan was to lay a one hundred yard long pontoon bridge at Kelly's Ford, since the Rappahannock there was too deep and swift for Slocum's infantry to wade across. Through careful planning, the canvas pontoon boats arrived from Washington at Kelly's Ford at about 1730 on the 28th. The army's skilled

*Hooker's right wing crossing the Rappahannock at Kelly's Ford on 29 April.*

engineers, assisted by infantry volunteers from the *XI Corps*, at once sent about constructing the bridge and had it in place in a couple of hours. The *XI Corps* began crossing at 1000, preceded by the *17th Pennsylvania Cavalry*. Their movement was so quick that all the Confederate pickets nearby were captured, and no one was able to send word of the crossing to the rear. Stuart, who was at Culpeper, heard through other sources about 0900 that there was a Yankee force at Ely's Ford, but he wrongly assumed it was a diversion in favor of Stoneman's raid. Hooker's campaign plan was working to perfection so far.

The remainder of the *XI Corps* crossed at Kelly's Ford just before dawn on the 29th, followed by the *XII Corps*. Some time was lost as Slocum directed the *XI Corps* to stand aside and let his *XII Corps* lead the march to Germanna Ford. As a result the *V Corps* did not begin crossing until 1030; its progress was delayed still more by a rainstorm that started up, delaying the completion of the crossing until past noon.

Jeb Stuart was by now well aware that the Yankees were crossing in force at Kelly's Ford. Early in the morning a staff officer from Schurz's division was captured, who freely boasted that the whole *XI Corps* was across the river. Stuart promptly notified Lee that at least a Federal division was on the march, and then prepared to meet their expected movement towards Gordonsville. He sent the 13th Virginia towards Kelly's Ford and ordered one of Fitz Lee's regiments to Stevensburg. He kept the rest of his men on the railroad line, with Rooney Lee's brigade at Culpeper and Fitz Lee's at Brandy Station.

Stuart's misconception of the size and goal of Slocum's column permitted the Yankees to march unimpeded to Germanna Ford on the Rapidan. The ford was held by a Confederate picket force of just over 100 men, with another fifty men working on a partially completed bridge. Their commander strengthened his picket line at 1000 when he received word of the Yankee crossing at Kelly's Ford. Even so, the

*R.F.Z.sb.*

*Union troops crossing the Rapidan River at Ely's Ford on 29 April.*

Confederates were in no position to meet the Yankee onslaught that struck at mid-afternoon. Brigadier General Thomas Ruger, who commanded Slocum's advance, sent his skirmishers forward so stealthily that they were able to capture the entire Confederate detachment that was working on the bridge. Ruger then sent an entire brigade splashing across the ford and captured most of the Confederate picket force. The surviving pickets retreated six miles to Wilderness Tavern, where they informed the closest infantry commander, Brigadier General William Mahone of Anderson's Division, of what had happened.

On the afternoon of the 29th, Stuart had learned of the size of Slocum's column, and sent his two brigades forward to probe it. The *17th Pennsylvania Cavalry* was not strong enough to stop him, and Stuart broke through to pierce the Union infantry

column at several places. In the process he took a number of prisoners from all three Federal corps present. He continued to harass Slocum's column until 1530, when some of Stoneman's cavalry came up from their marching position behind the *XI Corps,* and drove Stuart back. By then Stuart was aware that Slocum's column was headed for Germanna Ford, but it was too late to help the picket force there.

*Meade's* V Corps *crossing the Rapidan at Ely's Ford on April 29.*

Ruger's men now set to work completing the bridge so nicely begun for them by the Confederates. It was soon completed, and the *XII Corps* was totally across the Rapidan by 2100. Howard began crossing his *XI Corps* at 1600, and had them on the other side by 0400 on the 30th. Meade's *V Corps* had a harder time getting across the river, due to an expected traffic jam on the way to Germanna Ford, Meade was instructed to march via a different road to Ely's Ford, five miles downstream from Germanna Ford. He arrived there at 1700, and had to send his men across without benefit of a bridge. The weary men strained to ford the icy cold river that was up to their armpits. They finished crossing after midnight and settled down for a few hours of rest, too tired to dry off.

Throughout the afternoon of the 29th, Confederate Brigadier General William Mahone received increasingly distressing reports of enemy movements converging on his position. He and Brigadier General Carnot Posey had been guarding U.S. Ford, and were the only Confederate infantry west of Zion Church. Mahone acted promptly when he first heard that the Federals were at Germanna Ford and Ely's Ford, the latter just two miles west of his camp. He speedily sent couriers flying to inform Lee at Fredericksburg, and ordered his men to break their winter camp as soon as possible.

By late afternoon Lee pieced together from various reports the location of Hooker's flanking column, and at once appreciated the threat if posed. About 1900 he sent orders for much of the reserve artillery to come forward from its winter camp; at the same time he began consolidating the troops in the Fredericksburg line. Since Hooker's most immediate threat was against Anderson's two brigades at U.S. Ford, Lee directed Anderson to have them withdraw south towards Chancellorsville. Anderson then ordered Mahone to form his men north of Chancellorsville to cover the approaches from Ely's Ford and U.S. Ford, with Posey to form west of Mahone so as to cover the approach from Germanna Ford. The two brigades were in position by midnight, when Anderson himself arrived at Chancellorsville. Anderson also ordered another of his brigadiers, Ambrose R. Wright, to bring his Georgia brigade west from Fredericksburg. Wright, who had been encamped the previous night at Massaponax Church south of Fredericksburg, did as ordered and brought his exhausted brigade forward to Tabernacle Church, having covered twenty-seven miles that day. He would continue on to Chancellorsville at dawn the following day. Anderson's other two brigades remained for the moment under Lee's direct command—Wilcox's Alabama brigade at Banks' Ford and Perry's Florida brigade opposite Falmouth.

When Mahone and Posey marched away from U.S. Ford that night, they left a combined force of about 600 men (the 12th Virginia and half of the 19th Mississippi) to watch the ford. This force was lucky it was not pressured by Couch's *II Corps*, which was poised across the river. Hooker had changed his plans and wanted Couch to force a crossing there instead of waiting for Slocum to arrive and clear the opposite bank. Couch, however, apparently did not receive Hooker's new orders and remained stationary.

Meanwhile Major General John Sedgwick was successfully carrying out his orders for the army's left wing. On the morning of 28 April he took his men into position

*Union troops crossing the Rappahannock on pontoon bridges below Fredericksburg.*

on Stafford Heights, opposite Fredericksburg, and made sure that Lee knew he was there with hostile intentions. A dense fog the next morning protected Brigadier General Henry W. Benham's skilled engineers as they erected two pontoon bridges at Deep Run and two more at Pollock's Mill. Sedgwick then sent troops across to secure the bridgeheads, while he held the remainder ready to cross. Lee chose to let the Yankees cross in peace, as he had before the battle of Fredericksburg, and held his men back in their prepared lines.

Lee was not at all pleased with his situation on the evening of 29 April. He realized that Sedgwick's crossing was only a diversion, yet it was clear that the Yankee force threatening Fredericksburg was too strong a menace to ignore. What most disturbed him was the fact that Joe Hooker had stolen a march on him and now had the upper hand. He had suspected that Hooker might try to cross the Rappahannock above Fredericksburg, but no farther up than Banks' Ford or possibly U.S. Ford, and he had positioned his troops on that premise. Now he had reports that a very strong force of at least three infantry corps plus cavalry was across the Rapidan at Germanna and Ely's Ford. Nor was he even sure how large the force was or where it was headed. Stuart had positioned his men to hold the railroad line from Culpeper to Brandy Station, so Hooker was apparently not headed west. The Yankees were going to strike Lee's army at once, or try to cut him off farther to the south. It was now that Lee greatly lamented the weakened condition of his cavalry—his only two brigades were on the west side of the Union flanking column, leaving only a few scattered detachments with the main army. Lee also regretted he did not have Longstreet present with the two divisions sent to Suffolk. In the afternoon he sent a telegram to Secretary of War Seddon, directing that Longstreet be ordered to return.

*Howard's second line. The Wilderness Church (in the left middle) and Hawkins' Farm ( on the right) as seen from the Plank Road in front of Dowdall's Tavern.*

# CHAPTER VIII

# Advance to Chancellorsville

## 30 April, 1863

*M*ajor General George G. Meade had his Union *V Corps* up before dawn on 30 April in order to continue his march towards Chancellorsville and Lee's rear. Even before his men left their makeshift camp near Ely's Ford, he sent three squadrons of the *8th Pennsylvania Cavalry* under Major Pennock Huey towards U.S. Ford to open it up for Couch to cross with the *II Corps*. As discussed in the previous chapter, most of the Confederate infantry that had been guarding U.S. Ford had been withdrawn the day before, leaving only about 600 men to guard the ford. At about 0500 the advance elements of the *8th Pennsylvania* surprised and captured the Confederate advanced picket post consisting of twenty-five officers and men of Company H, 12th Virginia Infantry. The Confederates had sought shelter in a brick schoolhouse during an earlier rain shower, and were unable to get off a shot in their defense because their powder was wet.

Major Huey now sent part of his command towards U.S. Ford and took the rest toward's Chancellorsville. About 0600 his vedettes ran into two figures riding north from Chancellorsville—Confederate Brigadier General Mahone and an aide—and fired at them. Mahone had no idea that the Union cavalry was so close and thought that the belligerent troopers were some of Fitz Lee's men. He told his aide, "I believe our cavalrymen are drunk." The general soon realized his mistake and turned back in haste to Chancellorsville. The Yankee cavalry followed them closely until they reached prepared lines held by the 12th Virginia north of Chancellorsville. The Confederate pickets vainly attempted to fire, but their guns were wet from the night's rain. A moment later a good portion of the regiment let loose a much more effective volley that sent the Yankee troopers running. The battle of Chancellorsville had officially begun.

Huey's report of Confederate troops at U.S. Ford and Chancellorsville persuaded Meade that the Confederates were preparing to defend the ford in strength. Accord-

*Major General R. H. Anderson commanded the first Confederate infantry engaged in the battle.*

ingly he sent his lead division, Sykes', towards U.S. Ford while Griffin's proceeded on the direct road towards Chancellorsville, followed by Humphreys'. They were not on the road long before Meade received word from Colonel Thomas C. Devin, Huey's brigade commander, that the Confederate defenders had been pushed away from U.S. Ford. Meade then directed all his force to proceed on directly to Chancellorsville.

While Meade's column was still advancing, Confederate General R.H. Anderson received orders to withdraw his three brigades from Chancellorsville before they were overwhelmed. Anderson began withdrawing up the Orange Turnpike towards Fredericksburg soon after the 12th Virginia of Mahone's brigade repulsed Huey's first probes, already described. The Union cavalry cautiously occupied Chancellorsville as soon as the Confederates left. After waiting for the lead elements of Griffin's infantry to arrive to hold the position, Major Huey sent his men forward to follow Anderson. Huey caught up with Anderson's rear guard, the busy 12th Virginia, about a mile east of Chancellorsville. He attempted to mount an attack, but was repulsed after a sharp fight, and withdrew to Chancellorsville.

Anderson marched his men another two miles to Zion Church, a more open area outside the dense woodland known as "The Wilderness," through which the Union force was then advancing. At about 0900 he posted Mahone's brigade astride a ridge that crossed the Orange Turnpike near Zion Church. Wright's brigade, which had arrived earlier, was already in line to the left along the Mine Road west of Tabernacle Church; Posey's brigade was assigned to fill the gap between the two positions. The troops felt the precariousness of their situation and began retreating at once. They were much relieved at 1000 to see Alexander's reserve artillery battalion of twenty-four guns come up.

Hooker's grand plan was still working, though it was beginning to run behind schedule. Griffin's division arrived at Chancellorsville at 1100, and Syke's division, which had taken a longer route via U.S. Ford, came up at 1300. Meade's *Third*

*Division*, Humphreys', was still standing on the road to Ely's Ford; its men had been up most of the night and were tired from marching in the dust of the rest of the column. Meade's advance had pressed the Confederates from their defenses at U.S. Ford, as directed, but Couch was very slow at getting his troops across. There had been no large Confederate force at the ford since late on the 29th, yet Couch was still cautiously scanning the opposite bank all morning of the 30th. He did not locate a good position for his pontoon bridge until 1300. The bridge was put up quickly enough, and the *II Corps* began crossing at 1530 to the tune of *Dixie* played by the Engineer Brigade band. Even then, Couch cautiously formed a broad skirmish line to probe the woods looking for nonexistent rebels. As a result of his slow advance, he would not reach the Chancellorsville area until well after dark.

Slocum's column, comprising the Union *XI* and *XII Corps*, had experienced a relatively easy time marching from Germanna Ford to Chancellorsville. He had his troops up at daylight, but for some reason did not get them underway until 0700 or so. Geary's division of the *XII Corps* led the infantry, preceded by a small cavalry screening force from the *6th New York*. Geary headed south on the Germanna Plank Road past Wilderness Tavern to the Orange Plank Road, where his vanguard turned left towards Wilderness Church and thence on to Chancellorsville.

At about 1000 Jeb Stuart formed up most of Fitz Lee's brigade (Rooney Lee had been sent to keep an eye on Stoneman) and struck Slocum's column near Wilderness Church. His advance was readily checked by Slocum's flank guard, the *28th Pennsylvania Infantry*, while the rest of the Yankee column continued moving. Stuart wrongly interpreted that he held up the whole Union column for two hours. Actually Slocum grew tired of the ongoing skirmish at Wilderness Tavern and at noon sent two more regiments to reinforce the *28th Pennsylvania*. The increased Union force convinced Stuart to break off the action. He then continued his probes, and determined that the Federals were concentrating in force at Chancellorsville.

*Troops of the* V *and* XI Corps *on the march to Chancellorsville, on 30 April.*

*Union troops at Chancellorsville.*

Stuart decided he better return to Lee's main force at Fredericksburg, since Lee had no cavalry with him and all the Confederate units west of Chancellorsville appeared to be in danger of being cut off for an extended period of time. In order to elude the Yankees and all their outposts, Stuart thought it necessary to swing south to Spotsylvania Court House before proceeding on to Fredericksburg. Nightfall overtook the tired command at Todd's Tavern, so Stuart put his men into bivouac while he and a few staff members rode east to locate General Lee, present their findings on the Yankee movements, and get new orders.

Stuart headed back towards Todd's Tavern and was pleased to out-distance the Yankee troopers. When he reached his camp, he alerted his old brigade and sent its lead regiment, the Fifth Virginia, dashing backup the road towards Spotsylvania. Two miles out, the Virginians ran into the New York troopers, who had taken up a prepared position in Alsop's Field. The Yankees emptied quite a few Confederate saddles and sent the 5th Virginia running. Stuart was not deterred and threw the 3rd Virginia into the fray. A sharp fight followed, made eerie by the light of a full moon filtering through the tree branches. At length Lieutenant Colonel Duncan McIvar, commander of the *6th New York*, sensed that he was outnumbered, and formed his men into a column of focus to charge through Stuart's regiments. The charge worked, though McIvar was shot dead leading it. Both sides suffered about equally in the affair. The Union regiment limped back to Chancellorsville, while Stuart continued on to Spotsylvania Court House, his return to the main Confederate force delayed by several precious hours.

On 30 April the head of Slocum's column reached Chancellorsville around 1400 and began taking up a position south of the Orange Plank Road west of Chancellorsville. The *6th New York Cavalry*, which had been screening Slocum's column during the march, was during the afternoon sent south to occupy Spotsylvania Court House. More will be heard from this unit later. Howard's *XI Corps*, which was following Slocum, reached Dowdall's Tavern, two miles west of Chancellorsville, about 1600.

It was now the critical point of the campaign. Hooker's flanking movement had caught Lee off guard, and a strong Union force was now perched at Chancellorsville ready to move into the more open country in the area of Zion Church, where Anderson's three small brigades were hurriedly preparing entrenchments. The troops arriving at Chancellorsville were well aware of their advantage, and many were jubilant. Among the most enthused was General Meade, who greeted Slocum with the following words when the latter arrived at Chancellorsville shortly after 1600. "This is splendid, Slocum; hurrah for Old Joe; we are on Lee's flank, and he does not know it. You take the Plank Road toward Fredericksburg, and I'll take the pike, or vice versa, as you prefer, and we will get out of this wilderness."

Meade could hardly have been more shocked to hear Slocum's reply: "My orders are to assume command on arriving at this point, and to take up a line of battle here, and not to move forward without orders." It was all too true, as Meade soon received confirming orders from Hooker's headquarters: "The general directs that no advance be made from Chancellorsville until the columns are concentrated. He expects to be at Chancellorsville tonight."

It is difficult today to tell what was on Hooker's mind when he stopped Slocum's and Meade's advance just when he had Lee on the ropes. Perhaps he was concerned about Confederate resistance near Chancellorsville, weak as it had been. He was not at all sure what sort of strength Lee had in that sector, and perhaps did not want Slocum and Meade to rush into a trap. Their divisions were a bit strung out from the

*Major General Jeb Stuart leading his cavalry.*

march, and Couch's corps was behind schedule coming down from U.S. Ford. Couch's lateness also delayed many artillery batteries that were backed up at U.S. Ford. Hooker apparently thought it would be better to concentrate his troops at Chancellorsville before moving on. He would also use the delay to transfer the *III* and *I Corps* from Sedgwick's wing to the growing force at Chancellorsville.

It may have been the case that Hooker actually believed he now had the campaign won. Some of his comments on reaching Chancellorsville that night suggest that he was over-rating his success to that point: "God almighty will not be able to prevent the destruction of the rebel army"; "God have mercy on General Lee, for I shall have none"; and "the rebel army is now the legitimate property of the *Army of the Potomac.* They may as well pack up their haversacks and make for Richmond. I shall be after them." His elation can also be seen in the following congratulatory order he wrote on the evening of April 30 at Falmouth before leaving for Chancellorsville. He ordered it to be read to the troops as if the campaign were over: "It is with heart-felt satisfaction the Commanding General announces to the army that the operations of the last three days have determined that our enemy must either ingloriously fly or come out from behind his entrenchments and give us battle on our own ground, where certain destruction awaits him. The operations of the *V, XI,* and *XII Corps* have been a succession of splendid achievements."

Upon receiving Hooker's orders to stop their advance, Meade and Slocum reluctantly and dutifully formed their troops at Chancellorsville. Meade formed most of Sykes' and Griffin's divisions facing east immediately east of Chancellorsville; Humphreys' division, which had been lagging behind all day, was permitted to encamp that night two miles north of Chancellorsville on the road to Ely's Ford. Despite Hooker's instructions, Meade's advance troops almost precipitated a larger engagement along the turnpike. Meade had sent Barnes' brigade of Griffin's division out front to support Devin's cavalry. When Griffin ran into Confederate outposts about one mile west of Zion Church at 1600, Meade sent another of Griffin's brigade to his support. The men fully expected to go into action, but eventually had to be withdrawn for fear of bringing on the engagement they wanted but Hooker did not. A member of the *118th Pennsylvania* later wrote of his disappointment that day: "After several hours of impatient waiting, in buoyant expectancy of a promised success, the whole force was withdrawn to the rifle pits near the Chancellorsville House. The soldiers were as discomfited as if they had been checked by a serious repulse."

Slocum formed up his *XII Corps* west of Chancellorsville and south of the Orange Plank Road. Howard, who had brought up the rear of the advancing column, continued Slocum's line west along the Plank Road to Dowdall's Tavern and from there another mile west in the direction of Wilderness Tavern. Part of his *Third Division* was posted facing west on the right of the line, and the *17th Pennsylvania Cavalry* was ordered to patrol the rear area between the *XI Corps* and the Ely's Ford Road. As already mentioned, Couch's two divisions came up after dark and camped at Chandler's, a mile north of Chancellorsville.

Sedgwick's wing opposite Fredericksburg remained largely inactive on 30 April. Lee had expected to see more troops cross the river, but none did. The front was in fact all too quiet except for occasional long range artillery duels. Hooker's decision to keep Sedgwick inactive was his second great mistake on 30 April. His lack of movement made it all to clear that the previous days river crossing was just a diversion. More aggression by Sedgwick would have greatly limited Lee's options at this critical opening stage of the battle.

Lee for his part was at first not quite sure how to deal with the Federal column at Chancellorsville. His first reactions had been limited to calling up reserve artillery from their camps and shifting Wright's brigade to help Mahone and Posey at Zion Church. At 1430 he wrote Anderson directing him to dig in, yet have the men prepare two days' rations and be ready to move out at a moment's notice with their gear packed. This order clearly shows that Lee was not yet certain whether he would stay and fight Hooker or withdraw.

Lee made up his mind not long afterwards. In one of his boldest decisions of the war, he decided to stay and fight Hooker despite the fact that the Yankees outnumbered his army by two to one. He would leave only five brigades at Fredericksburg (one of McLaws' and four of Jackson's) to face Sedgwick and would move the rest of his army to reinforce Anderson near Tabernacle Church. He would then "make arrangements to repulse the enemy." Lee's decision to engage Hooker was based on his confidence in his general and his men, as well as a certain disdain for the Yankees, particularly their commander, Fighting Joe Hooker.

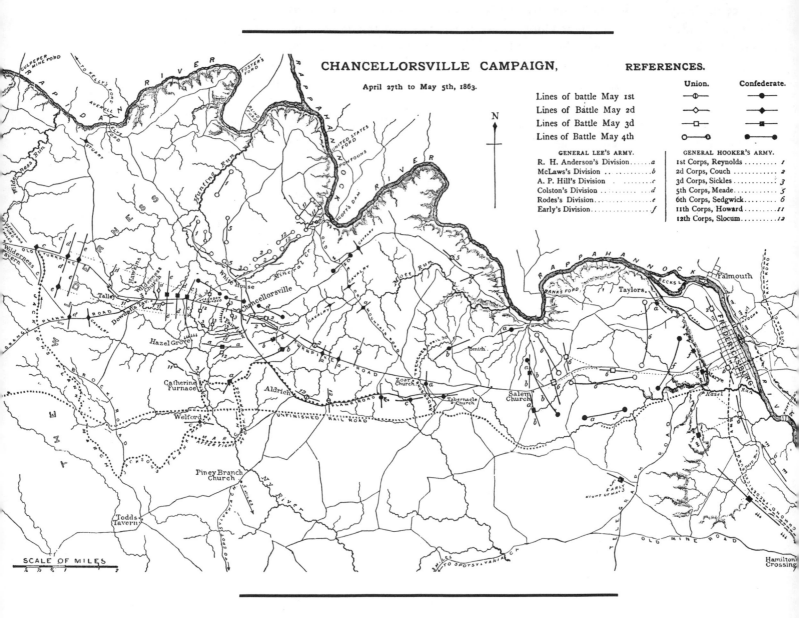

## CHANCELLORSVILLE CAMPAIGN,

April 27th to May 5th, 1863.

### REFERENCES.

|  | Union. | Confederate. |
|---|---|---|
| Lines of battle May 1st | | |
| Lines of Battle May 2d | | |
| Lines of Battle May 3d | | |
| Lines of Battle May 4th | | |

| GENERAL LEE'S ARMY. | | GENERAL HOOKER'S ARMY. | |
|---|---|---|---|
| R. H. Anderson's Division | a | 1st Corps, Reynolds | 1 |
| McLaws's Division | b | 2d Corps, Couch | 2 |
| A. P. Hill's Division | c | 3d Corps, Sickles | 3 |
| Colston's Division | d | 5th Corps, Meade | 5 |
| Rodes's Division | e | 6th Corps, Sedgwick | 6 |
| Early's Division | f | 11th Corps, Howard | 11 |
| | | 12th Corps, Slocum | 12 |

SCALE OF MILES

# CHAPTER IX

# Meeting Engagement—
# Hooker Loses His Nerve

## 1 May, 1863

*F*riday, 1 May 1863, began as a calm, cool, beautiful day, one of the nicest of the campaign. Despite the fact that the campaign was in its fifth day, there was no fighting going on. In fact, the only sector where the two armies had skirmishers in active contact was on the front of Sedgwick's bridgehead below Fredericksburg. There may also have been a few shots being fired between Anderson's skirmishers and vedettes of the *8th Pennsylvania Cavalry* along the Orange Turnpike west of Zion Church. Everything else was quiet, too quiet, the quiet before the storm.

As mentioned in the previous chapter, Hooker left Falmouth at about 1600 on 30 April and reached his right wing at Chancellorsville by 1800. He was overjoyed with the success of his flanking movement, and was especially glad to hear a report (later proved to be false) that Stoneman's cavalry had just cut Lee's communications with Richmond. For the moment Hooker was content to sit on the defensive, waiting for Lee to withdraw from Fredericksburg or attack at a disadvantage. He spent the morning consolidating his command as various artillery batteries came up to rejoin their corps and several rear detachments (most notably Humphreys' division of the *V Corps*) came up. His greatest concern was the arrival of the *III Corps*, which he wanted to have in hand before continuing the operation. Sickles' men had begun crossing at U.S. Ford at 0730, and Sickles himself reached Chancellorsville ahead of his men at 0900. His infantry began arriving two hours later.

Hooker's next concern seems to have been a movement to open up the approaches to Banks' Ford, a maneuver that would greatly shorten his communications with his left wing and allow reenforcements (Reynolds' *I Corps* and Gibbon's division of the *II Corps*) to reach him more easily. Such a move would also most surely force Lee out of his lines at Fredericksburg. During the morning he sent his chief engineer, Brigadier General Gouverneur K. Warren, to scout the enemy's positions and reconnoiter the roads towards Fredericksburg. Hooker had heard from Sedgwick's wing and Professor

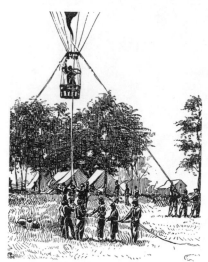

*Professor Thaddeus Lowe used an observation balloon tethered opposite Fredericksburg to keep Hooker posted on Lee's movements.*

Thaddeus Lowe's observation balloon tethered opposite Fredericksburg that Confederate forces were moving out of their lines at and below Fredericksburg. Since Warren and other scouts did not detect a reinforced Confederate presence in Hooker's front, the general falsely assumed Lee's troops were heading south. Even so, Hooker did not choose to move out aggressively, since he overestimated the strength of his position, now reenforced to 70,000 men and 184 cannons. He may also have been concerned about a rumor deliberately planted by Confederate "deserters" that Longstreet had arrived at Gordonsville from the south side of the James.

At mid-morning Hooker issued orders for the day to his corps commanders. Meade was to take the *V Corps* up the River Road towards Banks' Ford, while Slocum led the *XII Corps* up the Orange Plank Road towards the Confederate position at Tabernacle Church. Howard would move up a mile behind Slocum, and Couch would send one division to guard the right at Todd's Tavern. The remaining troops would form on the turnpike east of Chancellorsville, joined by the *III Corps* as it came up.

It is difficult to fathom the real intentions of Hooker's plan. His orders did not reveal the purpose of any of the movements, but only gave the positions he expected to be reached between 1200 and 1400, when further orders would presumably be given. Meade was probably going to be sent to Banks' Ford, but the purpose of Slocum's advance is not clear. He was directed to mass his *XII Corps* below the Plank Road, out of sight of the enemy. No mention was made of actually engaging the Confederates. Hooker probably intended to carry out the instructions he had given to Slocum the previous day, whereby he proposed for Slocum to proceed towards Banks' Ford if resistance was minimal, but "if the enemy should be greatly reenforced you will then select a strong position and compel him to attack you on your ground."

It may be true that Hooker was not certain exactly where Anderson's line was located. His orders directed Slocum to have the head of his corps "resting near Tabernacle Church," which was then well within Anderson's entrenched line. Slocum clearly could not have carried out Hooker's instructions without bringing on a sharp engagement. Hooker may have properly understood where Anderson was, and assumed the Confederates would withdraw without a fight before Slocum's advance. Chancellorsville historian John Bigelow, however, suggests that Hooker was mistaken about the location of Anderson's line, and may have thought that the Confederates were on a ridge near Salem Church, located two miles east of Tabernacle Church and two miles south of Banks' Ford. Bigelow's interpretation helps make more sense out of Hooker's orders to both Meade and Slocum.

While Hooker spent the first ten hours of 1 May in relative inactivity, Lee was rapidly shifting all the troops he could from Fredericksburg to the new front facing Chancellorsville. McLaws brought three brigades of his division up during the wee hours of the morning (his fourth brigade, Barksdale's, was left to help defend Fredericksburg). Semmes arrived at about 0100 and went into line north of Mahone's position at Zion Church. Kershaw and Wofford came up before dawn and extended Semmes' line eastward to Smith Hill. The whole position was entrenched under the skillful direction of Lee's engineers.

Stonewall Jackson arrived at Tabernacle Church about 0800, riding ahead of his men, who would not begin reaching that point until 1300. When the Second Corps (less Early's division, left at Fredericksburg) did arrive, they would increase Lee's strength on this front from 13,000 to 40,000 men, which he felt would be more than enough to defend against whatever force Hooker had at Chancellorsville. Lee understood quite well that the line at Tabernacle Church could be held only as long as Sedgwick made no serious attack at Fredericksburg. If he did, Lee's entire army would be in danger of being crushed between the two wings of Hooker's army.

Jackson was under orders from Lee to take charge of the troops at Tabernacle Church and "made arrangements to repulse the enemy." Jackson's instinct, though, was not to sit on the defensive unless he really had to do so. After surveying the situation on Anderson's front, he boldly decided to launch a spoiling attack against whatever Federal forces were on the Plank Road and the turnpike. It was a decision that would alter the course of the battle. Jackson might have chosen to hold Anderson's and McLaws' troops in their prepared defenses and await whatever attack Hooker might organize; he could then have launched counter attacks if he desired with the troops of his own Second Corps as they arrived. Instead he chose to employ the old adage "the best defense is a good offense" and throw the enemy's advance off balance or even drive it back. If the attack failed, Jackson could still withdraw back to the prepared lines already entrenched before Zion Church and Tabernacle Church.

Jackson chose not to wait until all his troops arrived at Tabernacle Church, since that would delay his advance until mid-afternoon at best. He drew up his plans during the morning, and sent the brigades forward at 1030. If he ran into trouble, he knew his reliable Second Corps would soon be available for assistance. Jackson directed Mahone's brigade of 2,000 men to lead the advance up the Orange Turnpike, followed by Wofford and Semmes with their combined 4,000. Brigadier General Carnot Posey would spearhead the attack up the Orange Plank Road, supported by Wright's brigade; the two units together totalled 3,000 men. Jackson's only available reserve, until his own corps came up, would be Kershaw's brigade of 3,000 men. The cavalry was divided into two parts. Stuart was told to cover Jackson's flank and accordingly sent the 2nd Virginia to the left and part of the 3rd Virginia to the right. Another two squadrons of the 3rd Virginia were to screen Mahone's advance up the turnpike. Fitz Lee was directed to take the rest of his brigades east to keep communications open with the troops at Fredericksburg.

In preparing for his advance, Jackson also ordered Posey's and Wilcox's brigades of Anderson's division to proceed to Zion Church. Posey had been recently posted opposite Falmouth, and Wilcox had been defending Banks' Ford. The decision was not a wise one because it stripped the Confederate river defenses just when a large part of the Union *V Corps* was heading for Banks' Ford from the west. Fortunately for the Confederates, Hooker never had a chance to exploit Jackson's error. When General Lee heard of Wilcox's withdrawal from Banks' Ford later that day, he at once ordered him to turn about and go back. Wilcox arrived in time to keep the ford in Confederate hands, though in this he had assistance from none other than Joe Hooker himself, as will be explained shortly.

Jackson's advance brought on all the elements of a classic meeting engagement. The advantage on paper seemed to be with the Federals, who had a total of 17,000 men on hand to oppose Jackson's 12,000. However, Slocum's large *XII Corps* of 13,000 would be slow to develop its advance on the Orange Plank Road. Sykes' *V Corps* division of almost 4,000 would be more active as it moved up the Orange Turnpike, about three-quarters of a mile north of Slocum's line of advance. Sykes for the moment would be out-numbered by the 6,000 men Jackson sent up the turnpike

*"Splendid advance of Sykes' Regulars" on the Orange Turnpike east of Chancellorsville on 1 May.*

towards Chancellorsville, though the Confederate column was still strung out along the road. Whatever engagement would arise on either or both roadways would begin independently, since the Turnpike and the Plank Road were separated by one-half to one mile of heavy woods. Once the fighting began, either side could reinforce its column on the other roadway. In addition, the Yankees had a large number of troops available at Chancellorsville, while Jackson knew that his own Second Corps would soon be up and available as reenforcements. The outcome of the approaching fight would thus depend largely on the skill of the opposing generals.

Jackson's advance had begun at 1030, as already noted. The first contact with Union troops was made near Mott's Run on the turnpike when skirmishers of Mahone's 12th Virginia ran into pickets of the *8th Pennsylvania Cavalry* about 1115. The Federals soon brought up four cannons of Watson's *Battery I, 5th U.S. Artillery*, and the Confederates countered with two guns of their own. When the first shell exploded over the woods, an officer of the *XII Corps* noted, "Twenty minutes past eleven; the first gun of the battle of Chancellorsville."

Major General George Sykes quickly brought up his infantry to support the *8th Pennsylvania Cavalry*. He sent the *17th U.S. Infantry* forward as skirmishers, and formed a battle line of Burbanks' and Ayres' brigades of U.S. Regulars; O'Rorke's New York brigade was held back as a reserve. Sykes had a numerical advantage over Mahone's advance elements, and the Yankees conducted a steady advance. A member of the *2nd U.S. Infantry* described the scene as follows:

> Not more than five minutes had elapsed after halting the line, before a volley of musketry was poured into our ranks by the unseen enemy, who had been hidden from our view by the heavy Hurber not more than two-hundred yards in our front. After the first fire was delivered by the enemy, we commenced to peg away at the rebels in the timber. In a few minutes the regiment with the brigade fell back about twenty-five yards and opened again on the enemy. The fire of the regiment had a telling effect on the rebels as they could be seen limping off the field every minute.

Sykes' men drove Mahone's Virginians back along the turnpike for an hour. As Confederate resistance stiffened, Sykes called his line to a halt at 1230 about one mile east of Mott's Run. He was becoming anxious about becoming isolated, since he had heard nothing from Slocum, now over a mile to the west on the Plank Road, and the rest of his own *V Corps* was over two miles to the north at some unknown spot on the River Road. And Sykes had a reason to worry. Major General Lafayette McLaws, now commanding the mixed Confederate force on the turnpike, was forming up six brigades of almost 10,000 men to face Sykes. McLaws' skirmish line was maintaining a heavy fire, especially against Sykes' flanks.

While Sykes' advance was brought to a standstill, Slocum finally began engaging the Confederates on the Orange Plank Road. Slocum had left his camp near Chancellorsville at 1030, and met Confederate skirmishers one mile to the south at the Decker farm. Here he should have formed up his lead brigade in battle line while keeping the rest of the Corps in columns on the road for faster movement. Instead, Slocum chose to form his entire corps in battle line, for he was not certain how many enemy troops he would face. His complicated formation in three lines took two hours to get into position. As a result, Slocum's line did not get moving until 1300; instead of moving parallel to Sykes' column on the turnpike and thus giving it support, Slocum was now over a mile behind Sykes' advance, a situation that would soon prove most perilous to Sykes' command.

When Slocum began advancing again at 1300, he had William's division in three lines north of the Plank Road and Geary's division similarly arranged south of the Plank Road. In the next half hour he advanced a mile to Aldrich, where he ran into the skirmishers of Wright's and Posey's brigade posted astride the roadway. Slocum by

*Hooker's* Army of the Potomac *in action near Chancellorsville on the first day of the battle there.*

his own account was not pressing his advance very aggressively. Up to this point he had lost only ten casualties.

Slocum's deliberate advance was putting Sykes into a desperate fix. By 1330, McLaws' had his line formed and was ready to begin a counter attack. In addition, Jackson now had Rodes' division up to fill the one mile gap between McLaws' left and the troops farther west on the Plank Road. Sykes felt the pressure growing more intense against him, and was not even aware that Jackson was then forming A.P. Hill's large division of six brigades behind McLaw's left.

It was now the crisis of the battle. Sykes was fearful of being overwhelmed, and sent back to Hooker at Chancellorsville to send forward some troops of the *II*, *III*, or *XI Corps*, all of which were available nearby. As Sykes later wrote, "I was completely isolated from the rest of the army, I felt that my rear could be gained by a determined movement of the enemy under cover of the forest. Griffin was far to my left, Slocum to my right, the enemy in front and between me and both those officers. In this situation, without support, my position was critical, still I determined to hold on as long as possible."

Sykes' call for help also found Hooker in an anxious mood. So far his plan of operations was going well, despite the loss of initiative when he stopped his column at Chancellorsville on the evening of 30 April. This was just the situation he was planning for—Lee's troops were abandoning Fredericksburg to attack him on his own ground. This was confirmed by a telegram Dan Butterfield sent from Falmouth at

*Near Chancellorsville, 1 May.*

*General Hooker's headquarters at Chancellorsville, 1 May.*

1230. Butterfield, who had been left behind to coordinate the movements of the two wings of the army, reported that all his sources indicated that Lee had stripped 10,000 to 18,000 men from Sedgwick's front and sent them west to meet Hooker's wing at Chancellorsville.

Hooker knew that he had more than enough men at Chancellorsville to deal with Lee's attacking force. He also had a trump card, the fact that Meade's two divisions on the River Road were on the verge of opening up Banks' Ford, which would enable Reynold's corps and much of the reserve artillery to join Hooker's wing. Yet, Hooker was uneasy. His plan called for Sedgwick to begin a major demonstration at Fredericksburg to tie down the Confederate defenders there and prevent them from further reinforcing the troops in Hooker's front. At 1130 he had sent an order for Sedgwick to engage, but not make a full attack. The appointed hour came, yet no sound of gunfire came from Sedgwick's line to signal any fighting there.

It is difficult today to tell what was on Hooker's mind when he received Sykes' appeal for help sometime after 1300. All we know for sure is that he sent Major General G.K. Warren, his chief topographical officer, back to Sykes with orders to withdraw to Chancellorsville. Perhaps Hooker was concerned with Sedgwick's inactivity, or perhaps he preferred to fight Lee on a more compact line closer to Chancellorsville. All we can be certain of is the fact that Hooker had Lee where he wanted him, and then flinched and ordered withdrawal. As Hooker later remarked to General Abner Doubleday, "for once I lost confidence in Joe Hooker."

Hooker sent out a flurry of orders when he decided to recall Sykes. He also ordered Slocum to return to Chancellorsville, and he directed Meade to return with his two divisions that had almost reached Banks' Ford. In addition, he told Howard, who had just begun moving to support Slocum, to stay put where he was. Hooker appreciated Sykes' critical situation, and ordered Couch to send one of his divisions (Hancock's) to cover Sykes' withdrawal. About 1400 he notified Butterfield at Falmouth of his change of plans "From character of information have suspended attack. The enemy may attack me—I will try it. Tell Sedgwick to keep a sharp lookout, and attack if can succeed."

No one was pleased to hear Hooker's withdrawal orders. The Regulars of Ayres' brigade were still full of fight, despite their exposed position. When the retreat order came, "there was heard cursing and grumbling from the Regulars...All knew too well that again somebody had blundered." Couch, Slocum, Meade, Hancock, Sykes and Warren all protested to Hooker that the army was surrendering valuable ground and giving up the initiative. Meade is said to have exclaimed to his fellow officers, "My God, if we can't hold the top of the hill we certainly cannot hold the bottom of it."

# The Battlefield Today

Just over 1100 acres of the large Chancellorsville battlefield are included in the present Fredericksburg and Spotsylvania National Military Park. Included within the park are most of the lines at Chancellorsville, Fairview, and the *XI Corps* position, part of Hazel Grove, almost the entire length of Jackson's flank march, and most of the positions at Fredericksburg. The house where Stonewall Jackson died, located at Guiney's Station, twelve miles south of Fredericksburg, is also owned by the park. A good driving tour of the battlefield is provided by *The U.S. Army War College Guide to the Battles of Chancellorsville and Fredericksburg* by Jay Luvaas and Harold Nelson (Carlisle, Pennsylvania, 1988). A detailed study of the important buildings and other locales related to the campaign is now available in *Chancellorsville Battlefield Sites* by Noel G. Harrison (Lynchburg, 1990).

# Chancellorsville

"Chancellorsville" was not a town or a village, but simply the name of the large brick house owned by the Guy family at the northwest corner of the intersection of Ely's Ford Road, the Orange Turnpike, and the Orange Plank Road, about eight miles west of Fredericksburg. It was constructed in 1816 to house a tavern, and had a number of out buildings. By the time of the war the building had been expanded to two and one-half stories with a two story inset front porch. The house received its name from Frances Chancellor, who ran the hotel there at the time of the battle.

Union troops passed by the Chancellorsville on 30 April 1863, and saw "quite a bevy of ladies in light, dressy, attractive spring costumes" on the upper porch. The scene became quite different the next day, when the hotel became a hospital for the wounded men of Sykes' Union division. The building then became Hooker's headquarters, and on the morning of 3 May, Hooker was wounded while standing on the house's porch when a cannon ball struck one of the porch's pillars. Later in the day the house caught fire and burned to the ground. A smaller house was built over a part of the original building's foundation in 1910, but it too, burned down in 1927. Today the house's foundations are preserved as part of the battlefield park.

*Ruins of the Chancellorsville house after it was burned at noon on 3 May.*

# The Nature of the Wilderness

The tangled woods called "the Wilderness" totally dominated the battle of Chancellorsville. The terrain of the Wilderness is wild growth, full of heavy woods, dense underbrush, and numerous streams, covering most of the ground south of the Rapidan from the western side of the battle area to a couple miles east of Chancellorsville. The Wilderness had only a few scattered small clearings, and even fewer locations where more than a battery of artillery could be brought into position. The ground was so densely wooded that infantry units had difficulty forming a line and could not keep it during movement. Units could not see much beyond their flanks, or hear much farther. Union general Alexander Webb wrote of the Wilderness, "Uneven, with woods, thickets and ravines right and left. Tangled thickets of pine, scrub oak and cedar prevented our seeing the enemy and prevented anyone in command of a large force from determining accurately the position of the troops he was ordering to and from. At times our lines while firing could not see the array of the enemy, not fifty yards distant. Union army engineer chief G. K. Warren

put it more succinctly: 'No one can conceive a more unfavorable field for the movements of a grand army'."

One of the major difficulties of the Wilderness was that the area contained very few roads. Most roads there were no more than wagon tracks leading towards the river fords, and there were very few connecting by ways. The only two roads of note through the area were the Orange Turnpike and Orange Plank Road, both of which ran west from Fredericksburg (do not be confused by the fact that the two ran concurrently from Fredericksburg to one mile west of Salem Church, and again for the two mile stretch from Chancellorsville to Wilderness Church). The two "highways" were described as follows in 1912 by an army officer:

The Turnpike was not a metalled road, but a graded dirt road, top-dressed with gravel, and corduroyed in the swampy bottoms which abound in that region. The corduroyed sections were graded and ditched and the road bed was then covered with corduroy or poles, varying from 3 to 8 inches in diameter and sixteen feet long, laid

transversely and covered with sand, gravel, and clay to a depth of 3 or 4 inches.

The Plank road was in fact a road covered with planks about two inches thick and sixteen feet long, laid transversely and spiked to two longitudinal sleepers buried in the prepared road bed.

At the time of the war this road had fallen into bad repair and was full of holes, where planks had broken through, exposing the soft clay bed beneath. These plank roads were primarily constructed for the hauling of tobacco to market. The tobacco was packed in huge hogsheads, through which an axle was placed. By attaching draught animals to the axle ends, the hogsheads were rolled to market along the plank roads, and arrived in much better condition that when rolled over ordinary dirt roads, and with the expenditure of less power that was necessary on poorer roads.

*The Plank Road, the path of Jackson's flank march through the Wilderness.*

Couch then finished withdrawing Hancock's men as directed. Then he went to see his commander: "Proceeding to the Chancellor House, I narrated my operations in front to Hooker, which were seemingly satisfactory, as he said, 'It is alright, Couch, I have gotten Lee just where I want him, he must fight me on my own ground'. The retrograde movement had prepared me for something of the kind, but to hear from his own lips that the advantages gained by the successful marches of his lieutenants were to culminate in fighting a defensive battle in that nest of thickets, was too much, and I retired from his presence with the belief that my commanding general was a whipped man."

The skirmishing along the turnpike continued until about 1800, when Hancock withdrew to a position on Sykes' left, north of the roadway. O'Rorke's New York brigade of Sykes' division then moved up to confront Heth, who then withdrew because of approaching darkness.

The only fighting still going on at dusk was at Hazel Grove, one mile southwest of Chancellorsville. At about 1600 Brigadier General A.R. Wright had swung to the left while the rest of Major General R.H. Anderson's command pursued Slocum's *XII Corps* up the Orange Plank Road. At about 1630 Wright ran into a horse artillery battery and Jeb Stuart near Catharine Furnace, two miles from Chancellorsville. The combined force decided to reconnoiter the Union position to the north, and at about 1730 began an artillery skirmish at Hazel Grove. Just then Stonewall Jackson and his staff rode up, as Jackson, according to his usual practice, was scouting his own front in order to make battle plans for the next day. When the Union artillery fire intensified and badly wounded one of Stuart's staff officers, Stuart astutely commented, "General Jackson, we must move from here." Jackson departed, only to scout the rest of his front all the way back to the turnpike. His habit of making personal front line reconnaissances was a most dangerous one, as events the next evening would show.

While Hooker's men were sullenly forming a defensive perimeter around Chancellorsville, Sedgwick was at last preparing to launch the holding attack that Hooker had wanted to take place at 1300. It seems that the telegraph lines to Falmouth were temporarily out of order that day, with the result that Sedgwick did not receive Hooker's order until almost 1800. As a result of the delay, Sedgwick was able to mount only a feeble demonstration before nightfall.

The scattered Union troops withdrew as best they could. Humphreys' division of the *V Corps* was within two miles of Banks' Ford when it received its withdrawal order about 1500. For some reason Griffin's lead division did not receive the order until close to 1700, when it was almost in sight of Banks' Ford. Both divisions returned along the River Road at the double quick, out of fear of being cut off or captured. Griffin would march to Chancellorsville, while Humphreys' exhausted men stopped for the night at Scott's Ford.

Slocum received Hooker's withdrawal order about 1330, when he was in the midst of an artillery duel near Aldrich. He was pursued by three brigades under R. H.

*The battle on 1 May.*

Anderson, but no major fighting developed until about 1530, when Rodes' division came up and was deployed. Rodes caused Slocum some anxiety until the Yankees reached their assigned position west of Chancellorsville about 1600.

There was more action in the center, where Sykes was trying to extricate his division after almost being cut off in his advanced position. Hancock skillfully deployed across the turnpike at Newton one and one-half miles from Chancellorsville, and helped Sykes withdraw to safety. The Confederate pursuit on this front did not begin in earnest until 1600, when McLaws received an order Jackson had sent at 1430 "to press on up the turnpike toward Chancellorsville." During his advance, McLaws was passed by Heth's fresh division of Jackson's Corps, which was just arriving via the turnpike. Heth was engaged with Hancock's skirmishers by 1630.

Hancock carried on his skirmish with Heth's advance even as he was withdrawing his regiments in accordance with Hooker's orders. At 1630, when all but two of Hancock's regiments had withdrawn, Couch received the following rather astonishing order from Hooker. "Hold on to your position till 5 PM, and extend your skirmishers on each flank, so as to secure yourself against being surrounded. General Slocum will hold a position on the Plank Road equally advanced." Hooker had belatedly decided to hold and fight! Couch, however, saw that it was now too late for this, and responded promptly to the courier who brought the message, "Tell General Hooker he is too late; the enemy are on my front and rear. I am in full retreat."

*Hooker's headquarters at Chancel-*
*lorsville, morning of 2 May.*

# CHAPTER X

# Jackson's Flank March

## 2 May, 1863

*T*he positions taken up by the Federal troops near Chancellorsville at dusk on 1 May 1863, were essentially those occupied the previous evening. Howard's *XI Corps* held the right of the line, being posted along the Orange Turnpike from Dowdall's Tavern to a position one mile to the west. Howard's line faced south, and gained some advantage from the lower ground of Scott's Run that ran along its front. Howard's right, however, was not anchored on any strong terrain feature, and was defended only by a few regiments posted perpendicular to the turnpike.

The center of Hooker's line was held by units of three different corps. Slocum's *XII Corps* occupied a broad arc beginning near Chancellorsville, and then stretched southwest towards Scott's Run before running back to reach the Plank Road one mile west of Chancellorsville. It was a strong line, supported by fourteen cannons posted at Fairview, behind the center of the position. Sykes' division of the *V Corps* and Hancock's division of the *II Corps* were posted east of Chancellorsville. Sykes was in a one-half mile line along the turnpike from Chancellorsville to the bridge over Great Meadow Swamp. Hancock's division was formed perpendicular to Sykes' making an angle at the bridge over the swamp. This angle formed a weakness in Hooker's line, since it was very much exposed and was largely unsupported by artillery. Griffin's division of the *V Corps* continued Hancock's line to the north towards Mine Creek; from here there was a half mile gap to the positions occupied near Scott's Ford by Humphreys' division of the *V Corps* and the *Irish Brigade* of the *II Corps*.

Despite the salient formed east of Chancellorsville by Sykes' and Hancock's divisions, and the gaps between Howard's and Slocum's Corps on the right and between Griffin's and Meade's divisions on the left, Hooker's position was not a weak one. He had four infantry divisions (all of the *III Corps* and French's division of the *II Corps*) massed in reserve north of Chancellorsville, along with over eighty pieces of artillery. Hooker ordered his generals to put their lines "in condition of defense without a moment's delay," and the Yankees were busy digging trenches and felling trees for much of the night. By some strange logic Hooker believed "that a suspension in the attack today will embolden the enemy to attack him." He clearly had no intention of taking the offensive anytime soon.

Lee's troops bivouacked that night on the ground they happened to occupy as dark fell. On the right, Mahone, Wofford and Perry held a line for a mile from the Orange Turnpike at Newton to the point where the Old Mine Road crossed Mott Run. Their front was well covered by the run and elements of the 2nd and 4th Virginia Cavalry regiments. The situation was more jumbled on the left between the turnpike at Newton and the Plank Road north of Decker. Here the First Corps brigades of Semmes, Kershaw, Posey and Wright were somewhat intermingled with the troops of Rodes' division that had fought Hancock's division and then O'Rorke's brigade late in the day. A.P. Hill's and Colston's divisions, along with much of the army's artillery, were piled up along the Plank Road for a mile on either side of Aldrich. Stuart with the remains of Fitz Lee's cavalry watched the army's left flank beyond Catharine Furnace, while Early's division and Barksdale's brigade were still keeping Sedgwick's command (*VI Corps*, *I Corps*, and Gibbon's division of the *II Corps*) in check near Fredericksburg.

Lee's troops were well positioned to launch a massive assault on the awkward salient occupied by Sykes' and Hancock's divisions. However, Lee was hesitant to launch a frontal attack on lines that were strongly held and being fortified. At dusk Posey's and Ramseur's brigades made a probing attack on the Union center, only to run into heavy artillery fire. As it grew dark, the sound of axes coming from the Union lines made it clear that Hooker was strengthening his position every moment.

These conditions persuaded Lee to turn his attention to the Federal left, where he had hopes of cutting off Hooker from his primary crossing at U.S. Ford. Lee investigated the terrain on his right personally at around 1830, and ordered scouts forward from Wilcox's brigade (then at Duerson's Mill near the River Road) and the 4th Virginia Cavalry. Everyone felt that the terrain there was too rough to mount an attack over, especially since there were few good roads available.

It was now clear to Lee that if he were to make an attack on Hooker's lines, it would have to be against the Federal right. Shortly after dark Lee rode to his left to meet with Stonewall Jackson and discuss the situation. Their conference, which took place at the Decker farm on the Orange Plank Road, began around 1930 and lasted almost to midnight. Some sources paint a picturesque scene, stating that both generals sat on empty Federal hardtack boxes next to a flickering fire on the edge of the woods. More accurate accounts relate that they sat side by side on a plain old log.

The conference opened with Lee asking Jackson what he knew about the Federal right flank. Jackson replied with an account of his reconnaissance near Catharine Furnace and along Slocum's front, which did not give him a grasp of where the Federal left was. Even so, he seemed to favor making an attack on Hooker's column, for fear the Yankees would retreat before they could be engaged again. Reportedly he stated, "By tomorrow morning, there will not be any of them on this side of the river."

Lee was also concerned about what Hooker's intentions were. While Jackson felt that Hooker was making a diversion in favor of Sedgwick, Lee more properly interpreted that Hooker's was the primary column. His major question, though, was what Hooker's intentions were. Captured prisoners made it clear that Lee had engaged the Federal *V Corps* that afternoon east of Chancellorsville. Where were the *XI* and *XII Corps*, which were known to have crossed the Rapidan with the *V Corps*? Were they at Chancellorsville, or were they heading towards Gordonsville, possibly in support of Stoneman's cavalry raid?

Lee now determined to try to get more information about the strength of Hooker's line at Chancellorsville, and sent two staff officers to reconnoiter in the moonlight (Major T.M.R Talcott of his own staff and Captain J.K. Boswell, Jackson's chief engineer). While these officers were gone, Jeb Stuart came bounding up about 2200 with exciting news from Fitz Lee that Hooker's right did not extend to the Rapidan, but was instead hanging "up in the air" a few miles west of Chancellorsville. Lee was now even more inclined to attack the Federal right, but he needed to know if roads were accessible for the purpose. Just after he sent Stuart to locate guides and reconnoiter the area, Talcott and Boswell returned to give their report. They observed that the Federal center was strongly posted, was being fortified, and had ample artillery support.

The report clinched the decision in Lee's mind. He got out a map and showed Jackson what he wanted to be done. Stonewall was to take his troops and swing around Hooker's right flank and attack him in the rear. He then added, "General Stuart will cover your movement with his cavalry." Jackson agreed to the movement, and rose up, touching his cap. "My corps will move at 4 o'clock," he replied as he went to get a little sleep.

Lee was not able to get to bed just yet. Not long after Jackson left, Reverend B. T. Lacy, a resident of the area who was serving as a chaplain in the Second Corps, arrived at General Stuart's orders to share what he knew of the local road net. Lee questioned him at length, and was assured that suitable roads extended to the army's left to enable Jackson to make the proposed attack. Lee then went to sleep, using his saddle for a pillow and his overcoat for a blanket.

It should be noted here that not all sources agree on this interpretation of events. Some historians, particularly Jackson's early biographer, Reverend R.L. Dabney, and Stonewall's mapmaker Major Jed Hotchkiss, felt that Jackson deserved the credit for planning the flank attack that would turn the cause of the battle. Douglass Southall Freeman, in his massive biography *R. E. Lee*, reexamined all the evidence to show that it was Lee alone who made the decision for the attack, though the route taken and organization of the assault were left to Jackson's control.

It should also be observed that Lee's bold decision to divide his army a second time in the face of a greatly superior enemy force, may have been based on a faulty and incomplete understanding of Hooker's position and strength. John Bigelow in his mammoth study, *The Chancellorsville Campaign*, argues rightly that no one in Lee's army had seen or located Hooker's right flank when Lee made the decision for Jackson to attack it. Bigelow doubts that Fitz Lee had probed Howard's entire picket line, and even suggests that Fitz Lee may have misrepresented Howard's flank as extending towards the intersection of the Orange Plank Road and the Brock Road, a line about one mile southwest of Howard's actual position. Lastly, it seems clear that Lee was not aware that Hooker had the *III Corps* and most of the *II Corps* with him at Chancellorsville. Had he known this, Lee might not have been so ready to release Jackson's corps for the flank attack.

Several accounts show that Jackson did not spend a comfortable night. At about 0200, only two hours after retiring, Jackson got up and went to warm himself at the camp fire. Soon he was joined by Reverend Lacy, who had met earlier with Lee, and the two began discussing the roads to the left. Jackson then sent Lacy off with his topographical officer, Major Jed Hotchkiss, to locate a suitable road for the advance. A short while later Colonel E.B. Long of Lee's staff awoke and found Jackson shivering by the fire, alone. As the two talked, Long noticed that Jackson had taken

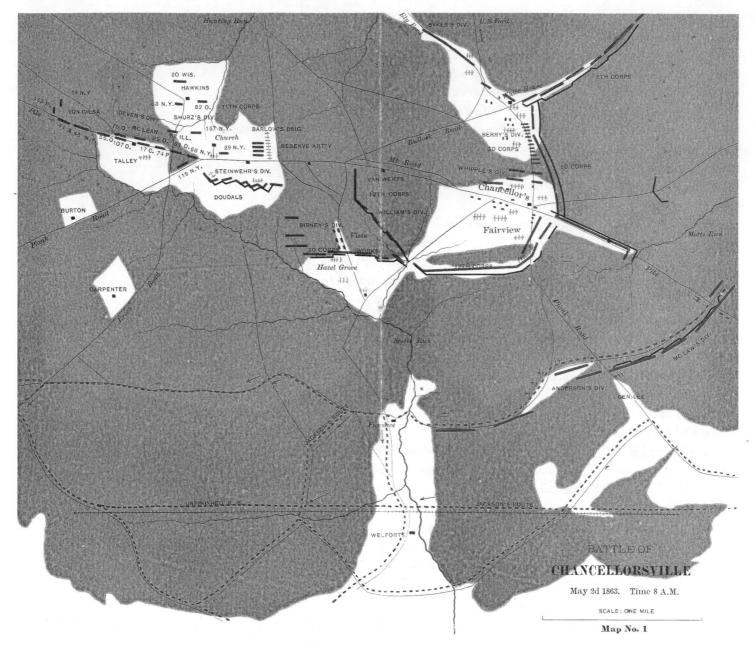

off his sword and leaned it against a nearby tree. All at once the sword fell over on its own with a crash, an ill omen indeed.

Lee woke up not much later, and the camp began to stir. Soon Hotchkiss and Lacy returned with the good news that they had located a route around Hooker's right, as well as a reliable guide to lead the column. Lee approved the route, and asked Jackson what troops he wanted to use. Jackson replied, "My whole corps," a response Lee was not quite expecting. Lee probably had planned to keep more than Anderson's and McLaws' divisions to face Hooker's large force at Chancellorsville, but he gave in to Jackson's desire to make the flank attack as strong and decisive as possible. He replied simply to Stonewall, "Well, go on."

It was now close to daylight. Jackson sent out orders for his line of march, which would proceed west to Catharine Furnace, south on the Furnace Road to the Brock Road to the Orange Plank Road on Orange Turnpike, a distance of about twelve miles right across the front of Hooker's army. Fitz Lee would proceed in front of Jackson's column to screen its movement. Next would come the infantry divisions of Rodes, Colston, and A. P. Hill, each followed by its own artillery and ammunition trains. Jackson's supply and ambulance trains would take a longer route, swinging through Todd's Tavern, in order to shorten the length of the main column while also keeping out of the enemy's range. Jackson took extra time to make sure everyone followed instructions during the march—there was to be no noise, no straggling, and officers could use bayonets to keep laggards moving. These extra preparations delayed the column's start until about 0700. Artillery commander Colonel E. P. Alexander wrote that "Two hours after sunrise, Lee, standing by the roadside, watched the head of the column march by, and exchanged with Jackson the last few words ever to pass between them."

As Jackson pulled out his troops and began his march, Lee extended Anderson's division (less Wilcox's brigade, sent to guard Banks' Ford) to cover the ground Jackson was vacating between the turnpike and the Plank Road. Lee had altogether only 13,000 men of all arms to hold a line over two miles long. Once skirmishers were posted, there were at some stretches only one man every six feet. Lee realized that Hooker was expecting him to attack, so he made every effort to give the appearance of doing so. The Confederate artillery opened up at several points when Jackson began moving, and continued to fire at intervals throughout the day. Likewise, the entire skirmish line was directed to be as aggressive as possible without bringing on a general engagement. Lee also ordered Early to keep a close watch on Sedgwick's force near Fredericksburg, with an eye to releasing troops to Lee if Sedgwick moved to recross the river.

Lee's heavy skirmishing had the desired effect on Hooker. He was indeed awaiting an attack by the Confederates, and during the night had taken several steps to strengthen the weakness in his line. The salient east of Chancellorsville was eliminated by pulling Hancock back half a mile and sending Sykes up to the Mineral Spring Road near Chandler's. Griffin's division of the *V Corps* was then moved north to a new position between Sykes and Humphreys' lines at Scott's Ford, so forming a continuous line along the Mineral Spring Road. When Birney's division of the *III Corps* was deployed in the gap between Slocum and Howard's Corps, Hooker had a

*Jackson's men conducting their
flank march on 2 May.*

# Stonewall's Faith

It would seem strange that so religious a man as Jackson was a general by occupation—how could he justify leading men to death and destruction if he were such a devout Christian? He was driven by motives different from those of Robert E. Lee, a devout Christian, who deplored war but fought because he thought it was his duty to defend himself and his home. It seems clear that Jackson was driven by an overwhelming sense of ambition to succeed and gain fame by force of arms. This explains why he so often pushed himself and his men beyond what was reasonable or even possible. We are not now in a position to judge what came first in Jackson's eyes, glory or God; most likely the two were one and the same.

Stonewall's feelings about glory and God are clearly shown in a letter to his wife on 22 July 1861, the day after First Bull Run: "My Precious Pet—Yesterday we fought a great battle and gained a great victory, for which all the glory is due to God alone. Although under a heavy fire for several continuous hours, I received only one wound, the breaking of the longest finger of my left hand; but the doctor says the finger can be saved. It was broken about midway between the hand and knuckle, the ball passing on the side next the forefinger. Had it struck the centre, I should have lost the finger. My horse was wounded, but not killed. Your coat got an ugly wound near the hip, but my servant, who is very handy, has so far repaired it that it doesn't show very much. My preservation was entirely due, as was the glorious victory, to our God, to whom be all the honor, praise, and glory. The battle was the hardest that I have ever been in, but not near so hot in its fire. I commanded in the centre more particularly, though one of my regiments extended to the right for some distance. There were other commands on my right and left. Whilst great credit is due to other parts of our gallant army, God made my brigade more instrumental than any other in repulsing the main attack. This is for your information only—say nothing about it. Let others speak praise, not myself."

Jackson was not deeply devoted to the Church until the prime of his life. In his early years he attended no particular church. His mother was reportedly a member of the Methodist faith, but young Thomas was affiliated with no specific church during his troubled early years. His first lengthy exposure to organized religion probably came at West Point, where he became accustomed to the Academy's Episcopal services. Nevertheless, he did not show deep interest in the Church until his stay in Mexico City in 1847-1848. There he experimented with several sects until he was reintroduced to Episcopalianism by Colonel Francis Taylor, the commander of the 1st Artillery. His dedication then became so deep that he was baptized under Colonel Taylor's sponsorship on 29 April 1849 at Fort Hamilton, New York, where he was on garrison duty.

On settling in Lexington, Jackson investigated the local churches and found himself attracted to the Presbyterian church, the largest and most influential in town. He particularly appreciated the church's simple style and the preaching of the devout minister, Dr. William S. White. Jackson made a public profession of his faith at the Lexington Presbyterian church on 21 November 1851. He entered the church with zeal, seeing himself as a warrior "clad in ministerial armor, fighting under the banner of Jesus." As evidence of his faith, he began a Sunday school for Negroes, to which he continued to contribute until his death.

As a devout Presbyterian, Jackson tried to avoid all military activities, especially fighting, on Sundays. Yet war allows no reprieves, and at times he had no choice but to make war contrary to his conscience. Particularly regretful to him were the Sunday battles at Kernstown (23 March 1862), Winchester (25 May 1862), and Port Republic (8 June 1862). To make amends for the Sunday battle at Winchester, he ordered his troops to observe a day of rest and thanksgiving, with church services, the following Monday. When reprimanded by his wife for fighting at Kernstown on a Sunday, he replied, "You appear much concerned at my attacking on Sunday. I was greatly concerned, too; but I felt it my duty to do it, in consideration of the ruinous effects that might result from postponing the battle until the morning. So far as I can see, my course was a wise one; the best that I could do under the circumstances, though very distasteful to my feelings; and I hope and pray to our Heavenly Father that I may never again be circumstanced as on that day. I believed that so far as our troops were concerned, necessity and mercy both called for battle. I do hope the war will soon be over, and that I shall never again have to take the field. Arms is a profession that, if its principles are adhered to for success, requires an officer to do what he fears may be wrong, and yet, according to military experience, must be done, if success is to be attained. And this fact of its being necessary to success, and being accompanied with success, and that a departure from it is accompanied with disaster, suggests that it must be right. Had I fought the battle on Monday instead of Sunday, I fear our cause would have suffered; whereas, as things turned out, I consider our cause gained much from the engagement."

Thus, Jackson was not above fighting on a Sunday if it were necessary or to his military advantage. Occasionally, though, he did put off necessary military activity that was called for on a Sunday. One notable case was on 22 June 1862, when he was pushing his troops hard to reach Richmond in time to attack the Yankees before they were aware of his arrival. Though time was of the essence in this movement, he kept his troops in camp all day. His reasons were those expressed to Reverend Dabney on another similar occasion: "The Sabbath is written in the constitution of man and horses as really as in the Bible: I can march my men farther in a week, marching six days and resting the seventh, and get through with my men and horses in better condition than if I marched them all seven days."

Jackson's ultimate wish was to die on a Sunday, a desire that was granted on Sunday 10 May 1863, when he succumbed to the effects of the wounds he received at Chancellorsville eight days earlier.

# Jackson's Horses

During the war Stonewall Jackson owned three horses of which he was especially fond. One, named Boy, was a carriage horse he bought for his wife shortly before the war. In July of 1861 he bought a small, rather rotund horse from those he captured abroad a Federal train on the Baltimore and Ohio Railroad. The horse was named Fancy, which was quite a misnomer because of its features and great size. The horse nevertheless became quite a pet, and had the strange habit of lying down like a dog when ordered to stop and rest. Jackson's favorite horse was the famous Little Sorrel, which he preferred because his gait was "as easy as the rocking of a cradle." Jackson rode him in nearly every battle, though he owned several larger steeds. Sorrel was lost for a while after Stonewall was mortally wounded at Chancellorsville, but was found and returned to Mrs. Jackson. The horse outlived its master by twenty-three years, dying in 1886 at an age of over thirty years.

*Stonewall Jackson's favorite horse, "Little Sorrel," in 1884.*

continuous line stretching six miles from the Rapidan to Howard's right on the Orange Turnpike.

The head of Jackson's column reached open ground near the Catharine Furnace around 0800. Here Jackson detached the 23rd Georgia of Colquitt's brigade to guard the flank of the passing column. He was especially anxious to move quickly so Lee would not be attacked or his own force be assaulted while it was all too strung out on the roadways. Jackson's medical director, Dr. Hunter McGuire, never forgot Jackson's eagerness and intensity that day. "His face was pale, his eyes flashing. Out from his thin compressed lips came the terse command, 'Press onward, press forward!' In his eagerness as he rode, he leaned over the neck of his horse, as if in that way the march might be hurried. Every man in the ranks knew that we were engaged in some great flank movements and they eagerly responded and pressed on at a rapid gait."

The open ground at the Catharine Furnace permitted Jackson's passing column to be seen clearly by Birney's division, posted one mile to the north. Birney saw the Confederates begin passing by shortly after 0800, and reported the fact to Hooker by 0900. Hooker did not have to go far to see the column himself. His first thought was that Lee was retreating, but on reflection he decided that this was not in Lee's nature. Instead, Hooker reckoned Lee was moving to attack the Federal line at another point, probably the right. Accordingly he sent the following warning to General Howard at 0930: "The disposition you have made of your corps has been with a view to a front attack by the enemy. If he should throw himself upon your flank, he wishes you to examine the ground, and determine upon the position you will take in that even, in order that you may be prepared for him in whatever direction he advances. We have good reason to suppose that the enemy is moving to our right. Please advance your pickets for purposes of observation as far as may be safe in order to obtain timely information of their approach." Hooker, though, did not go for a personal inspection of Howard's lines. Had he done so, he would have realized how exposed a position the *XI Corps* was holding. Even before Howard received Hooker's 0900 note, he wrote at 1050 that he saw a Confederate column moving across his front, and was making preparations to receive it.

Throughout the morning, Birney continued to send reports of Jackson's movement to his corps commander, Major General Dan Sickles. At about 1100 Sickles came forward to Birney's left at Hazel Grove to see the Confederate column for himself. He at once resolved to attack Jackson before the Confederates retreated to Gordonsville or attacked Hooker's right, whatever was their goal. At length he obtained permission from Hooker to take two of his division (Birney's and Whipple's) and "advance cautiously toward the road followed by the enemy and harass the movement as much as possible."

Sickles received Hooker's order to advance at about noon, and directed Colonel Hiram Berdan's elite green-uniformed sharpshooters to move out and lead the way. By 1230 Sickles' leading infantry brigade (Hayman's) was crossing Scott's Run. The heavy undergrowth and a certain degree of caution caused Hayman to consume over an hour to advance the one mile to the Confederate flank guard at the Catharine Furnace. When he arrived there, closely supported by five additional infantry brigades, he was opposed by only four Confederate artillery pieces, a detachment of the 3rd Virginia Cavalry, and the outmanned 23rd Georgia. This was all the force the Confederates had on hand to guard Jackson's rear trains, as all of Stonewall's infantry had long since passed by the furnace.

Had Sickles advanced earlier or more speedily, he would have caused great havoc to the tail of Jackson's column, and perhaps changed the course of the battle. As it was, he threw a great scare into the Confederate high command. Fortunately Lee and Jackson reacted quickly to the threat posed by Sickles' advance. Soon after noon, Lee ordered Anderson to send a brigade to move forward to check Berdan's advance. Anderson sent Posey's Mississippi Brigade to his left, and Posey's men fought so well against Sickles' left flank that they delayed the Yankee advance considerably. As the fighting grew heavier, Anderson sent Wright's brigade to support Posey at about 1300, and the 14th Georgia of Thomas' brigade was sent back "to the assistance of the artillery train," along with part of the 7th and 14th Tennessee.

The fighting at Catharine Furnace was closely contested for about an hour. The Federals held the upper hand at first, as Berdan's sharpshooters managed to capture a forty man detachment of the 23rd Georgia that was stationed at the furnace. The remainder of the Georgia regiment fell back over half a mile and barely held on until reinforced by the 14th Georgia and a few companies of the 7th and 14th Tennessee at about 1500. The line now began to stabilize as Posey and Wright started to pressure Sickles' left. About that time Sickles appealed to Howard for some supporting troops, but Howard said he had none to spare. An hour later Howard reluctantly sent Barlow's brigade to help Sickles when he was specifically ordered by Hooker to do so. Slocum was more cooperative, and sent Williams' division in to aid Sickles' advance. Hooker also sent Pleasanton's cavalry brigade to support Sickles at about 1600.

While Sickles' front was steadily expanding, a sharp contest began on two portions

# Dan Sickles, the One-Legged General

Major General Daniel E. Sickles, commander of the Union *III Corps* at Chancellorsville, was one of the more colorful characters to serve in the war. He was born in New York City in 1819, and had a successful pre-war career as a lawyer and Democratic politician in New York. In 1847, at the age of twenty-eight, he was named secretary of the American delegation in London. Later he was elected a New York Senator and served from 1857 to 1861 as a Congressman in Washington.

Sickles was by nature clever but impulsive, as is illustrated by the following incident from 1859 that earned him national notoriety. It seems that his wife Teresa was having an affair with Philip Barton Key, son of Francis Scott Key, author of "The Star Spangled Banner." Sickles was enraged, and proceeded to shoot Key dead in broad daylight in front of a number of witnesses across the street from the White House. The murder stunned all of Washington, and a sensational trial followed, with future Secretary of War Edwin M. Stanton as chief defense counsel. Sickles offered as his defense what would today be termed a plea of temporary insanity, and was acquitted—the first time this plea was successfully used in court. Sickles later astonished and enraged everyone by forgiving his errant wife and accepting her back into his house.

When the Civil War broke out, Sickles eagerly embraced the conflict, no doubt viewing it largely as a means for personal and political advancement. He spearheaded the raising of the *Excelsior Brigade* and so earned an appointment as colonel of one of its regiments. Despite his lack of West Point training and military experience President Lincoln nominated Sickles as a brigadier general in September 1861, seeking to cultivate the favor of Sickles' fellow War Democrats. The Senate rejected Sickles' nomination on political grounds in March 1862, but later accepted it when Lincoln reappointed him.

Sickles led his brigade well in the 1862 battles before Richmond, where it be-

*Major General Daniel E. Sickles, controversial commander of the Federal* III Corps.

longed to the *Second Division* of the *III Corps*. For this he was promoted to major general and given command of a division, which he led at Fredericksburg. Hooker then surprisingly appointed Sickles commander of the *III Corps*, despite his lack of seniority, when Major General George Stoneman was transferred to command of the newly formed *Cavalry Corps*.

At the battle of Chancellorsville, Sickles' corps was posted at the center of Hooker's line near Hazel Grove. Some of Sickles' men detected Jackson's flank march on the afternoon of 2 May, so Sickles sent Biney's division to investigate. Biney had a sharp skirmish with Jackson's rear guard near the Catharine Furnace, a fight that convinced Sickles that the Confederate army was in retreat. His false deduction may have played a major role at inducing Major General O. O. Howard, Commander of the *XI Corps*, to discount reports of a strong enemy force forming in his front that evening.

Early on 3 May Sickles was directed to withdraw against his wishes from a strong position at Hazel Grove. He became even more annoyed when the Confederates turned Hazel Grove into a strong artillery

position and began pummeling his new line at Fairview. Sickles remembered this lesson well in the second day of Gettysburg, when he was assigned a position on southern Cemetery Ridge that appeared to be dominated by higher ground three-quarters of a mile to the west at the Peach Orchard. At mid-afternoon Sickles decided to advance to the peach Orchard line, so changing the entire course of the battle. Army commander Major General George G. Meade would have liked to have court-martialed Sickles for disobeying orders, but Sickles, topnotch lawyer as he was, took the offensive first by charging that Meade's orders were unclear, and that Sickles' advance actually saved the battle because Meade was planning a retreat. These arguments today can be seen as more smoke than truth, but the Meade-Sickles controversy has continued to color interpretations of the battle to this day.

Sickles did not hold field command again after Gettysburg. During the evening's fighting he was badly wounded by a shell that hit his right leg. The leg was amputated, and Sickles ordered it preserved in a keg of whiskey; the bones can be seen today at a medical museum in Washington D.C. Sickles became a hero of sorts after the battle, and parlayed the fame into an appointment as a major general in the Regular Army. he was a supporter of the Congressional plans for reconstruction, and served as military Governor of South Carolina. In return for his loyalty, Congress voted him a Medal of Honor for his deeds at Gettysburg.

Sickles was active in politics for a number of years after the war. In 1869 President U.S. Grant appointed him U.S. Minister to Spain. Sickles then became a close friend of former Queen Isabelle, but had to resign his post when he became too involved in Cuban internal affairs. Sickles later was elected to serve as U.S. Congressman from New York from 1893-95. He died in 1914, a bitter and lonely man, the last surviving general of all who served at Chancellorsville or Gettysburg.

of the Union center near Chancellorsville. About 1515, Wofford's brigade of McLaws' division attacked up the turnpike and kept up brisk engagement for an hour. During this same time Brigadier General John Geary of the *XII Corps* led seven regiments and a battery in a probing attack towards the Orange Plank Road. He ran into strong enemy defenses and was forced to retire about 1630 after suffering reasonably heavy casualties. All this fighting convinced Hooker to keep an eye on what he thought was the main body of Lee's command facing Chancellorsville. It also prevented Hooker from reinforcing Sickles' advance more than he did.

About 1700 Sickles received orders from Hooker to attack the enemy on his right (Jackson's rear guard). Sickles delayed for awhile to mount the attack, as he needed to bring up some artillery and more time was needed for Whipple's and Williams' divisions to form on his left. Around 1730 some of his skirmishers captured some Confederate artillerymen who taunted, "You may think that you have done a big thing just now, but wait till Jackson gets in on your right." No one believed them, and Sickles continued his advance. By 1730, Sickles was receiving disconcerting reports that Howard's corps had collapsed on the right. He was just preparing to send Pleasanton's cavalry in pursuit of Jackson's rear trains, when orders came at 1830 to send the cavalry to the relief of Howard. By 1900 Sickles and Williams' received orders to retire because of Jackson's pressing threat to their rear, and Sickles' probing attack came to a halt. Nobody thought of informing Barlow of the change of plans, so the plucky brigadier continued his assigned march to the southwest, completely out of touch with his own troops and those of the enemy. He finally received a courier from General Birney at 1930, when he was almost two miles south of the Catharine Furnace. He hustled back north and did not reach the safety of Sickles' new lines at Hazel Grove until after 2100.

Jackson properly ignored all the firing that flared up when Berdan and Sickles moved against the rear of his column shortly after noon. He trusted A. P. Hill to deal with the attack, since there was not much he could do himself from a position four miles away from the point of conflict. Jackson proceeded with the 2nd Virginia Cavalry in advance, and did not run into any Union troops until the lead party reached the Orange Plank Road about 1300. Here the cavalrymen spotted one lone Union vedette, who promptly sped off to the east. They soon ran into a stronger Union cavalry picket force at a position in sight of Howard's main line along the Orange Turnpike.

Jackson was pleased to hear that the Union line had been located, and rode at once with Fitz Lee to a height three quarters of a miles west of Howard's position. All evidence showed that the Yankees were not aware of his flanking movement. Yet Jackson was very disappointed to find that he was looking at the center of Howard's main line, instead of its right flank. This meant that the Union right was on the turnpike, not the Plank Road as Jackson had anticipated. It also meant that Howard's right was farther west than Jackson wanted it to be.

Jackson stopped to think for only five minutes before ordering Rodes to continue marching north on the Brock Road until he reached the old turnpike. Fitz Lee had already assured him that there were no Union troops at Wilderness Tavern, so Jackson correctly assumed that Howard's flank was somewhere farther east on the turnpike. Rodes resumed his march at about 1400. The brief pause at the Plank Road, and the additional two miles that still had to be covered, would delay Jackson's flank attack at least two hours—a crucial two hours that possibly saved the Union Army from destruction and would also cost Jackson his life.

# CHAPTER XI

# Rout of the *XI Corps*

## Evening, 2 May, 1863

*M*ajor General Oliver O. Howard's *XI Corps* was in no position to receive a massive attack from the right. It was the smallest of Hooker's seven infantry corps, with around 11,000 effectives, and had been further weakened late that afternoon when Barlow's brigade was sent to reinforce Sickles' advance against Jackson's trains near the Catharine Furnace. Howard's remaining five brigades covered a line of one and one fourth miles, formed facing south along the Orange Turnpike with its center approximately at the point where the Brock Road met the turnpike. The position guarded this intersection well, along with the junction of the Plank Road and the turnpike at Wilderness Church. It was also in a relatively strong position on heights above Scott's Run, and may well have been able to repel an attack coming from the south.

Howard's line had several major weaknesses. One was that its right was not anchored on any naturally strong terrain feature. The line just ended a mile west of Wilderness Church where two guns of the *13th New York Battery* were placed on the turnpike facing west. The flank proper was guarded only by two infantry regiments, the *153rd Pennsylvania* and *54th New York*, which were placed at a right angle to the two guns on the turnpike. Howard's second weakness was that he had no reserves to speak of. Barlow's brigade, as already mentioned, was detached from the corps late in the afternoon. This left Howard with twelve of his seventeen regiments in the front line or picket line, and only five in reserve at various points on the line. Another weakness in the position was the fact that half of the corps' artillery was not in line, but was in reserve one-quarter mile east of Wilderness Church. Lastly, it should be noted that Sickles' advance to Catharine Furnace opened up a one mile gap between Howard's left and the *XII Corps* artillery position at Fairview. If the *XI Corps* got into any trouble, it would take awhile for supports to come up to help. The *XI Corps'* predicament was amply summarized by division commander Carl Schurz in his *Memoirs*: "As we were situated, an attack from the west or northwest could not be resisted without a complete change in front. It was almost impossible to maneuver some of our regiments, hemmed in as they were in the Old Turnpike by embarkments and rifle pits in front and thick woods in the rear, drawn out in long, deployed lines, giving just room enough for the stacks of arms and a narrow passage. This Turnpike Road was at the same time the only line of communications we had between the different parts of the front."

Despite Hooker's warnings to watch out for a Confederate attack from the right, Howard took few precautions to defend against the possibility. He posted pickets across his front, and sent out two squads of sharpshooters to a post on the turnpike 1000 yards west of the right of his line. No cavalry was available to screen his front, since Devin's brigade had been sent to help Sickles, and all of the rest of the army's cavalry was absent with Stoneman. The presence of the cavalry covering force would be sorely missed by the unlucky *XI Corps*. Had Union horseman been present and properly used on this flank, Jackson's flank movement and subsequent attack would not have been as successful as they were, if they could have been carried out at all.

Several of Howard's subordinate officers had strong indications during the day that a strong Confederate force was moving towards their flank. Their problem was that they could not convince their superiors—particularly Howard himself—of the seriousness of the situation. Brigadier General Charles Devens, Jr., commander of the *First Division*, had a very small cavalry force at his disposal, and used it to locate Confederate cavalry operating on his flank. He did not know what to make of the situation, and reported his findings to Howard. During the afternoon several large reconnaissance forces were sent up the Plank Road by Brigadier General Alexander Schimmelfennig. They located heavy Confederate skirmishers at a distance of two miles, but once again no one knew what to make of the information.

Additional reports of Confederate activity to the south and west of Howard's line continued to come in all afternoon. Between 1300 and 1400 skirmishers of the *55th Ohio* of McLean's brigade reported a strong enemy force moving across their front to the right. When Brigadier General Charles Devens heard this report, he declined to believe it because he had heard no confirmation of it from corps headquarters. Devens likewise was not inclined to believe a report from Lieutenant Colonel C. W. F. Friend, the officer of the day for the *First Division*, who had been to the front and seen large forces of the enemy there. Friend was so frustrated with Devens that he took his story to General Howard, who instructed him not to spread rumors and so cause a panic. Friend went back to his picket line and saw even more enemy activity, so he returned to Howard with the news. This time he was called a coward, and was sent back to his regiment. The corps command was sure that the Confederates were retreating, not making a flank march.

At 1445 Major Owen Rice of the *153rd Pennsylvania*, commander of Colonel Leopold von Gilsa's picket line, sent the following appeal to his brigade commander: "A large body of the enemy is massing in my front. For God's sake make disposition to receive him!" Von Gilsa was alarmed enough to take the report to Howard, but was sent away after being told that Rice was clearly mistaken because the thickets were too dense for the enemy to penetrate. Howard then showed his lack of concern for his far right flank by going to his left to join Barlow's brigade in pursuit of Lee's supposedly retreating army. During his absence, more reports of Confederate activity to the west were brought in but not heeded. About 1500 Major Gustav Schlieter of the *74th Pennsylvania* reported that he had conducted a reconnaissance up the Orange Plank Road and had found the enemy massed and preparing for an attack. His report was laughed off by Howard's staff members.

Later in the afternoon Captain Hubert Dilger of *Battery I, First Ohio Light Artillery* arrived at *XI Corps* headquarters to report that he had seen a large force of the enemy massing on Howard's exposed right flank. It seems that he heard reports of enemy activity to the west shortly after noon, so he went with an orderly to find out for himself what was happening. When he reached von Gilsa's front line, the colonel was agitated and warned him that it was too dangerous to ride to the west. Dilger nevertheless rode out a mile in that direction, until he ran into Jackson's column north of the Luckett farm. He then had to run for his life and barely escaped by using back paths that led to the rear of the Union army. By chance, he came out near Hooker's headquarters, so he went to the first officer he saw and explained that the enemy was massing to attack the army's rear. The officer shunned Dilger and suggested that he tell his story to General Howard. When Dilger reached Howard's headquarters, Howard was absent with Barlow, so he repeated his warnings to some members of Howard's staff. They scornfully replied that Dilger should have no concern because the enemy was in full retreat. The disgusted and by now exhausted Dilger now gave up and hurried back to his battery, which he reached just as the Confederate attack began about 1715.

Thus it is clear that a number of officers, Captain Dilger, Major Schlister, Lieutenant Colonel Friend, Colonels Lee and von Gilsa, and even Brigadier General Schurz, had good evidence that Jackson was massing to the right of the *XI Corps*. That their warnings were not believed by Brigadier General Devens, Major General Howard, or any members of Howard's or Hooker's staffs, was one of the great tragedies of the battle. Part of the reason was that Devens and Howard were new to their men and commands, and did not know whom to trust and whom not to trust. It also did not help that Howard was not present with his main line during those critical late

*Major General Carl Schurz, division commander in the* XI Corps, *wrote a very interesting account of the battle in his* Memoirs.

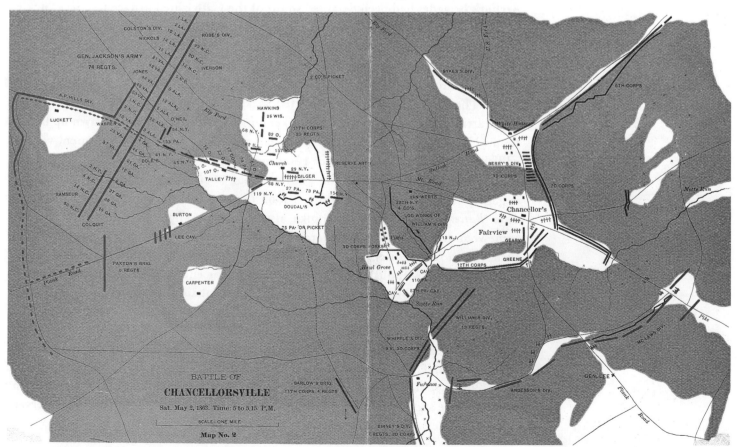

afternoon hours, since at 1600 he elected to go with Barlow's brigade to join Sickles' more promising advance. In the last analysis, responsibility for the disaster that would befall the *XI Corps* must be placed on Howard, and to some extent on Hooker. Howard had at least twice during the day received specific instructions from Hooker to watch his right flank, but he made only a few token efforts to do so because he interpreted Sickles' reports to show that the enemy was retreating. Hooker shares responsibility for the defeat by not being more aggressive in seeing that his orders to Howard were carried out. He had personally inspected most of his lines near Chancellorsville, but not Howard's. It should also be noted that Hooker had sufficient troops available to reinforce Howard's line or even form a strong picket line between Howard's right and the Rapidan, a move that would have helped prevent, or at least give more warning of, any Confederate advances in that sector.

Jackson's leading infantry unit, the 5th Alabama, reached the junction of the Brock Road and the Orange Turnpike about 1430. Jackson then directed his units to march east about one half mile to the Luckett farm, where he began forming his battle line perpendicular to the turnpike. He decided to form three battle lines, each about one and one-half miles long, with just a few hundred yards between each line. The front line was four brigades of Rodes' division (all units given north to south): Iverson, O'Neal, Doles and Colquitt. The second line comprised Jones' and Warren's brigades of Colston's division and Ramseur's brigade of Rodes'. Paxton's brigade of Colston's division had been left to guard the intersection of the Orange Plank Road and Germanna Plank Road, while Paxton's fourth brigade, Nicholls', mistakenly formed up on the left of the third battle line instead of the second line. To Paxton's right were Heth's, Pender's and Lane's brigades of A. P. Hill's large division. McGowan's brigade of Hill's division was still on the march behind all the artillery, while Thomas' and Archer's brigades had been detained south of the Catharine Furnace to check Sickles' advance. Jackson posted skirmishers 400 yards in front of his first line, and set up a strong guard line behind his third battle line to prevent stragglers. The left flank of the attacking force was guarded by the 2nd Virginia Cavalry and Ramseur's 23rd North Carolina, while Paxton's Brigade, already mentioned, would protect the left flank. The heavy underbrush permitted Jackson to form only two guns of Stuart's horse artillery facing east on the turnpike; four additional guns were drawn up behind them. His total force in the lines described amounted to over 26,000 men, with an additional three brigades and over 100 cannons on the way.

Jackson had sent his skirmishers out at about 1600, and they immediately became engaged with von Gilsa's skirmishers; soon the two Union cannons of the *13th New York Battery* posted in the turnpike also joined the fight. Things quieted down somewhat by 1620, when General Devens sent a small body of cavalry up the turnpike to reconnoiter. They soon returned, their captain reporting that he could not advance far without striking a large body of the enemy. Devens snapped back, "I wish I could get someone who could make a reconnaissance for me!," to which the cavalry captain replied, "General, I can go further, but I can not promise to return." Devens dismissed the squadron to go into bivouac.

At about 1630 a squad from von Gilsa's *45th New York* was sent west to see what was going on. They soon returned shouting that the enemy was in their front. In the *53rd Pennsylvania*, "Everyone was now on the 'qui vive'. That mischief was brewing became more apparent. Firing in front, which at first was only heard at long intervals,

# O.O. Howard, The One-Armed General

Major General Oliver Otis Howard, commander of the Union *XI Corps* at Chancellorsville, was born in 1830 in Maine. He attended Bowdoin College and then attended West Point in 1850, ranking fourth in a class that included Jeb Stuart and numerous other Civil War notables. Much of his pre-war service was spent as assistant professor of Mathematics at West Point.

At the beginning of the war, Howard was elected Colonel of the *3rd Maine Infantry*. By the time of First Bull Run he was commanding a brigade, only to see it melt away in the disaster that the Union army met that day. Quite surprisingly, he was promoted to brigadier general just six weeks later, in spite of his poor performance in his first battle. This was just the first of several instances in the war. Howard escaped personal blame for battlefield failures he was to some degree responsible for. How he managed to keep his reputation so clean under such circumstances is still not fully understood today.

Howard was transferred to command a brigade in the *II Corps* during McClellan's Peninsula campaign. He went straight to the thick of the fighting and lost his right arm at the battle of Seven Pines. Less than three months later he returned to action in time to take charge of the army's rearguard during the retreat from Second Bull Run. He was then given command of the *Philadelphia Brigade*, which he led at Antietam until he succeeded John Sedgwick as division commander after the latter was wounded. He was confirmed as division commander when he was promoted to major general in November, 1862.

During Hooker's reorganization of the *Army of the Potomac* in early 1863, Howard was quite annoyed that he was not promoted to corps command when two comrades of equal seniority (Reynolds and Sickles) received the honor. He finally got his wish when Major General Franz Sigel, commander of the army's *Reserve Grand Division*, resigned in a huff at being demoted to the command of the *XI Corps*. Howard's appointment was unpopular with the men of the new corps, who rightly viewed him as an outsider. Howard made no special effort to become more acquainted with his men, and was still becoming familiar with who his officers were when he entered the battle of Chancellorsville a little over four weeks later. Howard's failure to guard his right flank as directed by Hooker and his complete misreading of all the reports presented about Jackson's pending flank attack made him largely responsible for the disastrous rout his corps experienced on the evening of 2 May. Nevertheless, he escaped blame as all the fault for the rout was placed on his troops instead.

Howard's men performed equally poorly at Gettysburg. On 1 July, he posted two of his divisions on indifferent ground north of Gettysburg and then stayed in the rear to direct the entire battlefield as senior officer following the death of Major General John F. Reynolds. He actually had little control on the course of the battle, and once again his corps was badly defeated and routed. Before starting to rally the troops he got into an argument over seniority with Major General Winfield Hancock, whom Meade as army commander had sent with personal instructions to take command of the troops on the field. Somehow Howard managed to earn the thanks of Congress for his role in selecting the strong position on Cemetery Hill! All this in spite of the fact that part of his corps was routed for a second time during a Confederate attack on East Cemetery Hill on the evening of 2 July.

Howard somehow was still in corps command when most of his men were transferred to the war's western theater in the fall of 1863. When the *XI Corps* was consolidated with the *XII Corps* to form the new *XX Corps* under Joe Hooker, Howard was given command of the reconstituted *IV Corps*. By dint of his seniority he was named commander of the *Army of the Tennessee* when James McPherson was killed at Atlanta on 22 July 1864. He continued in this command until the close of the war, leading Sherman's right wing during the March to the Sea and the Atlanta campaign.

Howard was personally honest and quite religious, traits that led him after the war to become actively involved in supporting Negro causes. President Johnson appointed him the first director of the well-intentioned "Freedman's Bureau" in May 1865. His administrative in-efficiency and widespread corruption among subordinates soon soured this experience. He nevertheless continued to aid the Negroes by serving as director of a Negro bank. Howard also took up the cause of education, founding Howard University for Negroes and later establishing Lincoln Memorial University for the mountain people of eastern Tennessee. Howard's remarkable post-war career included a tour as superintendent of West Point. He remained in the army until his retirement in 1894 as a major general in the Regular Army. The year before he retired he was voted a Congressional Medal of Honor for the battle where he lost his arm. He died in Vermont in 1909.

Howard must have had a powerful and honest personality to escape blame for the poor performance of his commands at First Bull Run, Chancellorsville and Gettysburg. In any case, he might better be remembered for his significant contributions during the Reconstruction era rather than for his Civil War generalship.

---

became now frequent and was evidently nearing." Von Gilsa began scrambling for help, but the only troops that were made available to him were the men of the *75th Ohio*, posted one-quarter mile to his rear.

Jackson had most of his men formed for the attack by 1700. He gave careful orders to keep drums and bugles silent and make no cheering until the attack began. The brigades were to charge straight ahead, using the turnpike as their guide. There should be no stopping for any purpose, and commanders in the second and third lines should freely send reinforcements forward when requested.

At about 1700 Jackson asked Rodes, "Are you ready?" Rodes replied, "Yes," and at once sent his skirmishers forward. Due to some confusion on the left of the line, the attack did not get fully underway until 1715. Rodes' skirmishers immediately ran into the *XI Corps* skirmishers, and heavy firing at once broke out, made louder by the booms of Stuart's two guns on the pike. Soon drums and bugles were sounding and the men were screaming their unique rebel yell. Jackson's attack was no longer a secret.

The strength and suddenness of Jackson's assault took the *XI Corps* totally by surprise. The first real warning the Yankees had that Jackson's men were approaching came when a number of deer and rabbits came bounding towards their line, startled by the long advancing Confederate line. Major General Carl Schurz noted the appearance of these animals at 1720 and realized at once what it meant. Some of the Yankees had their arms stacked and were preparing supper when the attack came, and had to be hurriedly formed into line.

Devens' skirmishers and sharpshooters were easily overrun, and Rodes' line quickly closed in on von Gilsa's line. Von Gilsa actually had only two regiments (*153rd Pennsylvania* and *54th New York*) and two guns in position facing west. These men were formed in line in time to face Jackson's onslaught, but did not have enough strength to delay the Confederates long. Jackson had not actually expected to meet any defenders facing west since the woods had effectively concealed von Gilsa's right from observation. Brigadier General George Doles adjusted to the situation readily by sending two of his regiments straight at von Gilsa's right, while one regiment hit the left of the Union line and another swung behind von Gilsa's far right. The outnumbered Yankees could get off only a few volleys before being overwhelmed. Likewise the two cannons on the turnpike could fire only a few rounds before Doles'

*Stampede of the* XI Corps, *evening of 2 May.*

men were upon them. They tried to limber up to retire, when a volley from the 4th Georgia felled most of their horses. The guns were almost immediately captured.

Von Gilsa's two regiments on the turnpike (*41st* and *45th New York*) were also instantly overwhelmed. It appears from some sources that the two units received such a heavy fire from their right front that they began to melt away before firing a shot. About 300 men from the two regiments moved to the right to try to support the remains of the *153rd Pennsylvania*. They held on for three volleys until they were overwhelmed by Jackson's second line. The now jumbled Yankee command withdrew another 400 yards until it met the *75th Ohio*, which was advancing to their support. This makeshift line held for only ten minutes before it, too, was broken.

Jackson's lines continued to roll up Howard's flank. About 1800 they ran into four regiments of McLean's brigade formed up near the Taylor house, about three-fourths of a mile east of the *XI Corps'* original right flank. It took only a few minutes for three Confederate brigades to come up, envelop, and rout the Yankee line. It was about this time that General Howard belatedly arrived on the scene. He at once refused a suggestion by one of his staff officers to fire on his retreating men if they would not stand ("I will never fire on my own men.") Howard did not lack for personal bravery, and took up a flag, holding it across his chest with the stump of his lost arm while he held his horses' reins with his good hand. One of his staff officers was shot dead, and his own horse reared and fell over, without bad injury to the general. Within ten minutes he too was swept away in the rush for the rear.

The historian of the *153rd Pennsylvania* described how Devens' division now melted away: "Resistance against the fearful odds of the advancing foe was utterly hopeless; safety was only to be found in a hasty retreat, and when even the regiments sent to our support were seen in full flight, this retreat assumed the form of panic. All attempts to arrest the fleeing columns proved futile. Confidence had vanished. The panic had turned into a rout, and it was only after the retreating masses had found security within the lines of the corps in our rear, that order and discipline were restored...It was late in the evening before the various organizations were again in condition for active service. Everywhere men were inquiring for their regiments, while scores of officers were hastening to and fro in search of their commands."

Jackson's line pressed on and about 1750 encountered much of Schurz's division formed up in a half mile line from the high ground on Hawkins' farm to the turnpike. Schurz's command, and those members of other broken units who rallied on his line, numbered about 5000 men and would, if properly reinforced, perhaps have stopped Jackson's assault. It seems that the right wing of Jackson's force had lagged behind when Brigadier General Alfred Colquitt of Rodes' division stopped to deal with a Yankee force he thought he saw on his right flank. His delay stalled the brigaders behind him and to the right, a force amounting to some twenty percent of Jackson's strength. Colquitt, Ramseur, and Paxton thus would miss the heaviest fighting, and would be only briefly engaged after dark.

Jackson's center and left had too much momentum to be stopped for long before Schurz's line at the Hawkins' Farm. The Confederate left outflanked Schurz's right by some distance, and worked in behind the Yankee lines. In the front, Jackson's first and second lines were now intermingled but kept pushing forward. They overwhelmed Schurz's position in a sharp fight that lasted only twenty minutes.

The stouter elements of Schurz's command withdrew about one-quarter mile and fell in with Colonel Adolphus Buschbeck's fresh brigade, formed a couple hundred

# The Unlucky *XI Corps*

Without a doubt the most unlucky corps in the Union army was the *XI Corps* of the *Army of the Potomac*. The corps was never much trusted, due to its high proportion of foreign-born personnel, and its name was ruined by its collapse at Chancellorsville and Gettysburg. However, its bad reputation may not have been totally deserved. Study of the corps' battles and campaigns shows that the "German Corps" suffered more from bad luck and bad press than from bad ability.

When the war began, large numbers of foreign-born Americans, mainly Germans, did not hesitate to come to the defense of their adopted country. Many had come to America out of frustration and necessity after the unsuccessful German revolutions of 1848, and were grateful to the United States for offering them a new home. Many also strongly disliked slavery, an institution which, at least in the border states, helped deprive immigrants of needed jobs. At the opening of the war such foreigners, especially officers, were eagerly accepted into the army because of their European military experience.

It was only natural that foreign-born Americans would join friends of the same nationality when enlisting. In this way were formed such units as New York's *Garibaldi Guards* (*39th New York Infantry*, under Col. F. G. d'Utassy), and Adolph von Steinwehr's *Astor Rifles* (*29th New York*). Not so natural was the practice of grouping German regiments into predominantly German brigades. Logic suggested that foreign-born troops might fight better under foreign-born officers. In addition, putting foreign-born soldiers into their own brigades might also alleviate language problems, at least by creating common-language units, though one could imagine the hodge-podge of German, Polish, Italian, and French speaking units. Finally, the formation of these units may also have been influenced by not-so-latent racism. The Know-Nothings and other kindred nationalistic organizations had gained a great deal of political power in the decade before the war, spreading their doctrine of mistrust of foreigners. Such feelings could have led many Northerners to accept "foreigners" into the army, only if they served in separate units. This feeling was directed later in the war much more strongly against blacks, who not only had to serve in separate units but also were not permitted their own officers. The practice of separate units for some ethnic groups continued through World War II.

The first brigade of Germans formed in Virginia was formed in June of 1861. It was commanded by Colonel Louis Blenker, and consisted of the *8th, 29th,* and *39th New York* and *27th Pennsylvania* regiments. In December 1861 the brigade was expanded to a division, led by Blenker, by gathering together other regiments of German and mixed nationalities (*41st, 45th, 54th, 58th,* and *68th New York,* and *73rd, 74th,* and *75th Pennsylvania* regiments). The division's three brigades were commanded by Julius Stahel from Hungary, Adolph von Steinwehr from Prussia, and Henry Bohlen from Germany.

Blenker's division at first was praised for its discipline and the colorful uniforms of some of its units. Its abilities first came under suspicion when it was one of the many units defeated by Stonewall Jackson during his famous Valley Campaign. The division performed particularly poor at Cross Keys on 8 June, but here and during the campaign it and other units suffered much from the poor generalship of Major General John C. Fremont, one time "Pathfinders" and Republican candidate for president.

Later in June 1862, Blenker's division became the nucleus of the *I Corps* in the *Army of Virginia*. Most of the added troops were veteran "native" (non-German) troops from West Virginia and Ohio. Once again the "Germans" suffered from poor generalship, this time from army commander John Pope and corps commander Franz Sigel. At Second Bull Run alone, Sigel's corps lost 2,000 of its 11,000 men.

In September 1862, Sigel's corps was absorbed into the *Army of the Potomac* and renamed the *XI Corps*. The unit took no part in the great campaigns of Antietam and Fredericksburg, perhaps because of Washington's distrust of Sigel's abilities. Sigel finally left the corps in February 1863 because of bad feelings stemming from Hooker's reorganization of the army. He was succeeded by veteran commander Oliver O. Howard, a good leader who was not liked by his new command, most of whom wanted one of the corps' division commanders to succeed Sigel.

The corps' unfortunate positioning on the army's far right and its subsequent collapse under Stonewall Jackson's smashing flank attack have been fully discussed in the text. Most historians today agree that "it is doubtful if other troops under the circumstances could have held the ground." The blame for the rout of the corps on 2 May should most properly lie with Howard, for not heeding Hooker's warnings to watch out for his flank. At the time, however, Hooker's and Howard's shortcomings were overlooked as much of the blame for the loss of the battle was placed on the "Flying Dutchman." That, at least, was how Howard escaped personal blame for his corps' poor performance at Chancellorsville, and so was still in command during the Gettysburg campaign.

Gettysburg was the last battle fought by the entire *XI Corps*. Here again, the men of the corps were the victims of poor positioning and poor generalship. Assigned to John Reynold's advance wing of the *Army of the Potomac*, *XI Corps* on the forenoon of 1 July 1863 was rushed forward to support Reynold's *I Corps* west of Gettysburg. Howard posted his *First* and *Third Divisions* on open ground a mile north of town, at a right angle to ridges held by *I Corps* to protect it from Confederate reinforcements from the north. Von Steinwehr's *Second Division* was posted a mile south of town on Cemetery Hill.

In midafternoon, Howard's 5,000 men were struck in full force by 6,000 Rebels north of town. Dole's Brigade of Rode's Division hit the left side while Early's Division hit the far right of the corps' line. Francis Barlow, commander of *First Division* since Devens had been wounded at Chancellorsville, was also badly wounded, and the whole line pushed back through the town in disorder.

Once again, *XI Corps* was blamed for a Union defeat. Close examination, however, reveals that no Federal troops could have held the position assigned to the corps. While Steinwehr's division would have added to the corps line, it is possible that it could have held on until the arrival of *XII Corps* after 1700, if *I Corps* could also have held on longer on the left. While much of the post-battle literature blames the retreat of *XI Corps* for the collapse of *I Corps*, the truth is rather that the *I Corps* collapsed largely on its own from pressure from three Confederate divisions and from exhaustion due to the day-long fight.

The *XI Corps* spent the rest of the battle on Cemetery Hill, enduring another fight at dusk on 2 July, when two Rebel brigades broke through the remains of Barlow's *First Division* under Adelbert Ames at the base of the hill, just as Ames was rearranging his line behind a stone wall. The Rebels were driven off by darkness and by reinforcements from Winfield Hancock. This breaking of Ame's line is by far the most inexcusable defeat suffered by *XI Corps* troops; yet the units broken through were not "German," but Ohioan. Nevertheless, this was to be the last battle for the "German Corps" in the Eastern Theater.

After Gettysburg, the *Army of the Potomac* had had enough of *XI Corps*. In August the *First Division* was sent to join *X Corps* in the swamps off Charleston, South Carolina, stationed at a place called, appropriately enough, Folly Island. Later, its regiments were scattered in garrisons of the Department of the South.

In September 1863, the *Second* and *Third Divisions* of *XI Corps*, still under Howard, were transferred to the *Army of the Cumberland* in the Western Theater, along with *XII Corps*. While in Tennessee, a new *First Division* was formed for the corps from garrison troops at Nashville and Murfreesboro. Contrary to expectation, the corps fought reasonably well at Lookout Mountain and Missionary Ridge near Chattanooga in November.

The *XI Corps* retained its identity until 14 April 1864, when it was merged with *XII Corps* into the reorganized *XX Corps*. Perhaps because the *XI Corps* divisions were no longer trusted, they were broken up and their brigades distributed among the divisions of *XX Corps*: Schimmelfennig's old brigade (the *First* of the *Third Division* of *XI Corps*, 1-3-XI) became 3-1-XX, Coster's old brigade (*1-2-XI*) became 2-2-XX, Smith's old brigade (*2-2-XI*) became *3-3-XX*, and Krzyzanowski's old brigade (*2-3-XI*) was dispersed to the other brigades and to various guard stations. Most of the old "German" officers were relieved or else given new assignments. Howard was assigned to the revived *IV Corps*, and the *XX Corps*, after three months under Joe Hooker, was led by veteran *XII Corps* officers.

The men of *XI Corps*, then, appear to have been maligned by history much more then they deserve. Only once, on the second day at Gettysburg, did they fail to hold a defensible line. Their bad reputation stems almost entirely from their routs at Chancellorsville and the first day of Gettysburg. These disasters, however, were caused more by poor generalship and bad positioning than by lack of fighting ability. The fact that many of the corps' men (perhaps half) were German-born made it easy for the rest of the *Army of the Potomac* to make the "German Corps" the scapegoats for Chancellorsville and the first day of Gettysburg. The corps has never been able to clear its name of this bad press, which has been repeated in histories of the war. It might be closer to the truth to observe that the men of the *XI Corps* were the victims of poor generalship, bad luck, and a prejudice against foreigners rather than being unpatriotic or poor soldiers.

---

yards east of Dowdall's Tavern. Altogether Buschbeck had about 4000 men in a line about one thousand yards long. Some of the men enjoyed the protection of shallow trench line that had been prepared earlier on a line facing west, but the formation was weakened by the jumble of regiments and brigades that composed it.

Jackson's men approached the Buschbeck line about 1830 and immediately engaged it. Once again the Yankee position was outflanked at both ends of the line and overwhelmed by superior strength on the front. The Confederates carried the position after some sharp fighting, and by 1910 the entire *XI Corps* was in full retreat towards Chancellorsville.

Another crisis of the battle had now arrived. Because of Sickles' advance past the Catharine Furnace, there were no organized troops between Jackson's front and the rear of the Union lines at Chancellorsville, only a little more than a mile away. As the Confederates continued to press forward, the only determined resistance they met was firing from a single piece of artillery manned by Dilger's *9th Ohio Battery* on the Plank Road.

*General Howard striving to rally his troops near the Taylor House about 1800 on 2 July.*

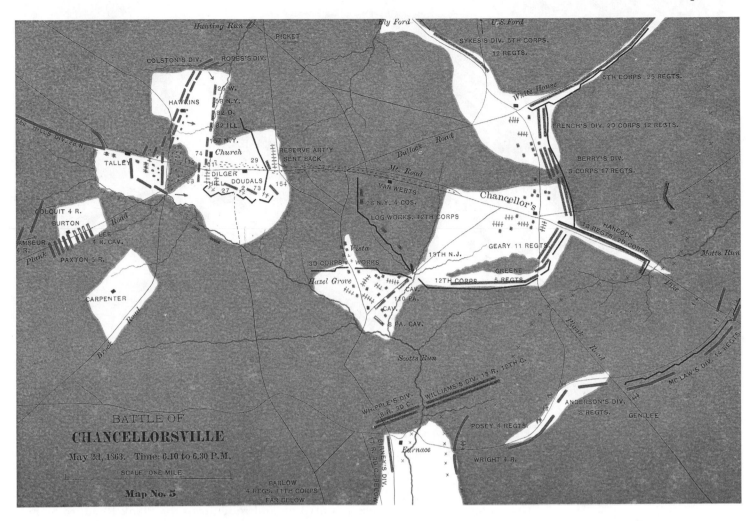

BATTLE OF
**CHANCELLORSVILLE**

May 2d, 1863.  Time: 6.10 to 6.30 P.M.

SCALE: ONE MILE

**Map No. 5**

*Union artillery attempting to delay Jackson's advance on the Plank Road, evening of 2 May.*

*Confederate attack on the Busch-beck line at 1830 on 2 May.*

*Major General A. P. Hill, Jackson's second-in-command, was wounded on the night of 2 May just after Stonewall Jackson was shot.*

It is most curious that Hooker seems not to have been aware of the fighting on Howard's front until over an hour after Jackson attacked. He was at his headquarters, the Chancellor house, and had heard faint sounds of cannon fire, but falsely interpreted that the noise came from Sickles' advance to the southwest rather than from Howard's front to the west. Since no one on Howard's front sent a report of what was happening there or asked for reenforcements, Hooker was unaware of Howard's disaster until 1830, when Captain Russell of his staff happened to look through his binoculars up the turnpike towards Dowdall's Tavern and exclaimed,"My God, here they come!" Hooker at once mounted up and rode down the Plank Road, to be met by an ever increasing stream of fugitives.

Hooker grasped the seriousness of the situation, and sent out a flurry of orders. Sickles, Williams and Barlow had to be recalled from the Catharine Furnace before they were cut off from Chancellorsville. Reynolds' *I Corps*, which had just crossed at U.S. Ford, was ordered to come forward with all speed. The more immediate problem was to form a line to stop Jackson. Fortunately he had Berry's division of the *III Corps* at hand. Sickles had several times requested Berry to be sent to him at Catharine Furnace, but Hooker had wisely held him back. He now formed up Berry's command facing west about one-half mile west of Chancellorsville, supported by Hays' brigade of the *III Corps*. On the left, Captain C. L. Best was realigning all the guns of the *XII Corps* at Fairview to face west. Hooker had to hope that these troops would stop Jackson, or else his whole command would be crushed.

Fortunately for the Federals, Jackson's front line had become so intermingled and confused that Rodes called it to a halt about 1915 on the edge of a woods just east of the recently captured Buschbeck line. He suggested to Jackson that A. P. Hill's fresher third line be brought forward to carry on the assault while he reformed his regiments. Jackson assented, and a comparative lull in the fighting followed for as much as an hour. While Hill's men came up, Sickles brought his two divisions to a comparatively strong position at Hazel Grove, three quarters of a mile south of the Plank Road. Berry advanced about a quarter mile to the west, and Williams returned to continue his line south of the Plank Road. Best by now had thirty-seven guns in line from

Fairview to the Plank Road, and the Yankee line was well appointed to receive Jackson's renewed assault. Nevertheless, the men had been unnerved by the stampede of *XI Corps* men and wagons they saw as they moved into position.

During this stage of the battle Colonel Pennock Huey's *8th Pennsylvania Cavalry* experienced quite an adventure. At about 1600 the regiment had been sent with its brigade to Sickles at Catharine Furnace, but Sickles had not used the unit. About 1845 Huey was ordered to ride to the right and report to Howard. None of the Union cavalrymen were aware of Jackson's attack, so they did not have their sabers or pistols drawn. As he approached the Plank Road, Huey saw some gray clad soldiers, but assumed they were disguised Union scouts. The unit rode on a little farther, and found itself within Jackson's front lines. Huey at once realized that he would have to fight his way through to reach Chancellorsville. He ordered his 350 men to draw their sabers, and led a charge to the Plank Road. Here he was shocked to see the roadway to safety blocked by Confederate infantry. The road to the left seemed more open, so the column slashed its way west for one hundred yards until it was rocked by a volley from a Confederate regiment concealed in the woods near the road. The regiment's Major, thirty other men and officers, and over eighty horses fell dead or dying. Colonel Huey, miraculously unhurt, informed his shattered command north of the road at about 1930, and eventually made his way to Chancellorsville. Huey's foray did not accomplish anything militarily except to make the Confederates jumpy about the presence of more Union cavalry.

As Rodes and then Colston began reforming their disorganized commands, A. P. Hill had more trouble than he anticipated bringing his three brigades forward. Lane's brigade was the first to come forward. It was formed across the Plank Road a mile east of Wilderness Church, with the 33rd North Carolina deployed as skirmishers. Heth's and Pender's brigades needed more time to form, since during the advance they had gone into column formation on the roadway, and now needed to be put back into battle lines. They were further delayed by a raking artillery fire received from the Union guns at Fairview. Hill finally got the Federals to cease firing by ordering his own artillery to stop shooting. Once they did so, the Yankee artillerymen were no longer able to get their range by observing their muzzle blasts, so they quit firing too.

Lane had his troops in position by 2030, and sought out his commander, A. P. Hill, for specific attack orders. Instead he met Jackson, who directed him to continue his attack straight down the Plank Road to Chancellorsville. Jackson had no idea how many Union troops were there, but hoped in all the confusion that Lane would be able to smash through and link up with Lee's two divisions on the other side of Chancellorsville. Meanwhile Jackson would lead Pender's and Heth's brigades, and any other available units, against Hooker's rear. Lane left Jackson at about 2100 to make final preparations for his attack. Soon afterwards Hill joined Jackson and

*Berry's division of the* III Corps *forming to cover the retreat of the* XI Corps, *evening of 2 May.*

*Stonewall Jackson going forward on the Plank Road in advance of his line of battle about 2100 on 2 May, just prior to his being wounded.*

*Repulse of Jackson's men at Hazel Grove, by artillery under General Pleasonton, evening of 2 May.*

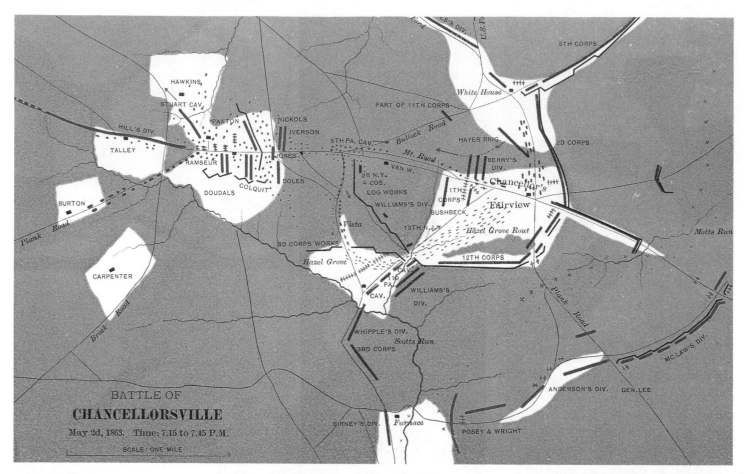

BATTLE OF
**CHANCELLORSVILLE**

May 2d, 1863.   Time: 7.15 to 7.45 P.M.

SCALE: ONE MILE

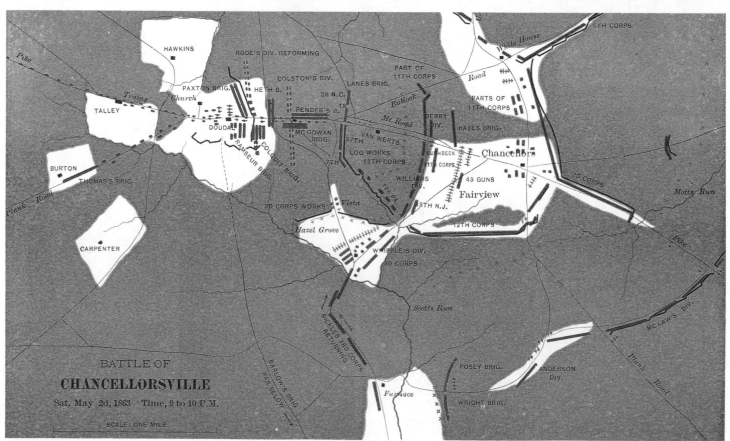

BATTLE OF
**CHANCELLORSVILLE**

Sat. May 2d, 1863   Time: 9 to 10 P.M.

SCALE: ONE MILE

# Young Stonewall

Thomas J. Jackson was born at Clarksburg in western Virginia on January 1824. His family was of Scotch-Irish lineage and had been settled in western Virginia since about 1750. Various ancestors had served in civil and military posts in the Colonial period, the Revolution, the early years of the Republic, and the War of 1812. One of four children, Thomas' father died when he was three, leaving the family destitute. His mother—to whom he remained very devoted—remarried but died in childbirth when Thomas was seven. Thomas and his siblings then lived with various relatives, including an uncle who was particularly fond of the young boy. When he reached adulthood—only Thomas and his sister Laura survived to see twenty-one—Thomas had acquired a rudimentary education and had worked in a variety of jobs. When his uncle died during the California gold rush, Thomas decided to apply to West Point.

Thomas had actively pursued his West Point appointment. When he heard that a cadet from his congressional district had resigned soon after entry, Thomas sought the support of his most influential relatives and went personally to see his congressman, Samuel Hays, in Washington. Hays was concerned about Thomas' lack of formal education, and arranged an interview with the Secretary of War. Here Jackson's determination won the day, and the secretary approved the appointment, saying, "Sir, you have a good name. Go to West Point, and the first man who insults you knock him down, and have it charged to my account!"

Jackson soon felt his lack of academic background for a program difficult as West Point's. He was not a quick learner, but worked hard and retained well what he studied. As he himself put it, he "studied very hard" for what he got at West Point. A classmate said of him, "He had a rough time in the Academy at first, for his want of previous training placed him at a great disadvantage, and it was all he could do to pass his first examination. We were studying algebra, and maybe

analytical geometry, that winter, and Jackson was very low in class standing. All lights were put out at "taps," and just before the signal he would pile up his grate with anthracite coal, and lying prone before it on the floor, would work away at his lessons by the glare of the fire, which scorched his very brain, till a late hour of the night. This evident determination to succeed not only aided his efforts directly, but impressed his instructors in his favor, and he rose steadily year by year, till we used to say 'If we

*Thomas J. Jackson as a First Lieutenant in the artillery during the Mexican War.*

had to stay here another year, Old Jack would be at the head of the class'."

Jackson's behavior at West Point was exemplary. He picked up only a few demerits, and generally kept to himself, having but few close friends. He matured in body as well as mind while attending the Academy. His frame filled out, and his performance and confidence in his work improved yearly. He fully expected to be expelled after his first year, but ended up ranking seventeenth in a class of seventy when he graduated in 1846. His class included such future notables as generals McClellan, Foster, Reno, Stone-

man, Couch, and Gibbon of the Union army; and generals A. P. Hill, Pickett, Maury, D. R. Jones, W. D. Smith, and Wilcox of the Confederate army.

Jackson graduated from West Point at the beginning of the war with Mexico, and immediately entered the action. As a lieutenant in the 1st Artillery, he fought in almost every battle from Vera Cruz to the fall of Mexico City. So eager was he for advancement that he sought and received an appointment to the battery of the aggressive Captain John B. Magruder. Jackson soon rose to be Magruder's second in command, and won the rank of brevet captain for his gallantry at Cherubusco on 20 August 1847. At Chapultepec on 13 September, Jackson's handling of himself and his section under fire won the praise of Magruder and generals Scott, Pillow, and Worth. One of these friends described the scene as follows: "Lieutenant Jackson's section of Magruder's battery was subjected to plunging fire from the Castle of Chapultepec. The little six-pounders could effect nothing against the guns of the Mexicans, of much heavier calibre, firing from an elevation. The horses were killed or disabled, and the men became so demoralized that they deserted the guns and sought shelter behind a wall or embankment. Lieutenant Jackson remained at the guns, walking back and forth, and kept saying, 'See, there is not danger; I am not hit!' While standing with his legs wide apart, a cannon ball passed between them..." This bravery earned him a promotion to brevet major.

When the fighting ended, garrison life in Mexico City enthralled the new major. After great pains he learned to speak Spanish, and he also developed a zest for dancing. But the greatest event of his sojourn in Mexico was his introduction to the Episcopal religion by Colonel Francis Taylor, commander of the 1st Artillery Regiment.

After the Mexican War Jackson did garrison duty in New York and Florida for a time, before accepting a post at Virginia Military Institute in Lexington.

# Stonewall Jackson's Last Days

Soon after Stonewall Jackson was wounded shortly after 0900 on 2 May, he was carried by litter to a waiting ambulance in the rear of the Confederate lines. The ambulance then proceeded west to Dowdall's Tavern, where Dr. Hunter McGuire inspected Jackson's wounds and readjusted the sling on his shattered left arm. After Stonewall was administered whiskey and morphia to dull the pain, he was carried three miles farther to the rear to a field hospital near Wilderness Tavern.

Sometime after midnight facilities were finally ready for Dr. McGuire to examine the general's wound in detail. He administered some chloroform before probing, and Jackson was heard to mutter, "What an infinite blessing!" McGuire first examined Jackson's right hand, and removed a round bullet of the type used in Confederate smoothbore muskets. His left arm had two wounds—one in the lower arm, and another that shattered the upper arm and broke the main artery. The good doctor at once realized that the arm could not be saved and had to be amputated, about two inches below the shoulder. It was a routine operation, completed in minutes. (The next day, Stonewall's severed arm was respectfully buried one-half mile away from the hospital in the family burial plot at the Lacy home "Ellwood," where it remains today. The blood soaked table on which the operation was made is still preserved today, as is the torn overcoat Jackson was wearing that unfortunate night.)

When he awoke after the operation, he had enough energy to issue a few orders and notify General Lee of his accident. Lee was noticeably affected by the sad news and remarked, "He has lost his left arm, but I have lost my right." To Jackson he wrote with all sincerity, "Could I have directed events, I should have chosen for the good of the country to be disabled in your stead."

On the afternoon of 3 May, as the battle focus moved eastward from Chancellorsville, it was decided best to move

*The Chandler office at Guiney Station, where Stonewall Jackson died on 10 May 1863.*

the wounded general to a safer locale. Jackson himself suggested Guiney Station where he had encamped briefly the previous December. This small cluster of houses was well situated ten miles south of Fredericksburg on the main railroad line to Richmond, near the army's supply depot and artillery park. Jackson's party left on the morning of 4 May, for the twenty-five mile trip to Guiney Station. The general was conveyed in an ambulance and was accompanied by Dr. McGuire, engineer Jed Hotchkiss, his chaplain and one aide.

Chaplain Lacy rode ahead of the party to make arrangements for Jackson's accommodations. He spoke to the Chandler family about using part of their large home "Fairfield," but the house was judged to be too crowded with family. Instead, they settled on a small two-room office, one of the farms several outbuildings. A bed was set up for the general in one of the rooms, and his staff members prepared to bunk down in two small attic rooms.

Dr. McGuire changed the bandages on Jackson's arm stump on 5 May, and noted that the wound was showing good signs of healing. Jackson grew stronger on the 6th, but developed nausea and sharp pains in his side early on the 7th. It was pneumonia. The seeds of the disease

may have been planted the night before Jackson was shot. Several accounts relate that he was unable to sleep well that night, and got up several times to try to warm himself by the fire before rising very early to begin preparations for his flank march. Physical and mental exhaustion from the strains of the campaign did not help his weakened condition much, either.

Jackson's wife Anna arrived from Richmond later on the 7th, bringing along her baby, Julia. She was not pleased to see him breathing so laboriously or so dopey from the morphia he was being given for the pain. In those days doctors did not have penicillin or other drugs to deal directly with the pneumonia. Instead they used ineffective methods like cups to his chest. Jackson grew steadily weaker on the 8th and 9th, though during periods of lucidness he spoke clearly and delighted in seeing his baby. On the 9th he noted, "I see from the number of physicians that you think my condition is dangerous but I thank God, if it is His will, that I am ready to go."

Stonewall's mind now began to wander from the combined effects of his weakness, the disease, and the medicine. At one point he cried out, refighting some past battle, "Order A. P. Hill to prepare for action...Pass the infantry to the front." His wife sang and read the Bible for him, and he reassured her, "I think I will be better by morning." He failed still more on Sunday the 10th, and sensed the end was near. He even observed, "My wish is fulfilled. I have always desired to die on Sunday." At 1515 he spoke his last words and expired: "Let us cross the river and rest under the shade of the trees."

Jackson's body was taken to Richmond that evening, and lay in state in the capitol. Burial was made in his hometown of Lexington on 15 May, not far from his home and his beloved Virginia Military Institute where he taught before the war.

received the terse command, "Press them; cut them off from the United States Ford, Hill; press them."

Jackson now decided to reconnoiter Lane's front before the advance began. It was definitely not a wise decision because of all the scattered firing that was going on there. The skirmishers of Lane's 33rd North Carolina were jumpy because of the closeness of the Federal lines and because of anxiety over another enemy cavalry charge such as the *8th Pennsylvania* had conducted ninety minutes before. Since they had come into position, a Federal Colonel, Joseph A. Matthews of the *128th Pennsylvania*, had wandered into their lines while looking for his regiment, and so was captured. This prompted Lane to send out a patrol to his right to see what Yankees were positioned there. Then another Union officer, probably Brigadier General Joseph A. Knipe, rode into the woods calling for General Williams. His presence provoked a volley from Lane's front line that caused several casualties among his own skirmishers. All the racket persuaded the Federals that an attack was being made, so they began to open fire.

*Major Peter Keenan of the* 8th Pennsylvania Cavalry, *killed during his unit's famous charge on the evening of 2 May.*

Such was the confusion in Lane's front when Jackson and some staff members rode ahead into the woods a little after 2100. A bright moon was casting eerie shadows in the darkness. Jackson's intention was to see if there were any roads running to the Federal rear. He rode up to the rear of the 33rd North Carolina's skirmish line and heard trees being chopped down; the Federals were there and fortifying their lines. At about 2115 Jackson turned back, as a burst of firing erupted on the picket line.

The party was now north of the roadway, opposite the van West House. Suddenly a few shots, then a volley, came crashing out of the Confederate line south of the road. Lane's troops had mistaken Jackson's party for Federal cavalry! Officers in the rear and someone from Jackson's staff cried out, "Cease firing, you are firing on your own men." Back came the query, "Who gave that order? It's a lie! Pour it into them, boys!"

A volley now poured forth, probably from the 18th North Carolina. The bullets struck several members of Jackson's group, just twenty paces away. Captain J. K. Boswell, Jackson's chief engineer, and his horse were killed instantly. One orderly was killed and another wounded. Jackson himself was struck by three balls—one in the palm of his right hand, one through the wrist of his left hand, and the third and worst blow broke his left arm between the shoulder and elbow. Jackson's horse, Little Sorrel, was terrified by the volley, and ran into the woods, where Jackson was almost thrown to the ground by some low hanging boughs. The frantic horse might well have run off towards the Union lines if Lieutenant J.M. Wynn of his staff had not intercepted it only one hundred yards from the Union position.

Wynn and Captain R. E. Wilbourn, the only two members of Jackson's party who were not struck or dehorsed by the destructive volley, got Jackson down from his horse and placed him under a tree. Wynn then went to find A. P. Hill, who was also reconnoitering nearby, and then an ambulance. Wynn found that Hill's party had also been struck by a volley of musketry, probably the same that felled Jackson. Hill had hit the dirt when the firing started, and then rose to help his aide-de-camp, Captain Murray Taylor, who was pinned under his fallen horse. Hill left Taylor's side to help Jackson as soon as he heard his commander had been hit. He arrived to find Wilbourn examining Jackson's wound and attempting to improvise a sling. Hill expressed regret that the wound had been caused by accidental fire from his own troops. Hill then removed Stonewall's belt and saber, and gently took off his now blood soaked gauntlets. Jackson was offered a shot of brandy, which he reluctantly drank, and he seemed to perk up for a few minutes.

It was by now obvious that Jackson had to be moved to the rear and taken to a hospital. The following graphic account was written by Captain James Power Smith, one of Jackson's aides, who arrived on the scene after his commander was wounded:

The writer reached his side a minute after, to find General Hill holding the head and shoulders of the wounded chief. Cutting open the coat-sleeve from wrist to shoulder, I found the wound in the upper arm, and with my handkerchief I bound the arm above the wound to stem the flow of blood. Couriers were sent for Dr. Hunter McGuire, the surgeon of the corps and the general's trusted friend, and for an ambulance. Being outside of our lines, it was urgent that he be moved at once. With difficulty litter-bearers were brought from the line near by, and the general was placed upon the litter and carefully raised to the shoulder, I myself bearing one corner. A moment after, artillery from the Federal side was opened on us; great broadsides thundered over the woods; hissing shells searched the dark thickets through, and shrapnels swept the road along which we moved. Two or three steps farther, and the litter-bearer at my side was struck and fell, but, as the litter turned, Major Watkins Leigh, of Hill's staff caught it. But the fright of the men was so great that we were obliged to lay the litter and its burden down upon the road. As the litter bearers ran to the cover of the trees, I threw myself by the general's side and held him firmly to the ground as he attempted to rise. Over us swept the rapid fire of shot and shell—grape-shot striking fire upon the flinty rock of the road all around us, and sweeping from their feet horses and men of the artillery just moved to the front. Soon the firing veered to the other side of the road, and I sprang to my feet, assisted the general to rise, passed my arm around him, and with the wounded man's weight thrown heavily upon me, we forsook the road. Entering the woods, he sank to the ground from exhaustion, but the litter was soon brought, and again rallying a few men, we essayed to carry him farther, when a second bearer fell at my side. This time, with none to assist, the litter careened, and the general fell to the ground, with a groan of deep pain. Greatly alarmed, I sprang to his head, and, lifting his head as a stray beam of moonlight came through the clouds and leaves, he opened his eyes and wearily said: "Never mind me, Captain, never mind me." Raising him again to his feet, he was accosted by Brigadier-General Pender: "Oh General, I hope you are not seriously wounded. I will have to retire my troops to re-form them, they are so much broken by this fire." But Jackson, rallying his strength, with firm voice said: "You must hold your ground, General Pender; you must hold your ground, sir!" and so uttered his last command on the field.

Again we resorted to the litter, and with difficulty bore it through the brush, and then under a hot fire along the road. Soon an ambulance was reached, and stopping to seek some stimulant at Chancellor's (Dowdall's Tavern), we were found by Dr. McGuire, who at once took charge of the wounded man. Passing back over the battle-field of the afternoon, we reached the Wilderness store, and then, in a field on the north, the field hospital of our corps under Dr. Harvy Black. Here we found a tent prepared, and after midnight the left arm was amputated near the shoulder, and a ball taken from the right hand.

# CHAPTER XII

# Hooker Is Rendered Senseless

## Morning of 3 May, 1863

Stonewall Jackson was not the only high ranking Confederate officer wounded on the night of 2 May. Not long after he was hit, his artillery chief, Colonel Stapleton Crutchfield, was wounded by Federal artillery fire; Stapleton would ride to the rear in the same ambulance that carried Stonewall. Just after Jackson was sent to the rear, Hill returned on foot to the scene of his wounding, probably to make sure that Jackson's haversack full of letters and dispatches had not been left on the ground for the enemy to find. While searching the ground, he was struck by a minie ball that went through the calves of both legs. It was a painful wound, and the general hobbled to the rear, unable to walk or get into a saddle. He would not fight any more during the rest of the battle.

Hill's wounding caused a command crisis on the Second Corps front. As the corps' senior division commander, A.P. Hill succeeded to corps command when Jackson went down. When Hill was wounded, the next senior corps officer was Jubal Early, but he was absent at Fredericksburg. Command then had to devolve on the corps' senior brigadier, Robert E. Rodes, who was that day commanding a division for the first time in battle. Rodes had not been aware of Jackson's plans to attack Hooker's rear, so he made preparations for a direct attack on Chancellorsville. About 2145, Pender formed on Lane's left, and Thomas deployed his Georgia brigade on Lane's left by 2300. These three brigades fell under the direct supervision of Brigadier General Harry Heth, Hill's successor as commander of the Light Division.

While Rodes was forming for his attack, preparations were being made to transfer command of Jackson's corps to none other than Jeb Stuart, commander of the army's cavalry division. Even though Stuart had not previously commanded infantry, the choice was a good one. He was well known and well respected for his cavalry exploits, and as Major General outranked all the brigadiers still unscathed in the corps. With Stuart in temporary command of the corps, Rodes could return to lead his division, so allowing his senior brigadier, Stephen D. Ramseur, to return to his brigade. Stuart at the time was very available, since he in effect had no command to lead—he had only one of his brigades on the field, ably led by Fitz Lee, and sometime after dark had taken a small force to guard the Ely's Ford Road "as there appeared nothing else for me to do." The idea to send for Stuart was probably Hill's, but may have originated with Jackson. Since neither Jackson nor Hill survived the war, it is difficult today to resolve the question. Stuart says that the request to come forward was delivered by Captain R. H. T. Adams of Hill's staff. Stuart rode up as fast as he could, and conferred briefly with Hill, who was being carried to the rear on a litter. Stuart later reported that it was shortly before 1000 when Hill formally turned over command to him. Stuart wrote, "I sent also a staff officer to General Jackson to inform him that I would cheerfully carry out any instructions he would give, and rode immediately to the front."

When Stuart arrived at the front, he conferred with Rodes and several of the brigadiers, and the consensus was to suspend operations until dawn. There was simply too much confusion on the front to mount a solid night attack, and many of the troops were disheartened by the loss of Jackson and Hill, as well as by the repeated Union artillery fire from Hazel Grove and Fairview. Stuart's decision was a good one, for by that time Hooker had stabilized his line west of Chancellorsville, and Sickles' troops were well positioned at Hazel Grove. The Confederates' best move might have been to move up the Bullock Road toward the Union rear, as Jackson had been planning, but even so they would have run into fresh troops from Berry's division. The fact of the matter was that Jackson had dealt a terrible blow to Hooker's army when he routed Howard's corps, but it was not a deadly blow. The critical moment had come and passed at 1915, when Rodes halted to reform his division, which was tired but certainly not routed and disorganized like the Yankee troops in his front. Had Jackson insisted that Rodes press on at 1915, the road to Chancellorsville was pretty much open. By the time Jackson got ready to renew his advance at 2100, the door of opportunity was closed by Hooker's adjustments and Sickles' return.

While Stuart was still learning the positions his new troops occupied, a ruckus arose on his right as Dan Sickles began a night attack from his lines at Hazel Grove. Night attacks were seldom attempted during the war, and this case amply illustrates why. Sickles sent two brigades forward through the woods, deployed in a mixture of line and column formations. The men had their bayonets fixed, and their guns loaded but not capped, so they would not be inclined to stop and start a firefight before reaching the Plank Road. Sickles was unsure of the Confederate position, and neglected to send skirmishers or scouts forward. As a result, the center of his advance struck the openground between Heth's front and Hooker's lines. Sickles' left obliquely hit the right of Lane's line, but Sickles' right ran right into the center of Williams' Union division. To put it mildly, all hell broke loose. While the center of the attacking line advanced unopposed to the Plank Road, the men on the left and right began firing indiscriminately at whatever troops were in their front. Some units on the right began charging a battery until they found out it belonged to the *XII Corps*. The attack confused Williams' Union troops, with the result that the *13th New Jersey* fired into the rear of the *3rd Wisconsin*. On the left, Lane's troops eventually repulsed those of Sickles' men who reached their lines. At length Sickles retreated from his fiasco, having accomplished no military objective other than providing

Stuart additional reason to delay the Confederate attack until dawn.

Stuart spent much of the night completing the formation of his forward battle line. At about midnight, McGowan's brigade came up and was placed on Lane's right to face Sickles. As already noted, Pender and Thomas were already posted north of Lane to complete the front line. Stuart brought up Brockenbrough's (formerly Heth's) brigade to back up Lane in the center of the line, and resupplied the battery posted on the Plank Road. At midnight he ordered Archer to bring his men out of bivouac and form on McGowan's right to extend the line facing Sickles' front. Colston's division was brought up to back up the front line, while Rodes was still reforming at Dowdall's Tavern where he had stopped at 1915. Altogether Stuart had slightly over 40,000 men in his command, facing Hooker's wing of 75,000.

General Lee was able to be much more communicative when he learned of Jackson's accident at about 0200. He was awakened by Captains Wilbourn and Hotchkiss to hear the sad news, and at once exclaimed, "Thank God it is no worse! God be praised he is still alive! Any victory is a dear one that deprives us of the services of Jackson, even for a short time." At 0300 he wrote instructing Stuart to press on to Chancellorsville. Lee promised to join Stuart's wing personally as soon as he could. Newer orders sent at 0330 were more specific, directing Stuart "to slide to his right, turning the positions of the enemy so as to drive him from Chancellorsville, which will again unite us."

Jackson had his left arm amputated during the wee hours of the morning, and was in no condition to give orders. When a messenger arrived from Stuart to brief him and ask advice at about 0330, all Jackson could respond was, "I don't know, I can't tell; say to General Stuart to do what he thinks best."

During the night the Federals worked hard to fortify their entire line, which now sported logworks three feet high, designed for the men to fire over while kneeling. Hooker intended to hold his troops on the defensive while Sedgwick came up to strike Lee in the rear. He properly figured that Lee had stripped his defenses at Fredericksburg, and the moment was ripe for Sedgwick to attack. Late on 2 May, he finally established a reliable communication line with his left wing commander, and had given him clear orders to push forward.

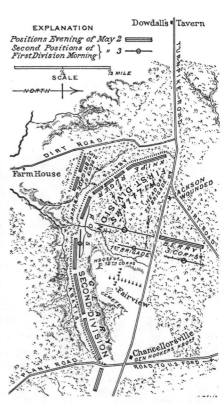

These orders clearly show that Lee was unaware that Sickles' two divisions were at Hazel Grove, blocking the route he wanted Stuart to use. Nor could Lee have been aware that Meade had made major readjustments to his lines so as to face Stuart's threat. Hooker shifted Sykes' and Griffin's divisions of Meades' corps from their now fortified lines on Mineral Spring Road to a new position along the Ely's Ford Road north of Chandler; their place on the Mineral Spring Road was taken up by Howard's reforming corps. During the early morning hours Reynolds' exhausted troops began to come up, having marched twenty-three miles since the previous morning. These were placed at an angle along Hunting Creek Run from Meade's right northeast to the Rapidan. At last Hooker's wing was occupying a more compact line with its apex at Chandler and both wings anchored on the river. The only problem with this position was that half his force was compressed into a bulge that extended south from Chandler, past Chancellorsville. The *II Corps* was still facing McLaws' earlier lines on Mott's Run (even though Lee had shifted McLaws south of the turnpike when most of Anderson's men were sent to face Sickles at Catharine Furnace), and Geary's division of the *XII Corps* was in a long arc south of Fairview.

*Confederate defenses on Willis'
Hill behind Fredericksburg, now
the site of the national cemetery.*

*The* 29th Pennsylvania *of Geary's
division under artillery fire,
morning of 3 May.*

As already mentioned, Williams' division of the *XII Corps* and Berry's of the *III* were facing west toward's Stuart's troops, and Sickles was at Hazel Grove with Whipples' and Birney's divisions of his corps, along with Barlow's brigade of the *XI Corps*.

Before daylight, Lee began pushing his left (Anderson's division, still without Wilcox's brigade) forward and to the west to feel out Federal positions and establish contact with Stuart. Stuart had his men up at dawn, but it took more time than anticipated to align the brigades once daylight came. The skirmishers along Stuart's first line did not move out until 0600. Many of the Confederates helped to cut off and capture Sickles' men in their exposed position at Hazel Grove. The men of Archer's brigade were surprised with the ease by which they moved right up to Hazel Grove, where they got into a fire fight with Graham's brigade. Graham's lines fired a few volleys and then withdrew to the north—the strong but exposed position at Hazel Grove was being given up without a fight! Hooker had visited Sickles at dawn, and decided that the position was too exposed to hold on to, despite the advantage it gave at flanking Stuart's lines. Sickles reluctantly obeyed, and soon had his troops marching north to Fairview. Graham's brigade, encountered by Archer, had been his rearguard, and withdrew under orders not to start a fight.

Archer's elated men thus occupied Hazel Grove after a brief skirmish, and paused to catch their breath. They then moved north against the *XII Corps* infantry posted in their strongworks southwest of Fairview, only to be repulsed by 0645. Meanwhile the Confederate command quickly realized the potential of using Hazel Grove to enfilade the *XII Corps* lines, and some thirty-one guns, including most of Colonel E. P. Alexander's battalion, were rolled into position at Hazel Grove. These, and another twenty guns posted in Stuart's lines near the Plank Road, would soon cause great havoc on the Yankee troops. The principal Union artillery position, the forty guns under Captain Best at Fairview, were not as advantageously posted. They were set up

*Repulse of the Confederate attack west of Chancellorsville, morning of 3 May.*

*Brigadier General Frank Paxton, commander of the Stonewall Brigade, was killed on 3 May.*

too far behind their infantry to give them any support without hitting their own troops, once the Confederates began advancing.

As the Confederates were massing their artillery at Hazel Grove, Stuart's front line was moving forward to attack. During the advance McGowan's and Lane's brigades became separated from each other, and met differing levels of success. McGowan struck the *37th New York* of the *III Corps* while its troops were forming into column to move back, and easily routed the unit. It then ran into Ruger's brigade of the *XII Corps* and the *7th New Jersey* of the *III Corps*, and became stalled in a firefight that lasted half an hour. Eventually McGowan was outflanked and forced to retreat in disorder. Lane, lacking McGowan's support on the right but having Pender on the left and Brockenbrough to the rear to give more weight to his attack, enjoyed much more success. This attack hit the *3rd Maryland Infantry (U.S.A.)*, a large green unit that promptly broke and fled. Lane now advanced until he was checked by the New Jersey regiments in the second line.

Confusion now reigned at the center of the Union line on the turnpike. Captain Poland of General Berry's staff could not get the *115th Pennsylvania* to advance, and Colonel Robert McAllister of the *11th New Jersey* likewise questioned Poland's power to issue orders (Poland later wrote "unfortunately my authority was questioned at an untimely moment.") Major General Hiram A. Berry now found it necessary to go in person to Brigadier General Gershom Mott, commanding the brigade that was now checking Lane south of the turnpike. Berry's staff members urged him not to ride across the exposed ground at the turnpike, but he did so anyway. He made the outgoing trip safely and had his say with Mott, only to be felled by a sharpshooter's bullet as he crossed the roadway on his return trip. The bullet struck him in the vitals, and he died instantly at 0726.

The Federal right fell into confusion as Pender pushed deeper into the Union lines, and Thomas and Brockenbrough added their weight to the attack. By 0745 the Confederates had punched a hole one-half mile deep in the Union lines immediately north of the turnpike. Unfortunately, Colston's second line was not yet up to help exploit their success, and the attack on the right was meeting trouble. Lane's brigade met severe resistance from the *XII Corps'* second line and was losing men to the Union artillery at Fairview. In addition, McGowan's repulse exposed his right flank. When Ruger's Union troops conducted a sharp counter attack, Lane's men were driven back beyond the line of Union works captured the previous day, from where they had started the attack. Soon Thomas' and Pender's Brigades suffered a similar fate as Hooker came up and personally sent French's division forward in a smashing counter attack against the Confederate left.

Stuart's front line was by now completely shattered; its brigades had not attacked in unison and Stuart had not used artillery support properly. His second line under Colston now entered the fray, more because the fighting rolled back to its position than through any advance of their own. It was all Colston could do to stabilize the front along the line of the previously captured Union works already mentioned. Paxton's "Stonewall" brigade found comrades packed six to eight men deep lined up behind the works. Colonel J.H.S. Funk of the 5th Virginia later reported, "We endeavored to persuade them to go forward, but all we could say was of no avail." The Virginians declared, "We will show you how to clear away a Yankee line" as they crossed the works and pressed forward. The next instant Paxton fell dead. The valiant men of the Stonewall Brigade charged to within seventy yards of Ruger's line before they were repulsed.

The length of the day's fighting, which now had been going on for close to three hours, and continuing command confusion following the death of General Berry, now began working to Hooker's disadvantage. Ruger's brigade, which had been fighting superbly, had to withdraw because it was out of ammunition. Likewise, most of the artillery at Fairview had used all its long range ammunition and had only shortranged canister in its caissons. About 0800 Brigadier General Joseph W. Revere heard of the death of his commander, General Berry, and falsely assumed he now led his division (the job actually fell by seniority to Brigadier General Joseph B. Carr). On his own impulse Revere decided to march his brigade and most of three other regiments out of the battle to reorganize and get fresh ammunition at the supply trains near U.S. Ford. (For this dereliction of duty, Revere would be convicted by a court martial after the battle. President Lincoln revoked the court martial verdict for reasons of political expediency, and then allowed Revere to resign his commission quietly.)

The tide of battle now began to shift in favor of the Confederates. French's Union counter attack was repulsed when he came face to face with ten cannons Lieutenant Colonel H. P. Jones had lined up across the Plank Road. At this opportune moment Stuart's third line—Rodes' refreshed division—at last entered the fray. Rodes' ad-

*The Chancellorsville House at the time of the battle. General Hooker was wounded while standing on the front porch on 3 May.*

*Rescuing the wounded from the burning woods on the morning of 3 May.*

vance hit the Yankees head on and then began exploiting their weaknesses. His attack found its greatest success on the right, where Geary's *XII Corps* division had begun pulling back at 0800 because of heavy enfilading fire from the Confederate guns at Hazel Grove. Brigadier General George Doles, leading a portion of his Georgia brigade that had become separated from the rest of Rodes' line, found an undefended seam in the Federal lines, and came up behind Colonel Samuel Ross' brigade of the *XII Corps*. Doles captured a large number of prisoners as he broke Ross' line and then continued slashing his way towards Chancellorsville, capturing seven cannons en route.

At this critical juncture, several of Williams' regiments had to leave for the rear because they, too, were out of ammunition. Their withdrawal exposed Geary's right flank even more, so Geary had to pull back part of Greene's brigade as a flank guard. As the Union infantry regiments north of Fairview retreated or were driven back, the Confederates came face to face with all the Union artillery massed at Fairview. The Union guns blasted away with their canister—the only ammunition they had left—as Confederate sharpshooters began picking off their horses. By 0900 the cannoneers figured they better retreat while they still had enough horses to do so, since Confederate infantry (Doles' command in particular) were in their rear.

As the Union artillery retreated from Fairview, the rest of the Union supporting infantry also withdrew from that sector. One of the few Union successes at this stage of the battle came when Colonel Louis R. Francine's *7th New Jersey* managed to capture the flag, Colonel, and a large number of men of the 2nd North Carolina. During the action Francine yelled himself hoarse, and was advised by his surgeon to go to the rear. For some reason he took his regiment with him and much of the rest of the brigade. Graham's brigade, the last big organized Union command in this sector, was forced into a disorderly retreat by a charge conducted by the Stonewall

Brigade at about 0915.

By now many of the Confederate troops were becoming exhausted from two days of heavy fighting. Stuart had driven most of three Union divisions (Berry, Whipple, and Williams) from the field, had taken the Union strong points at Hazel Grove and Fairview, and was on the verge of linking up with Lee's left at long last. Nevertheless, Hooker still had the *II* and *V Corps* intact and immediately at hand, more then enough troops to stop Stuart and still turn the tide of battle.

At this juncture yet another chance event intervened to alter the course of the battle. The fighting had drawn even closer to Chancellorsville, and Hooker was on the porch of his headquarters, preparing to speak to Major H. E. Tremain of Sickles' staff. It was about 0915. Just then a twelve pound Confederate solid shot struck the porch pillar against which Hooker had been leaning, broke it in two, and sent part of it crashing on the general's head and side. He was knocked out by the blow, and his staff members at first thought he was dead. They took him inside the house, where he was soon revived by his doctor. Because a rumor was spreading quickly that he had been killed, Hooker mounted his horse in order to be seen by his men. However, he soon became dizzy, and had to lie down. His doctor gave him some brandy to stimulate him—the only liquor he drank during the campaign. (Hooker had a reputation for being a lush, but swore off liquor during the campaign, a fact verified by and monitored by his second-in-command, Major General Darius Couch). The general then rose to ride to a less exposed new headquarters at the Bullock House. Right after he got up, another Confederate artillery shot struck the blanket where he had been lying.

Hooker was in severe pain from his wound for the rest of the day, and for the next several days to follow. His right side was partially paralyzed, and his thinking was cloudy for the rest of the battle. One of his aides wrote a few days later, "The blow which the General received seems to have knocked all the sense out of him. For the remainder of the day he was wandering, and was unable to get any ideas into his head excepting to remain in the extreme front and under as much fire as could possibly be found. In fact, at no time of trip after Sunday did he seem to be compos mentis." In this condition, he should have relinquished command of the army to his second-in-command, Couch, at once, but he declined to do so, and nobody dared to suggest the idea to him. As he rode to his new headquarters, Couch noted, "This was the last I saw of my commanding general in front."

A number of pressing matters needed attention at this time, and had to be tabled or handled behind the scenes by Couch. Sickles wanted to mount yet another counterattack, but was refused by Couch. Meade wanted to strike a blow at Stuart's left, which appeared to be vulnerable. He had already sent a brigade (Tyler's) to French's division in a successful limited counterattack that crossed Hunting Run. Reynolds likewise wanted to form a massive assault on Stuart's left. The two corps commanders met with Hooker, and were definitely refused permission to mount an attack. Hooker even specifically instructed Meade not to send any more troops to help French. To the south, Geary's division was now withdrawing towards Chancellorsville, and would need instructions on where to form.

Couch and Hancock now took charge of the lines behind Chancellorsville. Franklin's brigade made an attack that recovered Fairview and captured the battle flags of the 5th and 26th Alabama regiments, while Caldwell's brigade and the *Irish Brigade*

*Major General Winfield S. Hancock ably covered the army's withdrawal from Chancellorsville.*

counter attacked north of the turnpike. Most of the Confederate regiments, now low on ammunition themselves and disorganized by heavy losses, retreated to a line of captured Union works one-quarter mile west of Fairview. Their only energetic units still on the field were the Stonewall Brigade, which made yet another attack on Fairview, and the 26th Alabama, which charged in a successful attempt to recover its lost flag.

By 0930, the left of Anderson's division (Perry's brigade) had finally worked its way through the underbrush to Fairview, and at last the two wings of Lee's army were reunited. Anderson's comparatively fresh troops helped drive back the last of Sickles' men, and pushed forward all along their front as Geary's division finished its withdrawal. Soon the Confederates were forming their batteries at Fairview to blast away at the eighteen Union guns still in line at Chancellorsville. The few Union troops here were now being hit in front and rear from Fairview to the west and McLaw's artillery on the Plank Road to the east.

About 1000 the Confederate troops on the entire line were surprised to see all the Union infantry in their front begin heading for the rear. Unknown to them, Hooker at 0930 had finally decided to give Couch command of the army. As he did so he gave Couch orders to withdraw the troops near Chancellorsville to the line north of Chandler. Couch well understood that he would be "simply acting as executive officer to General Hooker in fulfilling his instructions, which were to draw in the front, and make some new dispositions." As such, he would not be able to order any movements on his own initiative.

Orders now went out for Sickles to withdraw, then Geary. Their departure left Hancock virtually alone at Chancellorsville. He left part of his line facing east, and formed the rest of his command three quarters of a mile to the west, facing Stuart. The southern flank of his formation was covered by Geary's last brigade, acting as a rearguard. When Geary withdrew, Hancock himself began to pull back, calmly and slowly, even though he was pressed by Confederate fire coming from three different directions. The fire was so heavy that Hancock's mount was killed, and Couch lost his horse besides receiving two slight body wounds. Hancock's withdrawal was nobly covered by the reduced artillery force at Chancellorsville, which continued to fire though unsupported and heavily outgunned by opposing Confederate batteries. Most selfless of these brave Union artillerists was the men of Pettit's *Battery B, 1st New York Light Artillery*, and those of Leppien's *5th Maine Battery*. When Leppien's guns had to be abandoned because he had lost all his horses, they were bravely pulled away by volunteers from the *53rd, 116th* and *140th Pennsylvania* regiments. All Union troops were clear of Chancellorsville by 1030.

Couch formed the withdrawing corps the center of the line already formed leading from Chandler to the river on each flank. Couch and Slocum were massed in reserve immediately north of Chandler, while Sickles formed at the apex of the line, supported by a mass battery of forty-eight guns. The position was definitely well defended, and, unknown to Lee, had previously been fortified. As the Federals were withdrawing, Lee formed his five divisions along the Plank Road. Colston was placed in the center at Chancellorsville, with Rodes and Heth to the west; Anderson and McLaws were formed to the east. Altogether Lee had some 34,000 men in a line barely two miles long, facing 75,000 Yankees in prepared defenses over five miles long. Even so, Lee was pondering making an assault on Hooker's new lines, when deteriorating affairs to the east demanded his attention.

*Union line formed north of Chancellorsville near Chandler, where the army withdrew on 3 May.*

*Laying Pontoons for Sedgwick's Corps.*

# CHAPTER XIII

# Sedgwick at Second Fredericksburg and Salem Church

## 3 - 4 May 1863

*H*ooker's plan of operations for the Chancellorsville campaign assigned a key role to Major General John Sedgwick, commander of the army's largest corps, the *VI*. While Hooker took approximately half the army on a wide flanking movement west of Lee's positions at Fredericksburg, Sedgwick would hold the army's left wing (60,000 men in the *VI*, *I*, and *III Corps*, plus Gibbon's division of the *II Corps*) ready to cross at Fredericksburg and either help crush Lee's smaller army, or force the Confederates to retreat toward Richmond. The move was all the bolder because the army's two wings would be separated by ten or more miles, and maintaining communications would be essential to keep their movements coordinated.

In compliance with Hooker's orders, Sedgwick moved the *I*, *III* and *VI Corps* from their winter camps to Stafford Heights, opposite Fredericksburg, on the afternoon of 28 April. Gibbon's division was allowed to stay in its camps at Falmouth, where it was in clear sight of the Confederate lines. About 1600 on the 29th, Sedgwick sent 1,200 men in small boats across the river at Franklin's crossing to secure a bridgehead. This was safely done under cover of a heavy fog, and Brigadier General Henry Benham's skilled engineers put up three pontoon bridges in the next four hours. Two miles to the south, Brigadier General James Wadsworth of the *I Corps* sent his boats across the river at Fitzhugh's crossing at 0900, and the engineers constructed two bridges by noon. Additional infantry was then sent across the new bridges, and easily drove scattered defenders out of their rifle pits. To support them, Sedgwick moved more infantry up to the eastern approach of the pontoon bridges, which were also guarded by numerous artillery batteries. Stonewall Jackson, who commanded the Confederate troops camped near Sedgwick's crossings, was at first inclined to launch an attack on the first Yankee divisions that crossed. Lee, however, did not allow this out of respect

# Uncle John Sedgwick

Major General John Sedgwick, commander of the Union left wing during the Chancellorsville campaign, was one of the most competent and beloved generals in the Union army. He was born in Connecticut in 1813, and entered West Point as a member of the Class of 1837, having Joe Hooker and Jubal Early as classmates. Following graduation he served in the Seminole Wars and won two brevets during the War with Mexico. His military skills were great enough to win him appointment in 1855 as Major of the 1st Cavalry, a regiment led by Colonel Robert E. Lee and Lieutenant Colonel William Hartel.

Sedgwick was appointed a brigadier general in August 1861 and led a division in the *II Corps* ably until he was wounded in action at Frayser's Farm on June 30, 1862. He returned to action as a newly appointed major general in time to fight at Antietam. Here he marched his division into a trap in the West Woods, his worst tactical maneuver of the war. The mistake cost a loss of over 2000 men in just twenty minutes; Sedgwick himself was wounded three times and put out of action for three months.

When Sedgwick returned to duty he briefly held command of the *IX Corps*, and then was transferred to the *VI Corps*, with which he became most closely identified. He led the Union left wing during the Chancellorsville campaign, where he carried the Confederate works at the battle of Second Fredericksburg. He was then boxed in at Salem Church because of Hooker's defeat at Chancellorsville, and had to use all his skills to get out of the scrape.

Sedgwick's corps was the largest in the Union army during the Gettysburg campaign, and had to march long and hard to reach the battlefield, some units covering over thirty-five miles in one day. Once arrived, its brigades were sent to various reserve positions as needed, and did not see a great deal of action. Later that year, Sedgwick led the troops that captured almost 2000 prisoners in the well designed attack on Rappahannack Bridge in November.

Sedgwick continued in command of the expanded *VI Corps* when new army commander U.S. Grant reduced the *Army of the Potomac* from five to three corps in the spring of 1864. He fought well at the battle of the Wilderness in May, but became too careless about exposing himself to enemy fire at the battle of Spotsylvania. When warned to be more careful, he replied that "they couldn't hit an elephant at this distance." The next instant he was struck by a sharpshooter in the left eye and died instantly.

*Major General John Sedgwick, commander of the Union left at Second Fredericksburg and Salem Church.*

for the fire power of all the Yankee batteries lined up on Stafford Heights, which would surely blast any Confederate infantry that advanced in front of their trenches.

Sedgwick's crossing did not deceive Lee, who began shifting troops towards Chancellorsville as he learned of Hooker's flanking movement on the 30th. That morning Sedgwick received instructions from Hooker, sent at 0830, to "make a demonstration on the enemy's lines in the direction of Hamilton's crossing at 1 o'clock, the object being simply to ascertain whether or not the enemy continues to hug his defenses in full force; and if he should have abandoned them to take possession of his works and the commanding ground in their vicinity...If you are certain that the enemy is in full force in your front...the demonstration herein will not be made." When Sedgwick made a few probes, he determined the enemy to be still present and strongly posted, so, according to his discretionary orders, he did not make his full demonstration.

Sedgwick's lack of aggressiveness on the 30th convinced Lee that the force facing Fredericksburg was most likely a diversion, and that Hooker's flanking column was the more important menace. For this reason Lee took a major gamble on the morning of 1 May, and sent Jackson's Corps to face Hooker on the Chancellorsville front. Sedgwick was apparently not immediately aware of their departure, as he remained inactive during the day. Some fault must be his, however, for not being more aggressive to determine that the force opposing him had been reduced to about around 10,000 men.

Mechanical communication problems developed between Hooker and Sedgwick on 1 May. At 1130 Hooker sent a telegram to his chief of staff, Major General Dan Butterfield, who was stationed at Falmouth to coordinate the army's two wings, to direct Sedgwick to "threaten an attack in force at 1 o'clock, and continue in that attitude until further orders. Let the demonstration be as severe as can be, but not an attack." As the appointed hour came and went and no sounds of guns came from Fredericksburg, Hooker became anxious that Sedgwick's inactivity would not tie down Lee's force as planned. This failure to hear activity on Sedgwick's front was a contributing factor to Hooker's decision to pull back Sykes' and Slocum's commands that afternoon and go on the defensive at Chancellorsville.

The reason for Sedgwick's inactivity at Fredericksburg was the simple fact that he did not receive Hooker's 1130 attack order until close to 1900. It seems that the telegraph lines north of the Rappahannock were not functioning properly that day, and Hooker's order did not reach Butterfield at Falmouth until 1745. It then took another hour to reach Sedgwick at the front. When the order came, Sedgwick promptly directed his troops across the river to begin a demonstration and sent his Light Division across the river to help them. Even so, the demonstration was not pushed very aggressively, and at 2100 Sedgwick received an order via Butterfield to cancel the attack as coming too late.

More indecision tied Sedgwick down most of 2 May. Additional orders received late on 1 May directed him "in case of the enemy's exposing a weak point, to attack and destroy him; in case of his appearing to fall back, to advance in pursuit by the Bowling Green Road and Telegraph Road." Once again, Sedgwick did not have positive orders to attack, so stayed in position because the enemy still strongly held the works facing him. He operated under these instructions all morning and after-noon of 2 May, in spite of increasing sounds of battle coming from the west. That he did so was particularly awkward, since one of the primary purposes of Hooker's halting at Chancellorsville had been to wait for Sedgwick to come up against Lee's rear. That Sedgwick did not do so promptly was Hooker's fault for not sending more forceful instructions. Hooker clearly had the December disaster at Fredericksburg on his mind, and was not ready to take on the responsibility of giving Sedgwick unqualified orders to assault the deadly Confederate positions on the Fredericksburg

*Union soldiers crossing in small boats to establish a bridgehead for laying pontoons.*

*The pontoon bridges at Franklin's crossing, about a mile below Fredericksburg.*

heights. The resulting impasse has been aptly described by Chancellorsville historian John Bigelow, "Hooker was waiting for Sedgwick to do something, and Sedgwick was waiting for Hooker to do something."

At 1610 Hooker sent Sedgwick his strongest orders to date: "Cross the river as soon as indications permit; capture Fredericksburg with everything in it, and vigorously pursue the enemy. We know that the enemy is fleeing, trying to save his trains. Two of Sickles' divisions are among them." Sedgwick received the order at 1800 but was confused whether he should pursue the enemy towards Chancellorsville or to the south. He at once sent to Hooker for clarification, which arrived via Butterfield at 1905: "Pursue the enemy on the Bowling Green Road." Accordingly, Sedgwick sent his *Second* and *Third Divisions* across the lower pontoon bridges, and had his *First Division* begin pushing back Early's right in preparation for a march to the south.

Jackson's surprise attack and the collapse of the *XI Corps* that evening brought Hooker to give his first definite orders to Sedgwick, orders that also changed the left wing's objective from the Bowling Green Road to Chancellorsville. These orders unfortunately came twenty-four hours too late to have a decisive effect on the campaign as it was being waged: "The Major General commanding directs that General Sedgwick cross the Rappahannock at Fredericksburg on the receipt of this order, and at once take up his line of march on the Chancellorsville road until you connect with us, and he will attack and destroy any force he may fall in with on the road...He will probably fall on the rear of the forces commanded by General Lee, and between us we will use him up. Send word to General Gibbin to take possession of Fredericksburg. Be sure not to fail."

These key orders never reached Sedgwick directly. It seems that some supply wagons bouncing down the road from U.S. Ford to Chancellorsville banged into the telegraph poles by the side of the road, and knocked the line out of commission for awhile. This caused Hooker's crucial 2100 attack order to get lost during transmission. Sedgwick learned of the instructions second-hand after 2300 when Butterfield happened to send him a copy along with some other commands. Since his divisions were by then already in motion towards Hamilton's Crossing, as per his 1610 instructions, Sedgwick had to stop to analyze the content of the new orders. Should he recall his division, recross the river at the lower pontoons, and then cross again in front of the enemy at Fredericksburg in order to carry out the exact letter of Hooker's orders? Had there been a bridge at Fredericksburg, Sedgwick may have indeed done so. Instead, he chose to carry out the spirit of his orders by sending his troops up the west bank of the river to their jump off points for the attack.

Sedgwick had his troops marching to Fredericksburg a little after midnight. Due to the darkness and need to reform his troops before an attack could be made, he would not be able to make his assault until dawn (0500) at best. Hooker unrealistically hoped for Sedgwick to be arriving at Chancellorsville at dawn, and then spent all morning waiting for him to come up. Had Sedgwick been able to reach Lee's rear on the morning of 3 May, the battle may well have turned out differently. But Sedgwick would need a fair amount of time to make his plans, form his troops, defeat the enemy in his front, and march eight miles, probably with enemy resistance, to reach Chancellorsville. How Hooker expected Sedgwick to accomplish this with only half the force the left wing began the campaign with is uncertain. Sedgwick had sent the *III Corps* to join Hooker at 1330 on 30 April, and then released the *I Corps* early on 2 May. This left him with 27,000 men in his *VI Corps* plus Gibbon's *II Corps* division. Facing him were some 12,000 men in Early's division and Barksdale's brigade. Hooker doubtless believed Early's force was much weakened, as he received constant reports from Professor Lowe's observation balloon concerning Confederate troops marching away from Fredericksburg. Indeed, most of the Confederate defenders had marched out of Fredericksburg in the early afternoon of 2 May after they received orders from Colonel R. M. Chilton of Lee's staff to pull out. Early dutifully

*Marye's Heights and the western edge of Fredericksburg from a war time photograph. The portico of the Marye mansion can be seen at the top of the hill left of center.*

obeyed; leaving only 2500 men to hold the works as best they could. Chilton's order was clearly an error, and Lee quickly countermanded it as soon as he heard that Early was in motion. The troops promptly returned to their old positions, with the exception of a few artillery batteries.

Sedgwick's advancing troops had to contend with Confederate skirmishers during their march north, and so did not reach the outskirts of Fredericksburg until 0200. Newton's *Third Division* was the first to come up, and was sent into the streets of Fredericksburg. Howe's *Second Division* was drawn up behind the railroad lines immediately south of Hazel Run, while Brooks' first division remained near Franklin's Crossing. Gibbon's division (less one brigade left at Bank's Ford) was unable to cross until shortly after daylight, when the bridge from Fitzburgh's Crossing was brought up and relaid at the north end of Fredericksburg. Gibbon then crossed and formed north of Fredericksburg facing the canal line.

The Confederate forces defending Fredericksburg were substantially weaker then Sedgwick's command, but had an advantage in their strongly prepared entrenchments and prepared fields of fire. In addition, many of the Union troops were apprehensive about attacking over the ground that had seen so many casualties the previous December. Early's biggest problem was his lack of strength—he had less then one-sixth of the force Lee had used to defend the same lines just five months before. His lines were about six miles long, defended by about 1.1 men per yard, and he had no reserves.

The most famous and one of the strongest parts of Early's line, the Stonewall at the base of Marye's Heights, opposite Fredericksburg, was held by only 600 men of Barksdale's brigade (18th Mississippi and three companies of the 21st). To the north, four regiments of Hays' Louisiana brigade held Cemetery Hill. Fortunately for Early, the gap between Hays' line and the river was filled soon after dawn by Wilcox's Alabama brigade of Anderson's division. Wilcox had been guarding Banks' Ford and had been ordered to join Lee at Chancellorsville. When he learned that Gibbon was moving to cross at Fredericksburg, he took it on his own initiative to march to support Early.

The center of Early's position, Lee's Hill, was the strongest part of the line, and was held primarily by artillery, supported by three infantry regiments (two of Barksdale's and one of Hays'). Early had deployed over half of his force to face Sedgwick's troops after they crossed at Franklin's Crossing and Fitzhugh's Crossing (located one and one-half and three miles south of Fredericksburg, respectively). Hoke's and Gordon's brigades were in line along the vale of Deep Run, and Smith's brigade was deployed at Hamilton Crossing. Sedgwick's night march early on 3 May caught the Confederate commander by surprise, so that he was not able to transfer his forces from the right to the left in order to face Sedgwick's pending assault.

Sedgwick was cautious and careful in preparing his attack. He made his first probing attack about 0400, when the *62nd New York* and *102nd Pennsylvania* were sent forward in the predawn mist. They advanced only a short distance before meeting a terrible fire from artillery and small arms. Sedgwick watched the attack carefully, and was quick to realize that the heights were strongly defended. He now formulated his attack plans: Newton would demonstrate against Marye's Heights, Brooks would hold the enemy left in check, and the primary attack would be made jointly by Gibbon north of the town and Howe immediately south of the town.

Sedgwick's men were set to make their attack by 0730, but the general made the mistake of waiting for Gibbon's men to get into position, which they did not form until well after 0930. By then Sedgwick was forced to alter his attack plans. Gibbon reported that the canal in front of his position was thirty feet wide, and it would be suicidal to try to bridge it during the daylight. His attack would have to be scrapped. Then Howe reported that any attack he made up the gully of Hazel Run would be subject to severe flanking fire from Marye's Heights and Lee's Hill. Sedgwick's best shot now seemed to be a frontal attack from Fredericksburg by Newton's division, assisted by Burnham's "Light Division" (which was actually just a reinforced brigade).

Major General John Newton planned his assault carefully. He would use only ten regiments, some 4,700 men constituting just over half of his available force. On the left, four regiments would advance in two battle lines against the stone wall at the base of Marye's Heights. The key to the attack would be six regiments advancing in columns of fours, four using the Orange Plank Road on the right and two using the Telegraph Road in the center. The men in column were instructed not to fire a shot, but to use the speed of their formation to reach the enemy line quickly and then carry the line with bayonets. Sedgwick and Newton were well aware of the dreadful casualties the Union attackers had incurred when they tried to form line and shoot it out against the defenders of Marye's Heights at the Battle of First Fredericksburg, and they did not want to repeat those disastrous tactics.

Newton did not need long to form his men. The Confederates saw what was happening, but did not interfere, daring the enemy to make their charge. The attack stepped off at 1035, supported by the artillery barrage that had been ongoing since 0630. The assault began well enough, as the men advanced quickly and were soon so close to Marye's Heights that the Confederate artillery on the hill could not be depressed enough to hit them.

The next stage of the attack was much more costly. At about 300 yards the Confederates opened up with canister fire from two howitzers located near the northern end of the stonewall and with one gun placed on the Plank Road. The right column, commanded by Colonel George C. Spear of the *61st Pennsylvania*, was smashed to bits and Spear was killed. The center column pressed on. The Confederate infantry held their fire until the attackers were less than fifty yards distant. The

*Union troops attacking Confederate works on Marye's Heights behind Fredericksburg.*

*Confederate troops defending the stone wall at the base of Marye's Heights.*

tension was broken by one over anxious Mississippian who let go a shot. Then came the order "Fire!" The blast leveled the troops leading the assault. Colonel Thomas D. Johns of the *7th Massachusetts* rallied the column, and sent it forward again. Again it broke, as Johns and Colonel Burnham of the *Light Division* fell wounded.

As the Yankees sought cover, a brief lull in the fighting arose. Someone noted the weakness of the Confederate left flank, and sent a flag of truce forward to ask permission to remove the dead and wounded from the enemy front. Colonel Thomas M. Griffin of the 18th Mississippi innocently granted the request. During the short truce, Union officers confirmed the weak point in the Rebel line. As soon as the fighting resumed, the *7th Massachusetts* rushed forward to a wooden fence at the north end of Marye's Heights, and sent a withering enfilade fire against the defenders of the stone wall. At the same time the *5th Wisconsin* charged straight at the Confederate line. Their final rush carried the lines, and then swept over the top of the hill. The attack took only fifteen minutes, and cost over 1,000 casualties to capture the lines that 6,000 casualties failed to reach the previous December.

When Newton began his attack, Howe sent his division forward to support it. Five of his regiments veered north to help Burnham's attack on the stonewall, and in the process the *6th Vermont* became the second regiment to breach the Confederate line. Newton then sent in his reserves to secure the hill, and the Yankee victory was complete. Barksdale had sent for assistance as soon as the attack began, and Hays responded by sending four regiments while Wilcox sent one. However, the charge was over so quickly that the reenforcements did not have enough time to reach the threatened point before the fighting was over.

In a short time, the Yankees gathered up over 1,000 prisoners, several battle flags, and fifteen cannons. Remnants of the shattered Confederate regiments fled to the west and south. Wilcox headed for Chancellorsville, prepared to delay any Union forces that followed him. Early led most of his division south along the Telegraph Road, leaving Gordon's brigade as a rearguard. Barksdale rallied what troops he could on Lee's Hill, and also retired up the Telegraph Road.

Sedgwick's victory was now complete. All he lacked was a cavalry force to pursue and capture the scattered enemy. But he had none. He could have used his numerous infantry for the purpose, but felt that it was more important to follow Hooker's instructions and march for Chancellorsville. As soon as he could gather up Newton's division, he marched out the Orange Plank Road. Howe followed, delayed somewhat until Barksdale evacuated Lee's Hill. Brooks chose not to challenge Early's right, even though it was by then in retreat, and marched north into Fredericksburg. Gibbon moved onto the heights behind Fredericksburg and remained there. He declined to move further without orders, and Sedgwick did not feel authorized to command him forward (that was Butterfield's job).

Sedgwick, marching at the head of Newton's division, arrived about noon at the Guest Farm, two miles west of Fredericksburg. He thought it best not to proceed farther until he had support. The delay was a costly one, for Brooks' and Howe's divisions did not come up until 1400. Sedgwick and Newton had lost two valuable hours that could have been used to hunt down and destroy some of Early's troops, or to move closer to Chancellorsville. Brooks' division now at last took up the advance toward the west, formed in battle line with one brigade on each side of the Plank Road. Newton and Howe did not follow until 1515.

*Capture of the heights at Fredericksburg by the* 6th Maine Infantry *of Burnham's* Light Division.

Sedgwick's delay in advancing permitted the Confederates to form a viable defensive line at the Toll Gate one mile west of the Guest House and about one-half mile east of Salem Church. Wilcox was the first to form here as he retreated from Fredericksburg. He posted some dismounted cavalry and four cannons slightly to the east of the Toll House as an outpost. Wilcox anticipated making a fighting withdrawal before Sedgwick's advancing troops, but soon found that would not be necessary. About 1400, long before the Yankees came up, he was heavily reinforced by almost 8,000 infantry and 22 pieces of artillery. Lee had heard of the loss of Fredericksburg at about 1230, when he was debating whether or not to assault Hooker's new position at Chandler, north of Chancellorsville. Lee promptly decided that Sedgwick's column was the more immediate threat, and dispatched McLaws with three of his brigades, plus Mahone's Brigade of Anderson's Division and several batteries under McCarthy and Alexander, to stop the Federals advancing from the east.

McLaws placed his artillery on the Plank Road slightly west of Salem Church, and assigned two brigades to form on each side of the road—Mahone and Semmes to the left, and Kershaw and Wofford to the right. The whole line was about a mile long. Since the Yankees were so slow coming up, the Confederates even had time to dig in and fortify their line.

Sedgwick's advance did not engage Wilcox's outpost on the Plank Road until 1525. The firing they encountered there forced Brooks to redeploy into line formation, as his men had switched into column en route. As soon as they did so, Wilcox's outpost withdrew to the brigade's main line at the Toll House. The Federals reached this position at 1600, whereupon Wilcox fell back to the center of McLaws' line. His arrival raised the Confederate strength there to 10,000 men.

Brooks should have stopped to await the arrival of Newton's division, which was at least a mile behind him on the Plank Road. Instead, he formed his brigades and charged right at Wilcox's position. Bartlett's brigade shattered the 10th Alabama, and was on the verge of cracking the entire line. Wilcox desperately threw in his only reserve, the 9th Alabama. A fierce struggle ensued with charge and counter charge. By 1830 Bartlett was repulsed, just as Newton's lead units were coming up and forming on Brooks' right. All Newton could do now was stiffen Brooks' line and let darkness end the struggle.

Brooks' men slept that night on the battlefield "with the dead of the battle lying near us." The rest of the *VI Corps* was strung out along Plank Road. Sedgwick was anxious about being boxed in by the Confederates, and sent to Hooker for instructions. Hooker was in a deep sleep and groggy from his wound. When he was awakened, he said he had no instructions for Sedgwick. Major General G. K. Warren, the army's chief engineer, took it on himself to write to Sedgwick at 2300: "I find everything snug here. We contracted the line a little, and repulsed the assault with ease. General Hooker wishes them to attack to-morrow. If they will, he does not desire you to attack them again in force unless he attacks him at the same time. He says you are too far away for him to direct. Look well for the safety of your corps." Sedgwick would clearly be on his own. Even Gibbon had deserted him, as he was ordered to stay at Fredericksburg to guard the pontoon bridges.

Sedgwick's fears about being boxed in were totally justified. At 1900 Lee determined to suspend all operations against Hooker's wing, and concentrate on destroying Sedgwick. McLaws was ordered to hold his lines at Salem Church. Contact was reestablished with Early, who was directed to operate against Sedgwick's left and cooperate with McLaws. Shortly before dawn Lee directed Anderson to take three of

*Confederate prisoners captured at the battle of Chancellorsville being escorted to the Federal rear.*

his brigades (Posey, Perry and Wright) from their new position facing the *XII Corps* near Scott's Ford, and proceed to Salem Church. This would give the forces there about 23,000 men to deal with Sedgwick's 19,000. Stuart's command with 25,000 would keep an eye on Hooker's 75,000, who still showed no signs of aggressiveness.

At 0700 on 4 May, Lee sent three brigades of Heth's division to the Old Mine Run to prevent Hooker from marching to relieve Sedgwick, should he choose to do so. An hour later the planned encirclement of Sedgwick began as Early retook the heights at Fredericksburg. He left Barksdale to keep an eye on Gibbon, who remained in Fredericksburg, and began moving against Sedgwick's rear with the rest of his command.

Sedgwick was at once apprised of this new situation, and formed to meet the challenge. He formed Howe's division astride the Plank Road one mile west of Fredericksburg with instructions to watch for Early. Newton's division went into line north of the Toll House towards Scott's Ford, facing McLaws. Brooks' division was stretched out along the Plank Road covering the two miles between Newton's and Howe's lines. By noontime he was skirmishing with Anderson's division, which had arrived at Salem Church at 1100 and then been sent against Sedgwick's center. Thus Sedgwick's line formed three sides of a rectangle. The open side of the rectangle led to Scott's Ford, which was still guarded by Owen's *Philadelphia Brigade*. Sedgwick rightly judged this to be his best escape route in a pinch, preferable to fighting his way to join Hooker or being caught while trying to cross the pontoon bridges at Fredericksburg.

Lee arrived at Salem Church sometime before noon, and directed Anderson and Early to assault Sedgwick upon a given signal, three cannons fired in quick succession. His plan seems to have been to drive Howe's division back on McLaws'. Due to delays in establishing a continuous line of skirmishers around Sedgwick's position, Lee did not fire his signal guns until 1730. Hays and Hokes' brigades led the attack, but in the growing dusk became entangled with each other and had to withdraw. Gordon's brigade on the right made more progress until it was repulsed by Howe's main line. Meanwhile, Wright's brigade was repulsed by Brooks' artillery on the southern front. Perry and Posey took so long coming up in the brush that they did not become engaged.

*Confederate dead of Barksdale's Brigade along the stone wall at the base of Marye's Heights. The sketch was copied from a photo taken soon after the successful Union attack on the morning of 3 May.*

Thus Lee's feeble attacks were easily repulsed. Sedgwick nevertheless decided he had enough. He had no reason to expect any aid from Hooker, and he was apprehensive of being cut off from his escape route over the river. At 1845 he ordered a general withdrawal to Scott's Ford. Howe formed a rear guard, but was not challenged as the Confederates did not begin to pursue until 2130. Sedgwick formed his men on high ground near the ford while Army engineers constructed a pontoon bridge. At 2350 he asked Hooker for permission to withdraw across the river. Hooker sent his approval at 0100 on the 5th. Sedgwick received it at 0200, and promptly began the crossing. It is fortunate that he did so, for Hooker had changed his mind at 0320 and countermanded his permission to withdraw. Sedgwick received the order at 0230, when most of his command was across, and declined to recross to the southside of the river. He had had enough of the battle and Joe Hooker's wavering plans.

*Battle of Salem Church, 4 May.*

# CHAPTER XIV

# Conclusion

## 4 - 5 May, 1863

*H*ooker had been almost completely inactive on 4 May while Sedgwick was being hemmed in west of Fredericksburg. The only event of note on his lines was that Major General Amiel W. Whipple was mortally wounded in the stomach by a sharpshooter while directing the erection of some breastworks.

At midnight on 4-5 May, Hooker called his corps commanders to a meeting. All were present except Slocum, who arrived too late for the meeting, and Sedgwick. Warren and Butterfield also were in attendance. Hooker explained the army's situation, and posed the question whether the army should attack or withdraw. He and Butterfield then left. Couch, Meade, Reynolds, and Howard spoke in favor of advancing (Howard probably out of a desire to redeem his corps' reputation). Sickles favored retiring. The generals were discussing whether or not the army could retire in safety when Hooker returned, and stated he thought they should withdraw. The officers then held a formal vote. Meade, Reynolds, and Howard voted for an advance, while Couch joined Hooker to vote for a withdrawal. Couch apparently changed his mind because he felt it would not be safe to have the army fight again under Hooker in his present condition. Hooker then announced he would take it on his own authority to order a withdrawal, and adjourned the meeting. As the generals left, the annoyed Reynolds complained, "What was the use of calling us together at this time of night when he intended to withdraw anyhow?"

Hooker directed Warren as the army's chief engineer to prepare a defensive position covering U.S. Ford. His corps commanders were ordered to cut roads through the woods to the crossing area, so that then troops would not be jammed up on the few existing roads and so be made vulnerable to attack. The army withdrew later in the day (5 May), with the *V Corps* acting as rear guard. Hooker crossed the river during the day and intended to have the army follow, when a severe thunderstorm came up and began to swamp the bridges. Meade and Couch had an impromptu conference, whereupon Couch decided circumstances put him in command of the army, and he would stay to fight. His brief tenure as commander ended at 0200 on 6 May when Hooker sent a sharp message to bring the army across the river.

Thus the Chancellorsville campaign came to a damp conclusion. Couch complained about having to cross the river during a storm, and then proceeded to cannibalize one of his three pontoon bridges in order to stabilize the other two. The army began crossing, a process that was completed when Barnes' brigade of the *V Corps* passed over the river sometime before noon on May 6. The army then returned to its old camps near Falmouth. Most of the men knew that they had not been defeated in the field as much as they had been outgeneraled. When Lincoln heard the news of Hooker's withdrawal late that afternoon, he explained in disbelief, "My God! What will the country say? What will the country say?"

As Hooker's men crossed their pontoon bridges at U.S. Ford, Lee posted Early and McLaws at Fredericksburg and then ordered the rest of his army to march to Chancellorsville to rest and reorganize. His army had lost 12,821 men, some twenty-two percent of his 60,892 men engaged. These were casualties he could ill afford to replace, especially the loss of Stonewall Jackson. Hooker's losses were fewer, 17,287, some thirteen percent of his 133,868. The *Army of the Potomac* had been decisively defeated, but not destroyed, in spite of all the risks Lee had to take during the battle. It was now clear to Lee that he would have to adopt a markedly different strategy if he hoped to attain ultimate victory—a deeper invasion of the north.

*Union troops building corduroy roads prior to their retreat.*

# Bibliography

Several excellent studies of the Chancellorsville Campaign have been written. The best of these, and perhaps the most thorough study ever made of any Civil War battle, is *The Campaign of Chancellorsville* by John Bigelow Jr. (New Haven, 1910). This mammoth study (528 pages) covers every facet of the campaign and battle, and includes forty-seven maps and plans that are definietely the most detailed done on any battle of the war. There are only two problems in using Bigelow. One is that the work is arranged in segments organized both topically and chronologically, a structure that makes it difficult to follow the battle on a broader scope. The second is that the book is difficult to obtain—the original edition was printed in only 1000 copies, and the most recent reprint sells for $200.

Edward J. Stackpole's *Chancellorsville, Lee's Greatest Battle* (Harrisburg, 1958) is much more readily available than Bigelow and is also much easier to read through while still covering the battle on a detailed level. Stackpole is excellent at interpreting the battle in modern military terms, and his thirty maps (mostly based on Bigelow's) are much better than those in most campaign histories. The following studies are recommended for readers who desire well written accounts of the campaign that are not as full as Bigelow and Stackpole: *Lee's Lieutenant's, Vol. II*, by Douglas Southall Freeman (New York, 1943), *The Civil War, Vol. 2*, by Shelby Foote (New York, 1958), and *Glory Road* or *Terrible Swift Sword* by Bruce Catton (New York, 1962).

Four other campaign studies are worthy of note. *Chancellorsville* by Jed Hotchkiss and William Allan (New York, 1867; reprinted 1984) gives the battle from the Confederate viewpoint, while *Chancellorsville and Gettysburg* by Abner Doubleday (New York, 1886; several reprints) presents more of the Union viewpoint. August Hamlin in *The Battle of Chancellorsville* (Bangor, Maine, 1896) gives a detailed study of Jackson's flank attack with a view to defending the efforts of the *XI Corps*. *The Battle of Chancellorsville* by Samuel P. Bates (Meadville, PA, 1882; reprinted 1987) is a dated study that incorrectly challenges the fact that Stonewall Jackson was accidentally wounded by his own men.

No Civil War battle can be properly studied without reference to the battle reports, papers and dispatches compiled in *The War of the Rebellion, A Compilation of the Official Records of the Union and Confederate Armies* (Washington, 1880-1901, with recent reprints). This immense series contains 128 volumes, of which Chancellorsville is presented primarily in Series I, Vol 25, Parts I and II (serial numbers 39 and 40). Other excellent primary source material written by important participants in the battle (including Generals Couch and Howard) can be readily found in volume 3 of *Battles and Leaders of the Civil War* (New York, 1884, with several recent reprints). Other good critical primary accounts of the battle are harder to find. Best recommended are the following two studies by artillery officer E.P. Alexander: *Military Memoirs of a Confederate* (New York, 1907; reprinted 1962) and *Fighting For the Confederacy* (Chapel Hill, N.C., 1989).

There are a number of good studies of Lee and Jackson and their role in the battle. The best of the several biographies of Lee are Douglas Southall Freeman's multi-volume *R.E. Lee, A Biography* (New York, 1934), and *Lee* by Clifford Dowdey (New York, 1965), Stonewall Jackson and his last battle have long fascinated historians. G. F. R. Henderson's *Stonewall Jackson and the American Civil War* (New York, 1898) contains one of the best accounts written on Jackson's flank march and attack on the *XI Corps*.

Also recommended are *Mighty Stonewall* by Frank Vandiver (New York, 1957), and *They Called Him Stonewall* by Burke Davis (New York, 1954).

Besides Jackson, Lee's principal lieutenants at Chancellorsville were A. P. Hill, Stuart and Early. For good material on Hill, see *A. P. Hill, Lee's Forgotten General*, by Warren W. Hassler (Richmond, 1962), and *General A.P. Hill, The Story of a Confederate Warrior* by James Robertson Jr. (New York, 1987). The ever popular Stuart can be read about in *Jeb Stuart, The Last Cavalier* by Burke Davis (New York, 1957) and the more recent *Bold Dragon, The Life of Jeb Stuart* by Emory M. Thomas (New York, 1986). Early's account of the battle is available for study in his *War Memoirs* (Philadelphia, 1912; reprinted 1960). Biographies of other Confederate officers involved in the campaign can be found in Ezra Warner's *Generals in Gray* (Baton Rouge, 1959) and *Lee's Colonels* by Robert K. Krick (Dayton, Ohio, 1984).

For more on General James Longstreet's non-involvement in the campaign, see *The Forgotten Campaign* by Steven A. Cormier (Lynchburg, 1989), and Longstreet's autobiography, *From Manassas to Appomattox* (Philadelphia, 1896; reprinted 1960).

Literature on the Union generals in the battle is not as voluminous as for the Confederate side. There is only one good biography of enigmatic Joe Hooker, Walter H. Hebert's *Fighting Joe Hooker* (New York, 1944; reprinted 1987). Good biographies have been written of all of Hooker's principal subordinates except for Couch, Slocum, and Stoneman. The following are well recommended: *Toward Gettysburg, A Biography of General John F. Reynolds* by Edward J. Nichols (Penn State University, 1958); *Hancock the Superb* by Glenn Tucker (New York, 1960; reprinted 1980); *Sickles the Incredible* by W. A. Swanberg (New York, 1956); *Meade of Gettysburg* by Freeman Cleeves (University of Oklahoma, 1960; reprinted 1980); *General John Sedgwick* by Richard E. Winslow (Presidio Press, 1982); and *Sword and Olive Branch: Oliver Otis Howard* by John A. Carpenter (Pittsburgh, 1964). One of the most interesting autobiographies that covers the battle is *The Reminiscences of Carl Scmurz* (New York, 1907). The lives of other Union commanders may be read in *Generals in Blue* by Ezra Warner (Baton Rouge, 1964).

Of the numerous unit histories written of Confederate organizations that fought in the battle, the following may be of interest: *Up Came Hill, The Study of the Light Division and its Leaders* by Martin Schenck (Harrisburg, 1958); *The Stonewall Brigade* by James I. Robertson (Baton Rouge, 1963); *Lee's Tigers, The Louisiana Infantry in the Army of Northern Virginia* by Terry Jones (Baton Rouge, 1987); and *12th Virginia Infantry* by William D. Henderson (Lynchburg, 1984).

The following Federal unit histories may be of interest to students of the battle: *Carl Bornemann's Regiment, The Forty-First New York Infantry* (Dekalb Regt.) in the Civil War, by David Martin (Hightstown, NJ, 1987); *A History of the Forty-Fourth New York Volunteer Infantry* by Eugene Nash (New York, 1910; reprinted 1988); *Ten Months with the 153rd Pennsylvania Volunteers* by William Simmers (Easton, Pa., 1953); *Berdan's United States Sharpshooters in the Army of the Potomac* by C. A. Stevens (St. Paul, Minnesota, 1892; reprint 1984); *Sykes' Regular Infantry Division, 1861-1864*, by Timothy J. Reese (Jefferson, N.C., 1990); and *History of the Eleventh New Jersey Volunteers* by Thomas B. Marbaker (Trenton, 1898; reprinted 1990).

## UNION DIVISIONAL STRENGTHS AND LOSSES

| Unit | Strength | Losses K | W | M/C | T |
|---|---|---|---|---|---|
| General HQ | 5,384 | 1 | 7 | 1 | 9 |
| Staff | 66 | 0 | 1 | 0 | 1 |
| Provost Guard | 2,658 | | | | |
| Engineers | 807 | 1 | 6 | 1 | 8 |
| Signal Corps | 183 | | | | |
| Orderlies | 60 | | | | |
| Reserve Artillery | 1,610 | | | | |
| I Corps (Reynolds) | 17,183 | 9 | 80 | 46 | 135 |
| HQ | 81 | | | | |
| Wadsworth's 1st. Div. | 8,985 | 1 | 15 | 2 | 18 |
| Robinson's 2nd Div. | 4,612 | 7 | 42 | 6 | 55 |
| Doubleday's 3rd Div. | 3,507 | 1 | 23 | 38 | 62 |
| II Corps (Couch) | 17,012 | 149 | 1,044 | 732 | 1,925 |
| HQ | 104 | 0 | 3 | 0 | 3 |
| Hancock's 1st Div. | 5,645 | 78 | 445 | 601 | 1,124 |
| Gibbon's 2nd Div. | 5,442 | 8 | 90 | 12 | 110 |
| French's 3rd Div. | 5,598 | 63 | 504 | 119 | 686 |
| Reserve | 223 | 0 | 2 | 0 | 2 |
| III Corps (Sickles) | 19,185 | 378 | 2,645 | 1,096 | 4,119 |
| HQ | 6 | 0 | 1 | 0 | 1 |
| Birney's 1st Div. | 7,699 | 109 | 925 | 563 | 1,607 |
| Berry's 2nd Div. | 7,643 | 148 | 737 | 244 | 1,429 |
| Whipple's 3rd Div. | 3,837 | 111 | 682 | 289 | 1,082 |
| V Corps (Meade) | 17,865 | 69 | 472 | 159 | 700 |
| HQ | 61 | | | | |
| Griffin's 1st Div. | 6,817 | 17 | 108 | 13 | 138 |
| Syke's 2nd Div. | 6,700 | 27 | 167 | 91 | 285 |
| Humphrey's 3rd Div. | 4,287 | 25 | 197 | 55 | 277 |
| VI Corps (Sedgwick) | 24,190 | 485 | 2,620 | 1,485 | 4,590 |
| HQ | 185 | 0 | 1 | 1 | 2 |
| Brook's 1st Div. | 7,689 | 203 | 922 | 365 | 1,490 |
| Howe's 2nd Div. | 6,422 | 91 | 697 | 502 | 1,290 |
| Newton's 3rd Div. | 7,093 | 98 | 505 | 307 | 1,010 |
| Burnham's Light Div. | 2,801 | 93 | 395 | 296 | 798 |
| XI Corps (Howard) | 13,765 | 217 | 1,221 | 974 | 2,412 |
| HQ | 62 | | | | |
| Deven's 1st Div. | 4,753 | 61 | 477 | 432 | 970 |
| McLean's 2nd Div. | 4,123 | 27 | 248 | 244 | 519 |
| Schurz's 3rd Div. | 4,478 | 129 | 493 | 298 | 920 |
| Reserve | 349 | 0 | 3 | 0 | 3 |
| XII Corps (Slocum) | 13,466 | 260 | 1,411 | 1,121 | 2,822 |
| HQ | 168 | 0 | 3 | 1 | 4 |
| William's 1st Div. | 6,502 | 135 | 801 | 676 | 1,612 |
| Geary's 2nd Div. | 6,796 | 125 | 637 | 444 | 1,206 |
| Cavalry Corps (Stoneman) | 11,351 | 17 | 74 | 297 | 388 |
| HQ | 15 | | | | |
| Pleasonton's 1st Div. | 3,311 | 13 | 61 | 156 | 248 |
| HQ | 11 | | | | |
| Davis' First Brig. | 1,711 | 1 | 8 | 22 | 31 |
| Devin's 2nd Brig. | 1,589 | 12 | 53 | 134 | 200 |
| Averell's 2nd. Div. | 2,191 | 0 | 6 | 2 | 8 |
| HQ | 10 | | | | |
| Sargent's Brig. | 1,002 | 0 | 6 | 2 | 8 |
| McIntosh's Brig. | 1,179 | | | | |
| Gregg's 3rd Div. | 3,269 | 3 | 4 | 64 | 71 |
| Kilpatrick's 1st Brig. | 1,500 | 1 | 1 | 24 | 26 |
| Wyndham's 2nd Brig. | 1,769 | 2 | 3 | 40 | 45 |
| Buford's Reserve Brig. | 2,267 | 1 | 3 | 75 | 79 |
| Robertson's Horse Arty. | 298 | | | | |
| **Army Total** | **139,401** | **1,585** | **9,604** | **5,911** | **17,100** |

NOTE: Most sources agree that Hooker had over 130,000 men available for the battle. Bigelow gives 133,868; Stackpole gives 134,668; and the *Battles and Leaders of the Civil War* editors give 130,000. The total of 139,401 given in this chart should be reduced by five percent to give 132,430 available for battle duty. This may be the first time Union strengths have been published at the divisional level. Estimates of total Union losses range from Livermore's 16,792 to Stackpole's 17,287.

KEY:

| | |
|---|---|
| Arty. | Artillery |
| Brig. | Brigade |
| Div. | Division |
| NR | No Report |
| K | Killed |
| M/C | Missing or Captured |
| T | Total |
| W | Wounded |

## CONFEDERATE BRIGADE STRENGTHS AND LOSSES

| Unit | Strength | Losses | | | |
|---|---|---|---|---|---|
| | | K | W | M/C | T |
| I Corps | 17,900 | 413 | 2,395 | 687 | 3,197 |
| McLaw's Div. | 8,800 | 219 | 1290 | 380 | 1,889 |
| Barksdale's Brig. | 1,800 | 43 | 208 | 341 | 592 |
| Kershaw's Brig. | 2,700 | 12 | 90 | 2 | 104 |
| Semmes' Brig. | 2,000 | 85 | 492 | 26 | 603 |
| Wofford's Brig. | 2,000 | 74 | 479 | 9 | 562 |
| Cabell's Arty. | 300 | 5 | 21 | 2 | 28 |
| Anderson's Div. | 8,400 | 184 | 1,062 | 253 | 1,499 |
| Mahone's Brig. | 2,000 | 24 | 134 | 97 | 255 |
| Perry's Brig. | 1,200 | 21 | 88 | | 109 |
| Posey's Brig. | 1,500 | 41 | 184 | 65 | 290 |
| Wilcox's Brig. | 1,900 | 72 | 372 | 91 | 535 |
| Wright's Brig. | 1,500 | 25 | 271 | | 296 |
| Garnett's Arty. | 300 | 1 | 13 | | 14 |
| Reserve | 700 | 10 | 43 | 54 | 107 |
| Alexander's Arty. | 500 | 6 | 35 | 21 | 62 |
| Washington Arty.. | 200 | 4 | 8 | 33 | 45 |
| Jackson's Corps | | | | | |
| A.P. Hill's Light Div. | 11,000 | 426 | 2,354 | 213 | 2,993 |
| Archer's Brig. | 1,400 | 44 | 305 | 16 | 365 |
| Heth's Brig. | 1,700 | 33 | 270 | | 303 |
| Lane's Brig. | 2,000 | 161 | 626 | 122 | 909 |
| McGowan's Brig. | 1,800 | 46 | 402 | 7 | 455 |
| Pender's Brig. | 2,000 | 116 | 567 | 68 | 751 |
| Thomas' Brig. | 1,800 | 21 | 156 | | 177 |
| Walker's Arty. | 400 | 5 | 28 | | 33 |
| Rodes' Div. | 8,900 | 392 | 1,905 | 709 | 3,006 |
| Colquitt's Brig. | 1,700 | 9 | 128 | 312 | 449 |
| Doles' Brig. | 1,600 | 66 | 343 | 28 | 437 |
| Iverson's Brig. | 1,800 | 67 | 330 | 73 | 470 |
| O'Neal's Brig. | 1,900 | 90 | 538 | 188 | 816 |
| Ramseur's Brig. | 1,500 | 151 | 529 | 108 | 788 |
| Carter's Arty. | 400 | 9 | 37 | | 46 |
| Early's Div. | 8,300 | 125 | 721 | | 846 |
| Gordon's Brig. | 2,500 | 16 | 145 | | 161 |
| Hay's Brig. | 2,100 | 63 | 306 | | 369 |
| Hoke's Brig. | 1,800 | 35 | 195 | | 230 |
| Smith's Brig. | 1,600 | 11 | 75 | | 86 |
| Andrew's Arty. | 300 | | | | NR |
| Colston's Div. | 7,700 | 281 | 1,710 | 99 | 2,090 |
| J. Jones' Brig. | 1,800 | 52 | 420 | | 472 |
| Nicholl's Brig. | 1,800 | 47 | 266 | 10 | 323 |
| Stonewall Brig. | 1,600 | 54 | 430 | 9 | 493 |
| Warren's Brig. | 2,200 | 128 | 594 | 80 | 802 |
| W. Jones Arty. | 300 | | | | NR |
| Reserve | 700 | | | | NR |
| Brown's Arty. | 500 | | | | NR |
| McIntosh's | 200 | | | | NR |
| Army Reserve | 500 | | | | NR |
| Cutts' Arty. | 250 | | | | NR |
| Nelson's Arty. | 250 | | | | NR |
| Stuart's Cavalry | 3,300 | 8 | 13 | | 21 |
| F. Lee's Brig. | 1,200 | 4 | 7 | | 11 |
| W. Lee's Brig. | 1,800 | | | | NR |
| Beckham's Arty. | 300 | 4 | 6 | | 10 |
| **Army Total** | 58,400 | 1,645 | 9,908 | 1,708 | 12,151 |

NOTE: Most sources agree that Lee had about 60,000 men available for the battle. Bigelow gives 60,892; Stackpole gives 58,934; and Livermore in *Numbers in the American Civil War* gives 57,352. This chart may be the first published that attempts to break the army's strength down at brigade level. The loss figures are taken from *Battles and Leaders of the Civil War.* They are admittedly incomplete because some units did not report at all. Livermore estimates the total casualties to be 12,764 (1,665 killed, 9,081 wounded, 2,018 missing).

KEY:

| | |
|---|---|
| Arty. | Artillery |
| Brig. | Brigade |
| Div. | Division |
| NR | No Report |
| K | Killed |
| M/C | Missing or Captured |
| T | Total |
| W | Wounded |